Naval Aircraft

Hamlyn

LONDON · NEW YORK · SYDNEY · TORONTO

in association with Phoebus

Written by Louis S. Casey
Illustrated by John Batchelor
Edited by Christy Campbell
Designed by Jeff Gurney

Published 1977 by
The Hamlyn Publishing Group Limited
London · New York · Sydney · Toronto
Astronaut House, Feltham, Middlesex, England

ISBN 0 600 36583 2

This edition © 1977 Phoebus Publishing
Company/BPC Publishing Limited
169 Wardour Street, London W1A 2JX

Part published in *Naval Aircraft 1939–1945*
© 1975 Phoebus Publishing Company/
BPC Publishing Limited

Made and printed in Great Britain by
Waterlow (Dunstable) Limited

John Batchelor, after leaving the RAF, served
his 'apprenticeship' in the technical publications
departments of several British aircraft firms and
went on to contribute on a freelance basis to
many technical magazines. Since then, his work
for Purnell's *Histories of the World Wars* and subsequently the Purnell's World War Specials, has
established him as being one of the most outstanding artists in his field. A confirmed enthus-
iast, he takes every opportunity to fly, sail, drive
or shoot any piece of military equipment he can
lay his hands on.

Louis S. Casey is Curator of Aircraft, Department
of Aeronautics, National Air and Space Museum,
Smithsonian Institution, Washington DC. A pilot
in the USAAF during the Second World War, he
subsequently became Assistant to the Director
of Civil Aviation in Bermuda, and is a qualified
FAA instructor in several aspects of aircraft and
aviation. A regular contributor to aviation journals
both in the USA and elsewhere he is one of the
leading authorities in his field. His special interest
is the Curtiss Aircraft Company, of which he is
engaged in writing the definitive history.

ABOUT THIS BOOK

In 1914 the ultimate expression of naval power was the battleship. Already however, eight years after the Wright brothers first flight, courageous and daring pioneers in America and Great Britain had made the first landings on warships at sea. Naval warfare had been expanded into a third dimension and naval flying took off with the outbreak of war.

Shipborne fighters and Zeppelins duelled over the North Sea. Torpedo-bombers went into action, like the submarine, threatening the supremacy of the big-gun ship. By 1918 true aircraft carriers were in service and special classes of aircraft were being designed to equip them. Between the wars naval aircraft were amongst the most dazzlingly colourful machines ever to fly, but the Japanese attack on Pearl Harbor showed the real teeth of the new power at sea.

Carrier-borne aircraft revolutionised naval warfare during the Second World War. In the Atlantic and Mediterranean their work ranged from convoy protection to such dramatic actions as Taranto and the *Bismarck* and *Tirpitz* strikes; but it was in the vast reaches of the Pacific they came into their own.

With the Battle of the Coral Sea in 1942 a new era dawned: for the first time a naval engagement was fought by aircraft alone, without the surface ships of either side coming within sight of each other. Moreover, as the sinking of the *Repulse* and *Prince of Wales* in 1941, and of the *Yamato*, pride of the Japanese Navy, in 1945 demonstrated, the age of the battleship as king-pin of the fleet was over.

This is the story of naval aircraft from the beginning to the end of the Second World War. John Batchelor's illustrations show off the machines to perfection and Lou Casey of the Smithsonian Institution provides a fully researched and authoritative account of the development and application in combat of carrier aircraft.

CONTENTS

The Beginning of Carrier Aviation...6
Naval Aircraft: The First War...8
New Power at Sea..18
Fighters 1918–39..19
Threat from Above: Dive/Attack-Bombers 33
Strike from the Surface: Torpedo Bombers 40
Servicing the Fleet: Observation/Utility/Trainers 48
Armament 56

Sights 59
Flotation Gear 60
Powerplants 61
Wing Folding 63
The Carrier Grows Up 64
Eve of the Carriers War: State of the Art – 1941......................66
Catapults 70
Aiming a Punch Where it Hurts: Torpedo Bombers
    in Combat 72

'When We Say Dive We Mean Straight Down':
    Dive Bombers 83
Bomber Escort or Carrier Protector?: Fighters
    in Combat 94
Try Hards and Trainers: Useful Obsolescence...................113
Torpedoes 116
Bombs 118
The Long Arm of the Navy 121
USS Hornet and Doolittle's B25s 125

THE BEGINNING OF CARRIER AVIATION

The first aeroplane flight from a ship took place on November 14, 1910, when Eugene Ely flew a Curtiss Model D from an 83-ft ramp on the bows of the light cruiser Birmingham *off Norfolk, Virginia. The Curtiss' wheels, floats and propeller hit the water, but Ely retained control and landed ashore*

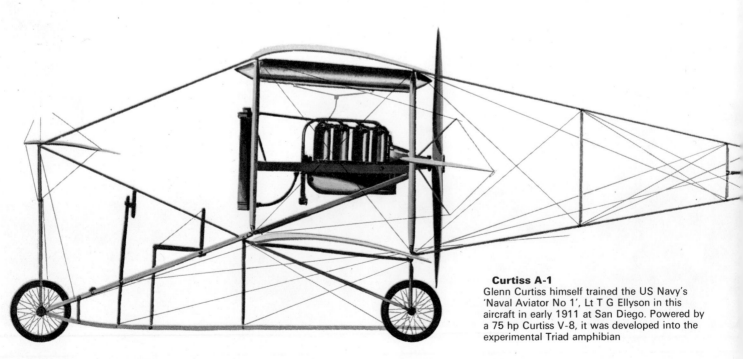

Curtiss A-1
Glenn Curtiss himself trained the US Navy's 'Naval Aviator No 1', Lt T G Ellyson in this aircraft in early 1911 at San Diego. Powered by a 75 hp Curtiss V-8, it was developed into the experimental Triad amphibian

When the Wright brothers made the first powered flight at Kitty Hawk in 1903, a new dimension was added to war. The potential of aircraft at sea was also made obvious to a courageous group of naval pioneers. The carrier aircraft was born.

Generally speaking, carrier aircraft are designed to operate from a platform rather than from the water surface itself. The first instance of such a flight occurred on 14 November 1910 when Eugene Ely flew a Curtiss Model D biplane from a platform specifically constructed on the foredeck of the US light cruiser, USS *Birmingham*. Over-water safety features had been developed for the spectacular Albany-New York flight made by Glenn H Curtiss on 29 May 1910. These consisted of a pair of canister-type floats mounted under the wings and a long bag of corks attached to the centre keel of the plane.

When Capt Washington I Chambers of the US Navy learned of the interest in ship-to-shore mail flights by the Hamburg-American Steamship Line, he obtained permission to fit a platform on the USS *Birmingham*. This platform, 83 ft long and 24 ft wide, sloped down toward the bow at a 5° angle, placing the leading edge of the platform 37 ft above the water at the bow. However, circumstances prevented J A D McCurdy, the pilot for the steamship line (formerly of the Aerial Experiment Assn, and later Governor General of Canada), from completing the mail flight.

The same Albany Flyer that Curtiss had used for the Albany-New York flight was at that time participating in an air meet at Halethorp, Maryland, and Eugene Ely, a Curtiss exhibition pilot who was also

Ely wore a football helmet and a bicycle inner tube for safety during his landing on the Pennsylvania. *Swimmers and life-boats also stood by*

taking part in the meet, volunteered to fly the plane. The plane was hoisted aboard the *Birmingham* with the front wheel positioned just 57 ft back from the front edge of the platform. Weather reports indicated the approach of strong winds for the following day, so the decision was made to attempt the flight on 14 November. After much delay due to low clouds, poor visibility and heavy rain showers, Ely climbed into the pilot seat of the Albany Flyer at about 1500. The *Birmingham* got under way and, while they still had 20 fathoms of anchor chain out, Ely gave the signal to the deck crew to let go. He cleared the deck at 1516 without benefit of much forward speed of the ship. Nosing down to gain the required

flying speed, he struck the water with the wheels, frame, canisters and propeller tips. The vibration resulting from the damaged propeller quickly convinced Ely that the prudent course would be toward the nearest land. In this instance it was a point of land, Willoughby Spit, two and a half miles distant, where he set the Albany Flyer down for a safe landing.

Unfortunately, like a good many other historic events it was much later before the importance of that flight was recognised. Ely's payment for the flight was a letter of thanks from the Secretary of the Navy, George von Lengerke Meyer. The aeroplane was not destined to revolutionise naval tactics – not at this date, anyway.

The second significant event involved the same pilot but a different ship, a different location and a different plane. The location was San Francisco Bay, the ship was the cruiser USS *Pennsylvania*, and the plane was a Curtiss D IV Military, the first of its kind, designed for the variable conditions of military aeronautics. In order to carry a second person for observation purposes, the wing area of the D IV was increased by the insertion of a 30-in panel in each wing cellule. So successful was this modification that varying sized panels up to a full extra panel or bay could be and often were added to increase the lifting capability of the otherwise standard Model D III Curtiss.

For this second experiment, a deck 120 ft long and 32 ft wide was constructed to cover the afterdeck equipment and turrets. This deck sloped upward at the forward end near the superstructure and after mast. As a further precaution canvas was laced to the front and sides of the deck, the for-

On January 18, 1911, Ely carried out the second half of his mission by landing aboard the cruiser Pennsylvania *in San Francisco Bay. He landed on a 120-ft wooden platform built over the ship's stern and after turret, using an arrester system of ropes stretched between 100 lb sandbags*

ward panel extending upward to screen the superstructure and the side panels extending downward to serve as a final barrier net should the plane veer out of control. In addition to these precautions, the first aircraft arrester system was developed and used. At least three claims for its design are known: however, the fact that it was ingenious and simple in construction made it a success, so much so that the modern-day systems bear a strong resemblance to this original. It consisted of 22 ropes stretched across the beam of the flight deck, supported by timbers which held the lines slightly above the deck and with each rope tied to two 50-lb sand bags, one at each end. The plane was equipped with three pairs of small grapnel hooks attached laterally to the landing gear between the main wheels. As in the case of the Albany Flyer, two canister-type floats were attached under the wings outboard of the main landing wheels, but this time the cork bag used for the Albany flight was missing. To complete the safety precautions, Ely used a pair of crossed, inflated motorcycle inner tubes around his neck and under his arms.

The day before the experiment a decision was made not to get the ship under way for the test flight. On 18 January 1911 Ely took off from San Francisco's Presidio Field and headed for the smallest field ever encountered to this date. Conditions were at their worst with the ship headed into an ebb tide and a light 10 mph wind blowing from the stern, necessitating a down-wind landing. The wind changed slightly as he approached the deck, producing a slight cross-wind. However, when less than 100 ft from the deck, the plane steadied. As he cleared the lip of the afterdeck Ely pulled the plane up slightly to lose some of the speed, estimated to be a staggering 39-40 mph. He skimmed over the first eleven athwartship lines, hooked the twelfth and added successive lines as the speed dissipated until it came to rest after contacting the 22nd line and 50 ft short of the forward end of the deck. The dawn of the aircraft carrier was at hand.

The take-off 45 minutes later was uneventful. The tailwind was now a headwind as the plane was turned around for departure off the stern of the ship.

With two successful demonstrations, one would think that this new technique would have gained instant acclaim or at least a

Cdr C R Samson's Short Hydroplane about to be launched from HMS Hibernia, *May 1912*

foothold – and be developed by the US Navy. Such was not the case, for the next step was taken by the British in making the first take-off from a ship under way. On 4 May 1912 Cdr C R Samson RN, and Lt Malone made two flights from HMS *Hibernia* while she was under way at an estimated 12 knots.

NAVAL AIRCRAFT: THE FIRST WAR

The first takeoff and landing aboard a navy ship by Eugene Ely and the first takeoff from HMS *Hibernia* while she was under way, demonstrated the basic techniques for aircraft launch and retrieval, as we know them today.

To the credit of the Royal Navy, they began experiments which eventually led to the development of shipborne aircraft and the techniques and ships to handle these planes. One wonders, when looking back over the development of naval aviation, why the navies of the world, particularly the British, United States, and Japanese, the major sea powers of that day, failed to grasp and perfect the techniques as demonstrated by Ely. Failure to utilize these techniques can probably be attributed to the battleship fixation of the senior naval personnel of these nations. The thought of having their ships' decks encumbered or obstructed by the gear necessary to handle aircraft was out of the question.

Development of ships' facilities for the handling of aircraft was accelerated due to the demand for some kind of ship with sufficient speed to accompany the fleet and to act as a carrier for the numerous aircraft required. The aircraft were desired for reconnaissance, offensive action and fire control for the heavy guns of the capital ships of the fleet. From these experimental installations, it became obvious that the aeroplane did indeed have a definite place in naval warfare.

It was also determined that something more reliable and efficient than seaplane tenders was required, for with seaplanes, frail as they were at this time, it was often impossible to launch and retrieve them under certain sea conditions. Often the

Avro 504
Remembered mostly as a trainer, the Avro 504 also saw service as a bomber and reconnaissance aircraft. On 21 November 1914, three aircraft of the Royal Naval Air Service bombed the Zeppelin sheds at Friedrichshafen in one of the most daring raids of the war. The Avro 504 was also used to attack Zeppelins in flight
  Span: 36 ft *Length:* 29 ft 5 in *Engine:* Gnôme, 80 hp *Max speed:* 82 mph *Range:* 250 miles *Armament:* Lewis mg (some) *Bombload:* 4 × 20-lb

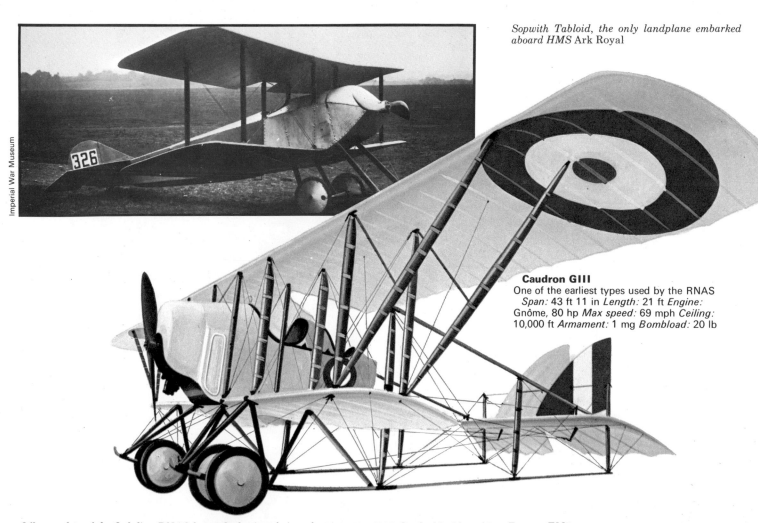

Sopwith Tabloid, the only landplane embarked aboard HMS Ark Royal

Caudron GIII
One of the earliest types used by the RNAS
Span: 43 ft 11 in *Length:* 21 ft *Engine:*
Gnôme, 80 hp *Max speed:* 69 mph *Ceiling:*
10,000 ft *Armament:* 1 mg *Bombload:* 20 lb

Officer cadets of the fledgling RNAS learn the basics of aircraft structure—1914. On the blackboard is a Farman FM7

Sopwith Pup (Type 9901a)

When Pups were first supplied to the early aircraft carriers, there was very little knowledge of the problems of deck flying. Experiments proved that a simple skid undercarriage could withstand the shock of landing better than wheels. The skid-equipped Type 9901a was built in some numbers for service throughout the fleet

Span: 26 ft 6 in *Length:* 19 ft 3·75 in *Engine:* Gnôme, 80 hp *Max speed:* 105 mph at 5000 ft *Ceiling:* 17,500 ft *Armament:* Vickers mg

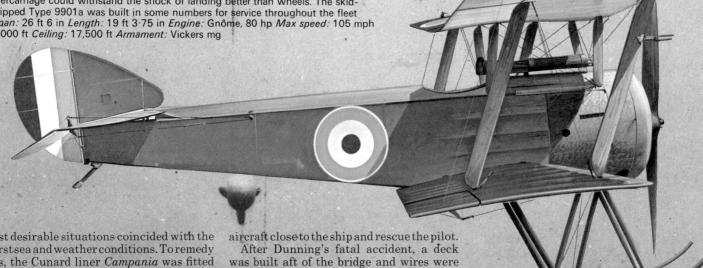

most desirable situations coincided with the worst sea and weather conditions. To remedy this, the Cunard liner *Campania* was fitted with a deck almost 230 ft long and seaplanes were launched under conditions which would have made operations impossible under the old system of hoisting aircraft over the side of the ship for a water takeoff.

Launching from the *Campania* was accomplished by use of the Gregory-Riley wheel gear. This interesting and successful gear consisted of a cross-axle which was fixed to the bottom of the floats. Outboard of the floats, an ordinary aircraft wheel was mounted. Incorporated in the device were springs which tended to force the wheels off but were prevented from doing so by a pair of safety pins, inserted into the axle, to which wires were attached leading to the cockpit. As soon as the aircraft lifted off the deck, the pilot pulled the pins clear and the wheels shot outward and off the plane.

The Gregory-Riley gear was also useful in making takeoffs from aerodromes, where they experienced no more difficulty than ordinary wheeled craft. An improved version of this system had a deck built over the

aircraft close to the ship and rescue the pilot.

After Dunning's fatal accident, a deck was built aft of the bridge and wires were strung fore and aft with ropes athwartship, similar to Ely's arresting system. As this system developed, hooks were attached to the axle which engaged the longitudinal wires to prevent a recurrence of Dunning's fate. It was, potentially, very wasteful of aircraft, however, and resulted in a short lifetime of only three landings using this system. This was the system developed on the Isle of Grain referred to elsewhere in the text.

A parallel development of short duration was barge flying. Commander C R Samson, RN, who, on 10 January 1912, made the takeoff from HMS *Africa*, produced an idea and developed it to a working system. He had a flat-bottomed barge towed behind a fast, powerful destroyer. Mounted on the barge was a Sopwith Camel which was equipped with a quick-release mooring. With the combined sea breeze and the top speed of the destroyer, the flying speed of the Camel was reached enabling the plane to lift off from the barge. This was another

appears to be a slightly modified Sopwith Baby) with a wing span 2 ft greater than the 25 ft 8 in of the Sopwith version. The Hamble Baby was powered by the 110-hp Clerget, the Sopwith by the 130-hp Clerget. The Fairey Campania seaplane was a two-place floatplane of 61 ft 8 in span (upper wing) and powered by a 275-hp Rolls-Royce engine.

Fairey Aviation produced the Type 3B powered by the 260-hp Sunbeam Maori engine. This, too, had biplane wings of unequal span, the upper span being 61 ft 0 in. Very similar was the Short 320, which was larger, 74 ft 6 in, and powered by the more powerful 320-hp Sunbeam Cossack engine. Last, but by no means least, was the Short Type 184, which proved to be one of the most durable of the lot. It was powered by a

forward hangar on HMS *Furious*. The deck was, in fact, the roof of the hangar and sloped downward towards the bow. Though this was something of an improvement, it left much to be desired, for the run available was only 200 ft.

It was on this deck that Squadron Commander Dunning made his ill-fated landing. His first landing on 2 August 1917, was successful. On this landing a deck crew assisted with the final touch-down of his Sopwith Pup. On the second landing, a tyre burst on touchdown, causing the Pup to swerve over the side of the ship and Dunning was drowned. Prior to this experimental landing, the usual procedure was to land the

short-lived experiment, but one that produced results, for shortly after Samson's experimental 'fly-offs', another pilot made a similar takeoff and shot down a far-ranging Zeppelin over the North Sea.

Aircraft involved in all these experiments were of wood and fabric structure and some, as in the case of the Camel and the Pup, were First World War fighters and well-known to anyone familiar with aircraft of that period. In addition, such aircraft as the Sopwith 1½ Strutter, P V N Griffin, Parnall Panther, Fairey Type 3A, Beardmore SB3D and the Hamble Baby were all used as ship's aircraft.

The Hamble Baby was a seaplane, (which

variety of engines, starting with the 225-hp Sunbeam engine.

Over 650 of these planes were produced during 1914-18 as torpedo reconnaissance aircraft and one is credited with the first successful aerial torpedo launching in the Sea of Marmara. It was also one of the early aircraft types sold to the Japanese navy in 1916 to begin their aviation training programme. Along with these, the Japanese acquired Sopwith Tabloid fighters and Deperdussin training seaplanes and the venerable Avro 504s.

Opposite is a comparison list of aircraft classified as ship's aircraft during this period of adapting aircraft to naval use.

From a barge towed behind a destroyer, a Sopwith Camel takes off into a North Sea headwind

Sq Cdr E H Dunning makes the first successful deck landing on HMS Furious in a Sopwith Pup, August 2, 1917. He had to fly around the bridge and funnel to land on the downward sloping deck

Sopwith 1½-Strutter

Deliveries to the RNAS began in the early spring of 1916, the aircraft being used as a bomber in its own right as well as an escort. The 1½-Strutter was the first British aircraft fitted with synchronizing gear to allow the guns to fire through the propeller, and its inherent stability compensated for a lack of manoeuvrability. A single-seat version was developed to carry out long-range bombing raids

Span: 33 ft 6 in *Length:* 25 ft 3 in *Engine:* Clerget or Le Rhône, 80—135 hp *Max speed:* 106 mph *Ceiling:* 16,000 ft *Endurance:* up to 4 hr *Armament (single-seat bomber):* forward-firing Vickers mg *Bombload:* 225 lb

The world's first true aircraft carrier, HMS Argus. She was completed in September 1918, could make 21 knots, had a displacement of 15,775 tons and could accommodate up to 20 aircraft in her hangars

	Span	Length	Height
Wight Seaplane	65 ft 6 in	44 ft 8 in	15 ft 10 in
Sopwith 2F1 Camel	28 ft 0 in	18 ft 9 in	8 ft 6 in
Sopwith Torpedo Plane	45 ft 9 in	28 ft 6 in	11 ft 0 in
Beardmore SB 3D	25 ft 1 in	19 ft 4 in	8 ft 8 in
Fairey Type 3A	61 ft 0 in	35 ft 6 in	13 ft 0 in
Parnall Panther	29 ft 6 in	24 ft 11 in	10 ft 9 in
PVN Griffin	41 ft 6 in	27 ft 3 in	10 ft 11 in
Sopwith 1½ Strutter	33 ft 6 in	25 ft 3 in	10 ft 3 in
Sopwith Baby	25 ft 8 in	23 ft 0 in	10 ft 10 in
Fairey Campania	61 ft 8 in	43 ft 3 in	15 ft 1 in
Fairey Type 3B	61 ft 0 in	35 ft 6 in	13 ft 0 in
Short 184	63 ft 5 in	40 ft 8 in	13 ft 2 in
Short No 320	74 ft 6 in	45 ft 9 in	17 ft 4 in

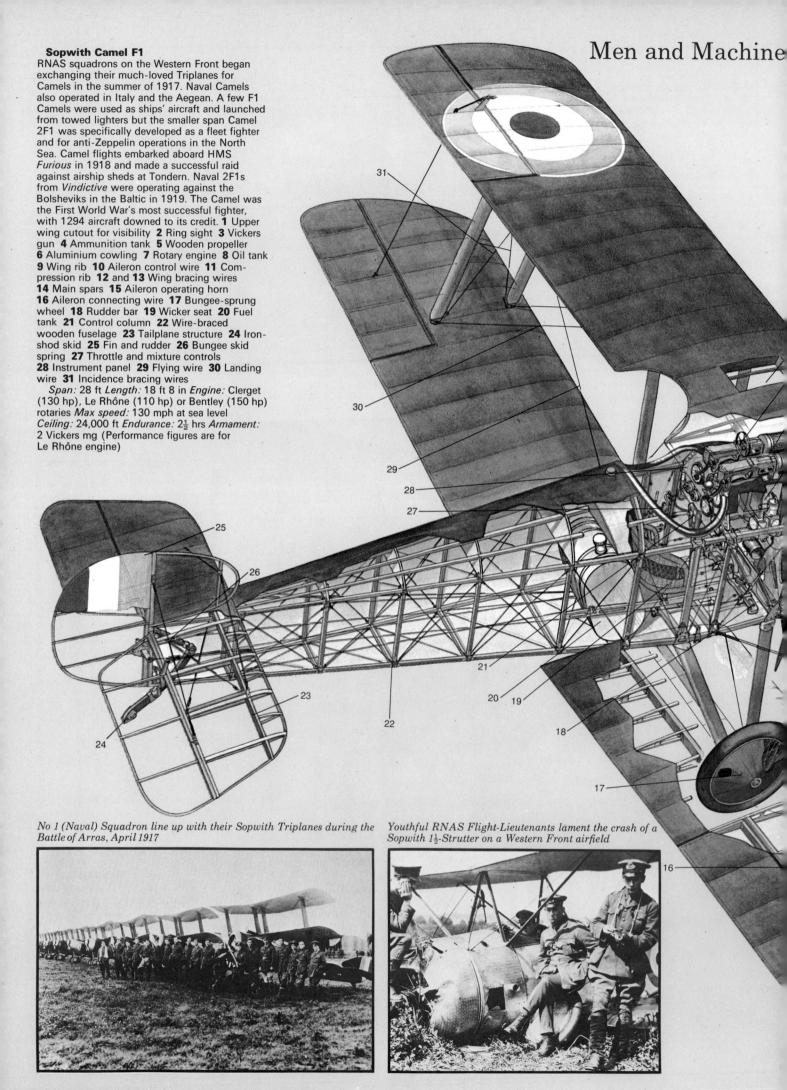

Sopwith Camel F1

RNAS squadrons on the Western Front began exchanging their much-loved Triplanes for Camels in the summer of 1917. Naval Camels also operated in Italy and the Aegean. A few F1 Camels were used as ships' aircraft and launched from towed lighters but the smaller span Camel 2F1 was specifically developed as a fleet fighter and for anti-Zeppelin operations in the North Sea. Camel flights embarked aboard HMS *Furious* in 1918 and made a successful raid against airship sheds at Tondern. Naval 2F1s from *Vindictive* were operating against the Bolsheviks in the Baltic in 1919. The Camel was the First World War's most successful fighter, with 1294 aircraft downed to its credit. **1** Upper wing cutout for visibility **2** Ring sight **3** Vickers gun **4** Ammunition tank **5** Wooden propeller **6** Aluminium cowling **7** Rotary engine **8** Oil tank **9** Wing rib **10** Aileron control wire **11** Compression rib **12** and **13** Wing bracing wires **14** Main spars **15** Aileron operating horn **16** Aileron connecting wire **17** Bungee-sprung wheel **18** Rudder bar **19** Wicker seat **20** Fuel tank **21** Control column **22** Wire-braced wooden fuselage **23** Tailplane structure **24** Iron-shod skid **25** Fin and rudder **26** Bungee skid spring **27** Throttle and mixture controls **28** Instrument panel **29** Flying wire **30** Landing wire **31** Incidence bracing wires

Span: 28 ft *Length:* 18 ft 8 in *Engine:* Clerget (130 hp), Le Rhône (110 hp) or Bentley (150 hp) rotaries *Max speed:* 130 mph at sea level *Ceiling:* 24,000 ft *Endurance:* $2\frac{1}{2}$ hrs *Armament:* 2 Vickers mg (Performance figures are for Le Rhône engine)

No 1 (Naval) Squadron line up with their Sopwith Triplanes during the Battle of Arras, April 1917

Youthful RNAS Flight-Lieutenants lament the crash of a Sopwith 1½-Strutter on a Western Front airfield

the Royal Naval Air Service

Sopwith Triplane

Designed for good visibility and manoeuvrability, the 'Tripehound' could out-climb its German contemporaries and gave rise to a whole family of German and Austrian triplanes designed to counter it. Deliveries began in late 1916 and the Black Flight of five Canadians, flying Triplanes, shot down 87 enemy aircraft between May and July 1917

Span: 26 ft 6 in *Length:* 18 ft 10 in *Engine:* Clerget, 110 or 130 hp *Max speed:* 117 mph *Ceiling:* 20,500 ft *Endurance:* 2¾ hr *Armament:* Vickers mg

Uniforms of the Royal Naval Air Service

Flight Lieutenant (left) wears army pattern field-service tunic, breeches and puttees typical of naval pilots serving on the Western Front. The RNAS cap badge is worn on the khaki cap and gilt eagle on the left breast. Rank is indicated by a cuff stripe with the executive curl. Flight Commander (right) wears navy blue jacket and trousers with flying helmet and coat. The gilt eagle badge is worn above the cuff rank insignia (inset) RNAS cap badge

When the Handley Page 0/100 heavy bomber, seen here outside the manufacturer's factory at Cricklewood, entered service in November 1916 it allowed the RNAS to step up its daylight bombing. The 0/100 could carry three times the load of the Short Bomber and six times that of the DH4

The Sopwith 1½ Strutter, and Sopwith Pup, in particular, and others on occasion, were fitted with skids which were mated with parallel U-shaped tracks which guided them down the sloping decks for their take-off 'run' and which, on landing, caused the aircraft to come to a halt after a very short run. In addition, they protected the propeller as the plane nosed down from this friction with the landing deck. These skids were also used on aircraft intended for takeoff from the turrets of battleships and cruisers during the early experimental stage of naval aviation both in Britain and the United States. The Japanese, who were at this time only beginning to adapt aircraft to naval use, apparently bypassed this stage on the advice of their British Technical Training Mission.

With the demonstration of the deck landing technique, the loss of aircraft with each flight was nearly at an end. Each flight had previously ended in a 'ditched' landing. Of

course, with the use of flotation bags much of the plane could be salvaged but, depending on the circumstances and sea condition, the probability of re-using the airframe more than once or twice was very slim, especially since the prevailing construction was of fabric-covered wood.

With this important milestone achieved, aircraft carrier development centred on landing decks which were built on the after-decks of the *Argus*, *Hermes* and *Vindictive* (originally the *Cavendish*). The latter was nearing completion and orders were given to include a landing deck aft, in addition to the flying-off deck forward.

These ships were a step along the way toward what we now know as aircraft carriers. The forward and aft flight decks were ponderous in the extreme. Aircraft would land on the aft deck and were then man-handled around the control bridge and

other superstructure on a trolley type arrangement to avoid damaging the wing or other flight components. After struggling with the aircraft past the bridge, it was positioned on the forward deck for takeoff. It was not long before the unpracticality of this arrangement became evident and the *Argus* was modified once again.

The cruiser *Hermes* had been fitted with a flying-off deck in 1913, but when war broke out, she was fitted with trackways over the foredeck. Unfortunately, little use was obtained from *Hermes*, for she was sunk by a German submarine in October 1914.

In 1913, a merchant ship, then under construction, was purchased and modified for the operation of seaplanes. Named the *Ark Royal*, she was fitted with a flying-off deck, 103 ft long, and stowage space for 10 seaplanes, plus shops for maintaining the planes. *Ark Royal* was launched in 1915 but

A Caproni Ca 5 fitted with torpedo shackles in place of its normal bomb racks. More than 250 of the type were built in 1918

Short Bomber

Developed from the Short 184 seaplane, the Bomber—which was never assigned an official name—was designed as a long-range heavy bomber and was used to attack targets such as Ostend and Zeebrugge. It was not a great success operationally, however

Span: 85 ft *Length:* 45 ft *Engine:* Rolls-Royce Eagle, 250 hp *Max speed:* 77 mph *Ceiling:* 9500 ft *Endurance:* 6 hr *Armament:* Lewis mg *Bombload:* 920 lb

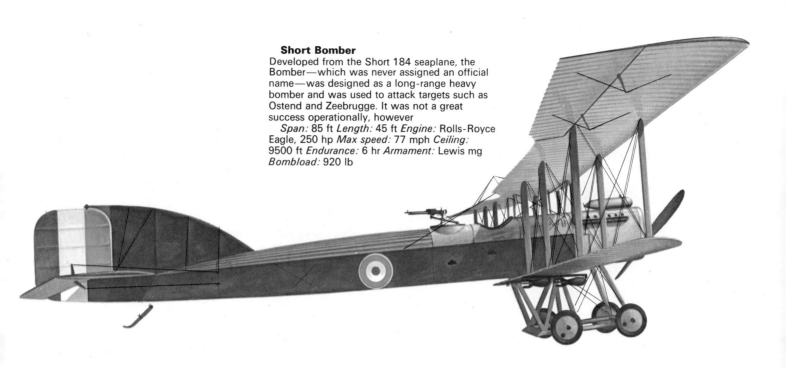

Caproni Ca 5

Caproni returned to the biplane layout for the Ca 5, having adopted a triplane configuration for the Ca 4s. The Ca 5s were beginning to replace the earlier Ca 3s as the war ended, and the type was regarded as Italy's best heavy bomber of the period. Capronis were used throughout the First World War to attack Austro-Hungarian targets such as the naval base at Pola and the seaport of Trieste

Span: 77 ft *Length:* 41 ft 4 in *Engines:* three Fiat A 12 bis, 330 hp each *Max speed:* 100 mph *Range:* 400 miles *Armament:* 2 Revelli mg *Bombload:* 2000 lb

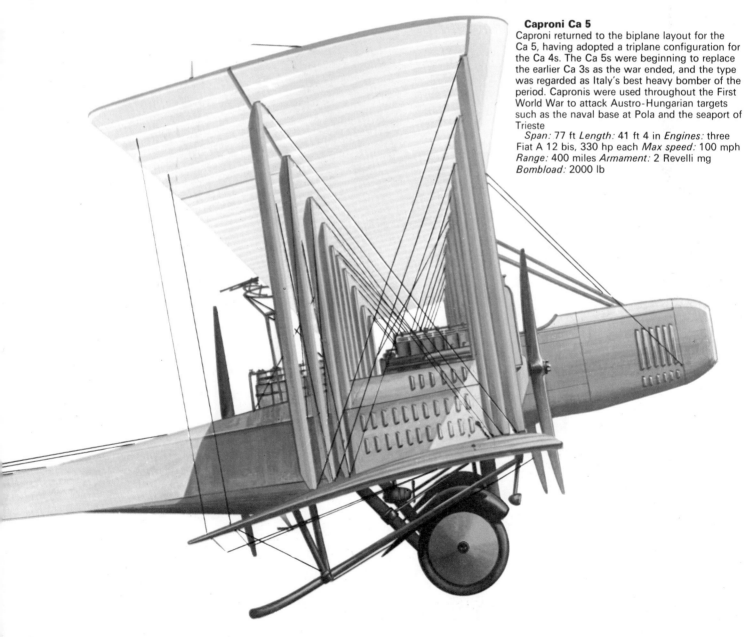

HMS Campania was fitted with a 120-ft flying-off deck forward, but this was never used in action. Seaplanes were hoisted overboard to take off from the open sea instead

Below: HMS Furious

When *Furious* joined the fleet in July 1917 it was as a hybrid vessel, aircraft carrier forward and cruiser aft. A hangar was built in place of the forward 18-in gun, the roof forming a flying-off deck. A landing deck was later added behind the funnel, but operations proved too dangerous and flying was confined to launching. Up to 12 Sopwith Pups and eight Short seaplanes could be accommodated in the two hangars
   Displacement: 22,000 tons *Length:* 786 ft overall *Max speed:* 32·5 knots *Armament (1918–1925):* 11×5·5-in guns, 18×21-in torpedo tubes, up to 33 aircraft

Below left: HMS Riviera

Converted into a seaplane carrier from a ferry. The aircraft were housed in a hangar at the stern, being hoisted out for launching and back in again after alighting
   Displacement: 1675 tons *Length:* 311 ft *Max speed:* 23 knots *Armament:* 2×4-in and one 6-pounder guns

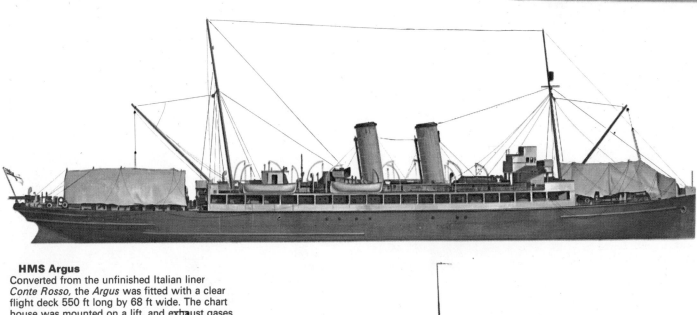

HMS Argus

Converted from the unfinished Italian liner *Conte Rosso,* the *Argus* was fitted with a clear flight deck 550 ft long by 68 ft wide. The chart house was mounted on a lift, and exhaust gases were ducted to ports in the stern. A squadron of Sopwith Cuckoos was embarked in late 1918, marking the first deployment of carrier-based torpedo bombers, but the war ended before the vessel could see action
   Displacement: 15,775 tons *Length:* 565 ft *Max speed:* 20·75 knots *Armament:* 6×4-in AA guns, up to 20 aircraft

her speed of 11 knots made her unusable with the fleet. She saw service in the Mediterranean as a base and maintenance ship.

At the beginning of the First World War, *Empress*, *Engadine* and *Riviera*, three cross-channel steamers, were fitted out to operate the ship planes and later the *Vindex*, in 1915, and *Manxman*, in 1916, were added to the list of ships converted to handle aircraft.

Prior to the commissioning of HMS *Eagle* in 1920, all the existing carriers had a level, squared-off flight deck at the stern. This resulted in a number of mishaps, usually the result of pilots approaching too high to assure their clearing the flight deck and the down-draught usually associated with it when the ship was operating at speed. To reduce or eliminate this problem, the *Eagle's* deck was constructed with a round-down to catch and correct for a low approach. Prior to this, a low approach often resulted in a sheared-off landing gear or worse. The round-down prevented further mishaps attributable to this.

The end of the First World War brought with it an economic retrenchment characteristic of post-war years when all the belligerents are physically and financially exhausted. This situation had its effect on carrier development which was reduced to experimental status which, in fact, it was.

The pressure to develop the equipment and operating techniques was no longer present. Great Britain had the *Argus* and the *Furious* operating in their earliest configurations. The United States was converting the collier *Jupiter* which became the first US carrier, *Langley*, and the Japanese were building their first carrier, from the keel up, to be christened *Hosho*.

Though the combinations varied from nation to nation and by date, the service functions for carrier aircraft were: fighters, torpedo-attack, bombers, reconnaissance, utility and trainers.

Below left, Sopwith Camels shelter behind the fold-down windbreak on HMS Furious. *Below right, a Sopwith Pup is lifted out of the hangar on* Furious

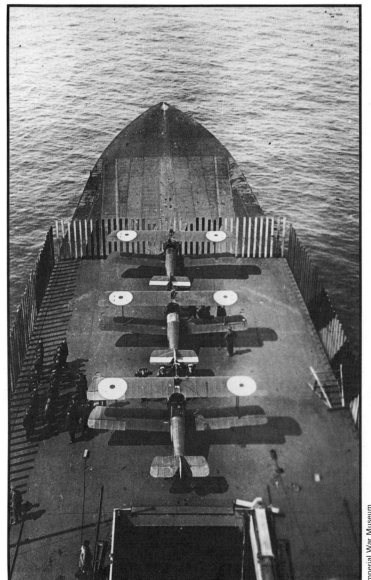

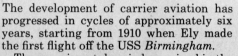

The development of carrier aviation has progressed in cycles of approximately six years, starting from 1910 when Ely made the first flight off the USS *Birmingham*.

The experimental period examined in the first chapter lasted up to 1915, when adapted landplanes were the dominant aircraft and flight decks were being installed fore and aft on battleships and cruiser hulls. Daring and courageous pilots were feeling their way with techniques that were eventually to bring the combination of aircraft and warship to its ultimate development and use during the Second World War.

For lack of better terminology, we will categorize the descriptions of further stages of development by 'generations' within the operational type groupings. The first generation, the period from 1915 to 1921, still relied on aircraft types developed in, and in many cases left over from, the First World War. They were still star performers, not because of their excellence, but because of their availability during a period of limited resources. The aircraft to dominate this period were the Sopwith Camel, Pup, and $1\frac{1}{2}$ Strutter; added to these were the relative newcomers, the Sopwith Cuckoo and Parnall Panther.

The second generation, 1922-1927, included US types, for with the conversion of the collier *Jupiter* into the carrier *Langley*, the United States began the long road to the mastery of carrier operations. Prior to this period, US Naval aviation had been concentrated on the flying boat and lighter-than-air craft to combat the submarine.

The third generation appeared in the years 1928-1933/4, the Depression years, but in aviation these were the golden years of the great air races and the smashing of one record after another. Great strides were made in the development of powerplants, airframes and overall designs. Fuels and lubricants were rapidly developed, largely in response to the racing activities where men, machines and motors (engines) were pushed to new limits.

The fourth generation, from 1934-1939, could be called the build-up years or the years of trial, when planes and aircrews were being tempered and tested as the world moved steadily toward conflict. The men that were destined to command the naval armadas of the Second World War were in training and developing the tactical and technical skills that were to be used in the war years. The transition to monoplanes was begun and the biplane, with the notable exceptions of the Fairey Swordfish and Albacore, disappeared from the decks of the carriers. With varying degrees of urgency, monoplane aircraft became the dominant first-line aircraft, just in time for the beginning of the Second World War and the fifth generation, the test of all that had gone before.

Whether by fate or pre-ordained destiny, all the lessons learned came to a focus during this period. The carrier task force replaced the dreadnought as the decisive weapon of naval warfare. One by one, the battleships slipped away, many the victims of carrier aircraft.

A Blackburn Dart torpedo bomber overflies HMS Hermes, the first vessel to be designed from the outset as an aircraft carrier

: FIGHTERS 1918-39

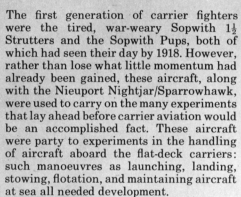

The first generation of carrier fighters were the tired, war-weary Sopwith 1½ Strutters and the Sopwith Pups, both of which had seen their day by 1918. However, rather than lose what little momentum had already been gained, these aircraft, along with the Nieuport Nightjar/Sparrowhawk, were used to carry on the many experiments that lay ahead before carrier aviation would be an accomplished fact. These aircraft were party to experiments in the handling of aircraft aboard the flat-deck carriers: such manoeuvres as launching, landing, stowing, flotation, and maintaining aircraft at sea all needed development.

The Sopwith aircraft – the 1½ Strutter and the Pup – were of conventional construction for First World War service. They were of wood and fabric structure, suitably braced by wires internally as well as externally. Both were powered by rotary engines. Their wing area was sufficient to give them a low wing loading and consequently low landing speeds. Coupled with these low landing speeds was good manoeuvrability which made them good, if not ideal, for deck flying. The low speeds made them appear to float from and particularly onto, the decks of the carriers, especially when the ship was underway producing a wind over the deck that approached in velocity the normal landing speeds of the aircraft.

Versatile 1½ Strutter

The development of flotation bags and early versions of the arrester gear were developed with the 1½ Strutter as was the technique of flying off a short forward deck.

It became one of the earliest multipurpose aircraft. At various times, sometimes interchangeably, 1½ Strutters were called upon to serve as fighters, reconnaissance aircraft, as well as single and two-seat bombers.

Performance was not spectacular. Speeds of nearly 100 miles per hour were all that could reasonably be expected. Armament, when it was carried, was limited to single rifle-calibre guns mounted on the cowling and on a flexible mounting in the rear cockpit.

The Pup, in addition to its wartime success, found use aboard ships. It was the first type used to take off from the turrets of battleships and return to short after-decks. These feats were performed on skids before wheel brakes and arrester hooks were standard naval aircraft equipment. The

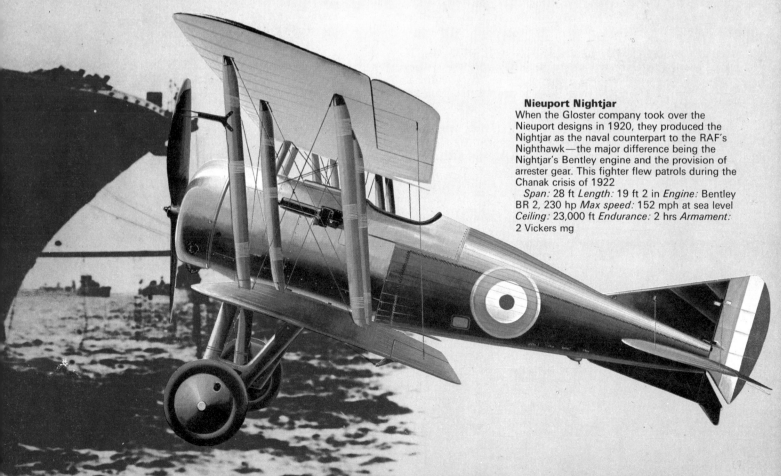

Nieuport Nightjar

When the Gloster company took over the Nieuport designs in 1920, they produced the Nightjar as the naval counterpart to the RAF's Nighthawk—the major difference being the Nightjar's Bentley engine and the provision of arrester gear. This fighter flew patrols during the Chanak crisis of 1922

Span: 28 ft *Length:* 19 ft 2 in *Engine:* Bentley BR 2, 230 hp *Max speed:* 152 mph at sea level *Ceiling:* 23,000 ft *Endurance:* 2 hrs *Armament:* 2 Vickers mg

Nakajima A1N1
The A1N1, a licence-built Gloster Gambet and closely resembling the Gamecock, was designated Type 3 by the Japanese Navy. It made extensive use of duralumin to combine light weight with high structural strength
Span: 31 ft 10 in *Length:* 21 ft 4 in *Engine:* Bristol Jupiter VI *Max speed:* 136 mph *Endurance:* $3\frac{1}{4}$ hr *Ceiling:* 23,000 ft *Armament:* 2 Vickers 7·7-mm mg *Bombload:* 4×20-lb

Pup was the aircraft type used by Lt S D Culley when he took off from a planing barge (lighter) in the North Sea to destroy the Zeppelin L53 at the end of July 1918.

The Nieuport Nightjar was another of the transition aircraft that used the rotary engine. It came into service in 1922 as a follow-on to the Sopwiths. Whether it used a rotary Bentley BR.2 engine because of familiarity with the type of engine in naval service, or because of shortage of funds dictating the rotary's continued use, is not known. The RAF used virtually the same airframe and installed either the Armstrong-Siddeley Jaguar or Bristol Jupiter radial engines, re-christening it the Nighthawk.

The name change was in itself worthwhile. The Nightjars were part of the first group of aircraft purchased by the developing Japanese naval aviation units. In spite of lack of arrester system or brakes, and in addition to the well-known torque from rotary engines, the Japanese mastered handling these Nightjars in their training programme. It is reported that 50 Nightjars and Sparrowhawks were consigned to Japan; however, it is unknown whether the Japanese Nieuports were the same as, or in addition to, those used by the Royal Navy. In any event, they served for a relatively short period until 1924.

The 'Unbreakables'
The second generation group of carrier fighter aircraft, while still predominantly of British design and manufacture, included in addition the Naval Aircraft Factory (US) TS-1 aircraft. The Fairey Flycatcher and Parnall Plover were readied to replace the Nighthawk in British carrier service.

The Flycatchers served long and well and were often called the 'Unbreakables', as they survived all that the Fleet Air Arm pilots and conditions could offer. They went on board HMS *Argus* for deck-handling trials in early 1923 and served until the early 1930s.

They were of conventional construction for their time, primarily wood with metal fittings and fabric covering. Though on close examination the fuselage profile was conventional, the addition of a rather odd shaped fin and rudder reminds one of a hobby-horse.

All pilot reports for the Flycatchers were very favourable. They were able to execute and survive virtually everything they were called on to perform. For their day, they were the ultimate carrier fighter. They were compact, with a span of 29 ft and length of 23 ft. They fitted the carrier aircraft lift with room to spare. In addition, they had built-in fixtures for float attachment and were often used in this configuration, particularly during Mediterranean cruises. They were very responsive to the controls, and visibility, particularly for deck landings, was excellent, in spite of the air-cooled radial Armstrong-Siddeley Jaguar engine. A robust, if ungainly-looking landing gear assured a reasonable landing. In conjunction with this, their specially patented camber-changing wings served as flaps during the landings. These, or equivalent systems, in varying combinations with other high-lift devices, are now being adapted to a wide range of military and civil types of aircraft, particularly the category now known as V/STOL aircraft.

Unlike the Nightjar/Sparrowhawk, the Flycatcher did not get a second innings in another naval service. They were used only by the Fleet Air Arm until they were declared obsolete in 1935.

One of the many guises allowed the Flycatcher was that of an amphibian. In this form, the floats, which were rather ordinary fitments to these aircraft, were suitably sprung with shock absorbers and wheels were installed in pockets within the floats just forward of the step. This installation permitted very little ground clearance when the Flycatcher was taxiing about the airfield or the deck, but did make them amphibious by definition.

Practically, however, they experienced considerable difficulty in getting 'unstuck'. This phenomenon was experienced previously in 1913 when Glenn H Curtiss, at the insistence of Captain W I Chambers, constructed the OWL (for Over Water and Land). The results were the same, water

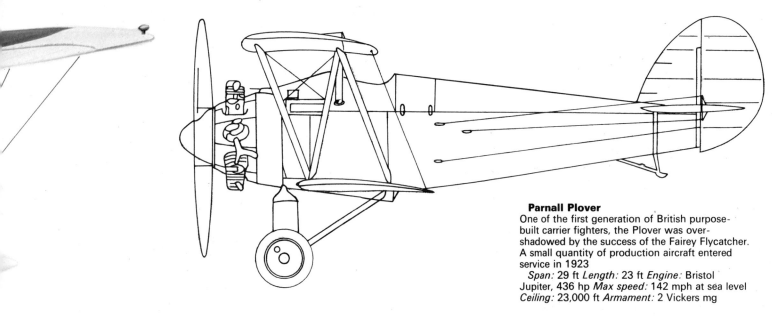

Parnall Plover
One of the first generation of British purpose-built carrier fighters, the Plover was over-shadowed by the success of the Fairey Flycatcher. A small quantity of production aircraft entered service in 1923
Span: 29 ft *Length:* 23 ft *Engine:* Bristol Jupiter, 436 hp *Max speed:* 142 mph at sea level *Ceiling:* 23,000 ft *Armament:* 2 Vickers mg

cavitating in the wheel pockets did little to help the cause of getting airborne.

Built to the same specifications as the Flycatcher (6/22), the Parnall Plover did not enjoy the same degree of affection as did the Flycatcher, partially due, no doubt, to word getting around about a weakness of the centre section. In any event, their service life was limited, as was the production run. Unlike the Flycatcher, the Plover did not have the patented drooping ailerons though it did have full-span ailerons on both upper and lower wings.

On the other side of the Atlantic, the US Navy was completing the *Langley* and with it the Naval Aircraft Factory was designing a single-place fighter not unlike its British counterparts. The resulting carrier fighter was designated the TS-1. It was designed by NAF and 34 were built by the Curtiss Aeroplane and Motor Company. Five planes were built by NAF as a financial check on the contract-built planes.

The TS went through a number of modifications, all part of the experimentation so necessary to this early phase of development. The first models had the fuselage suspended slightly above the lower wing.

The centre section of the lower wing served as the fuel tank.

About this same time, A V 'Fred' Verville had returned from an inspection tour of European aviation manufacturers with General 'Billy' Mitchell. One of the items reported on was an aerofoil-shaped fuel tank suspended on the landing gear axle of a Fokker aircraft. The idea seemed good from a safety point of view, since a crash would surely sever the tank from the fuselage and reduce the risk of fire. The principal short-coming was that the steady shocks of taxiing and landing continually ruptured

Fairey Flycatcher I
The first post-war quantity production naval fighter, the Flycatcher, was a superbly rugged, compact and manoeuvrable machine ideal for carrier operations and was the mainstay of FAA fighter squadrons in the 1920s and early '30s
Span: 29 ft *Length:* 23 ft *Engine:* Armstrong Siddeley Jaguar IV, 425 hp *Max speed:* 133·5 mph at 5000 ft *Ceiling:* 20,100 ft *Armament:* 2 Vickers mg

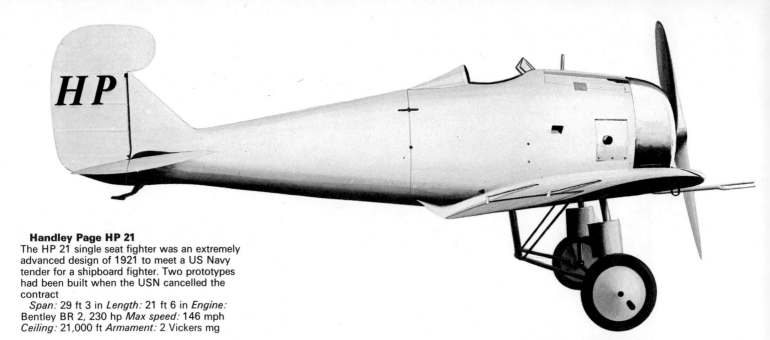

Handley Page HP 21

The HP 21 single seat fighter was an extremely advanced design of 1921 to meet a US Navy tender for a shipboard fighter. Two prototypes had been built when the USN cancelled the contract

Span: 29 ft 3 in *Length:* 21 ft 6 in *Engine:* Bentley BR 2, 230 hp *Max speed:* 146 mph *Ceiling:* 21,000 ft *Armament:* 2 Vickers mg

the soldered joints of the fuel tank, resulting in a high maintenance commitment. On the TS-1 the addition of arrester hooks would have also taken their toll on the tank. As a result, the tank, incorporated in the centre section of the lower wing, was a compromise – not on the axle, but still not in the fuselage.

The TS-1 was an extremely rugged machine which featured a wide gear tread and could also be fitted with floats. The structure was still wood and fabric, though a contract was negotiated with Curtiss to produce an all-metal version which was designated the F4C and built by Charles W Hall as part of continuing experimen-

tation with carrier-type aircraft. The results of this latter experiment, constructing the design out of metal, produced a weight reduction of 300 pounds but, by itself, was not sufficient grounds for further orders. Time had run out for the TS-1/F4C and European designs were surpassing it in performance.

US Naval Fighters

Like its British contemporaries, the TS-1 was fitted for float gear in addition to its wheel landing gear. Also it served as a test bed for the 240-hp water-cooled Aeromarine engine (TS-2) and 180-hp Wright-built Hispano Model E (TS-3). As if these changes were not enough chopping and changing,

the TS-3 was further modified by streamlining the fuselage, lowering the upper wing flush with the top of the fuselage, and changing the aerofoil – no small chore – all in the interest of making a trainer for the US 1923 Schneider Trophy team.

The third generation of carrier aircraft were among those to benefit from the increased development impetus of the golden years of aviation between 1928 and 1933/4. Certainly these were the fun years and yet they were also the years of learning, and carrier aviation development advanced considerably during this period.

Both Boeing and Curtiss had succeeded in capturing contracts with the Army Air

Curtiss F6C-2

Two examples of this shipboard fighter were ordered by the United States Navy in March 1925, in addition to seven F6C-1s. A variant of the Army's Hawk fighter, the F6C could be fitted with either wheels or floats. The USN later ordered 35 of the F6C-3 model, with arrester gear added, and 31 F6C-4s with Pratt & Whitney engines

Span: 31 ft 6 in *Length:* 22 ft 8 in *Engine:* Curtiss D-12, 400 hp *Max speed:* 159 mph *Range:* 330 miles *Ceiling:* 22,700 ft *Armament:* 2 × 0·30-in mg

A Nieuport 17 flies off the French sloop Bapaume. *Catching up with US and British experiments, the French began a series of flying-off tests in 1920. As a result the French Admiralty decided to complete a battleship hull as the* Béarn *— France's only carrier*

Corps for the production of sleek fighters based on the proven Curtiss D-12 liquid-cooled in-line engine. Boeing produced the PW-9 for the Air Corps, and not to be out-done, the Navy ordered 16 planes, which for practical purposes were the same, designated FB-1s. The first ten went to Marine squadrons without deck landing gear installed. After that, the deck landing equipment, including axle hooks and strengthened fuselage, were incorporated in the FB-2.

A succession of model modifications ensued, changing from D-12 water-cooled engines to radial air-cooled engines and back to the Packard water-cooled engines. Like the TS, time and design improvements overtook the FBs, but fortunately a successor was ready – the F2B – to start a new performance escalation in company with the rival Curtiss F6C series.

The FBs left their mark though, with a good production record for their day of 43 planes. Fortunately, one still survives, an FB-5 which one day will inspire current and future generations. They also marked the early stage of optional armament installation, permitting the substitution of a ·50 calibre machine-gun in place of one of the two ·30 calibre guns.

The Curtiss F6Cs, dubbed Hawks by their manufacturer, began this series and were powered by the Curtiss D-12 liquid-cooled engine. With the completion of the F6C-3s the change was begun to air-cooled engines, and the -4s, powered by the Pratt & Whitney R-1340, finished the series. Here again the technology of the times was passing them by, in spite of their aesthetically attractive lines.

Learning the Lessons

A specially modified and redesigned F6C-3 was fitted for racing purposes and was piloted by Captain Arthur H Page, USMC. A high-wing monoplane, redesignated as XF6C-6, it featured racy lines which were accentuated by elongated, streamlined wheel pants, which made this plane the talk of the US National Air Races in September, 1930. Page was off to an early lead in the race and continued to gain until the 17th lap of a 20-lap race. He then crashed, a victim of carbon monoxide poisoning. This was one of many such lessons learned during this period, too often at the cost of the life of a courageous pilot.

Though greater in span than the 29 ft of the Flycatcher, the Boeing at 30 ft and the Curtiss at 37 ft 6 in were still small and readily accommodated on the aircraft carrier lifts. The time was not right for folding wings, at least not for the fighters.

As evidence of increasing interest in naval aviation, appropriations were forthcoming to purchase no less than 75 of the Curtiss F6C series in addition to 76 aircraft combining the earlier FBs and F2Bs, really a breakthrough in the mid-1920s. The carriers *Langley*, *Lexington*, and *Saratoga*

The Americans too began with fighters on big ships, a Nieuport 28 up on the flying-off platform of the battleship USS Oklahoma, *1920*

were by now in commission and we were seeing the last of the tube-and-fabric aircraft and the end of the convertibility requirements (convertible to floats or wheels as the need arose, but always provided for in the design specifications).

Boeing, still adhering to the 30 ft span, produced an improved aircraft, the F3B-1. in 1928. An order for 74 insured that the fighter groups aboard the carriers would receive the improved models though the service life was to be shortened by the development of the Boeing F4B, probably the

most famous and appealing US carrier fighter of all time.

The F4Bs, in their developmental sequence, topped the list for orders of a single type and its variants. A compact, handsome biplane, the F4B was built with semi-monocoque fuselage and corrugated metal control surfaces in contrast to the bolted square-section aluminium frame as used in the F3Bs. Like the Fleet Air Arm's Flycatcher, these F4Bs caught the fancy of the pilots who flew them, and most of those who didn't as well. Performance-wise, they were good for their day. Powered by a Pratt & Whitney R-1340-16, the F4B-4 had a top speed of over 185 mph. As a series, F4B-1 to F4B-4, they remained operational over a seven-year period until 1937, when they were replaced by the Grumman fighters.

About this time (1928), decisions were

Boeing F4B-4
The second in the series to have an all-metal fuselage, the F4B-4 introduced the broad-chord tail and an enlarged head-rest for the pilot. The US Navy bought 74 of these single-seat fighters, and a further 14 were exported to Brazil
Span: 30 ft *Length:* 20 ft 5 in *Engine:* Pratt & Whitney R-1340-16, 550 hp *Max speed:* 187 mph *Ceiling:* 27,500 ft *Range:* 400 miles
Armament: 2×0·30-in or 1×0·50-in and 1×0·30-in mg

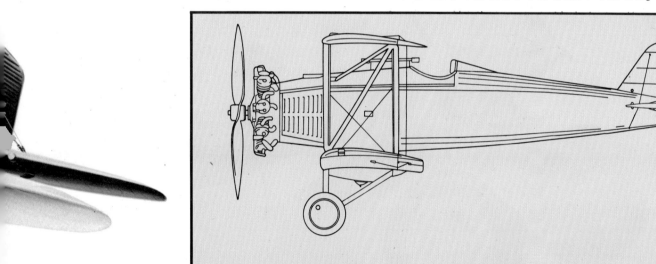

Curtiss TS-1
The first fighter designed specially for the United States Navy, the TS-1 was delivered from December 1922 for operations aboard the USS *Langley*. In an unusual arrangement, the fuel tank was mounted under the fuselage so that it could be jettisoned in an emergency. Curtiss built 34 of the aircraft, which was later redesignated FC-1, and the Naval Aircraft Factory assembled a further five
Span: 25 ft *Length:* 22 ft 1 in *Engine:* Wright J-1, 200 hp *Max speed:* 125 mph *Ceiling:* 16,250 ft
Range: 480 miles *Armament:* 0·30-in mg

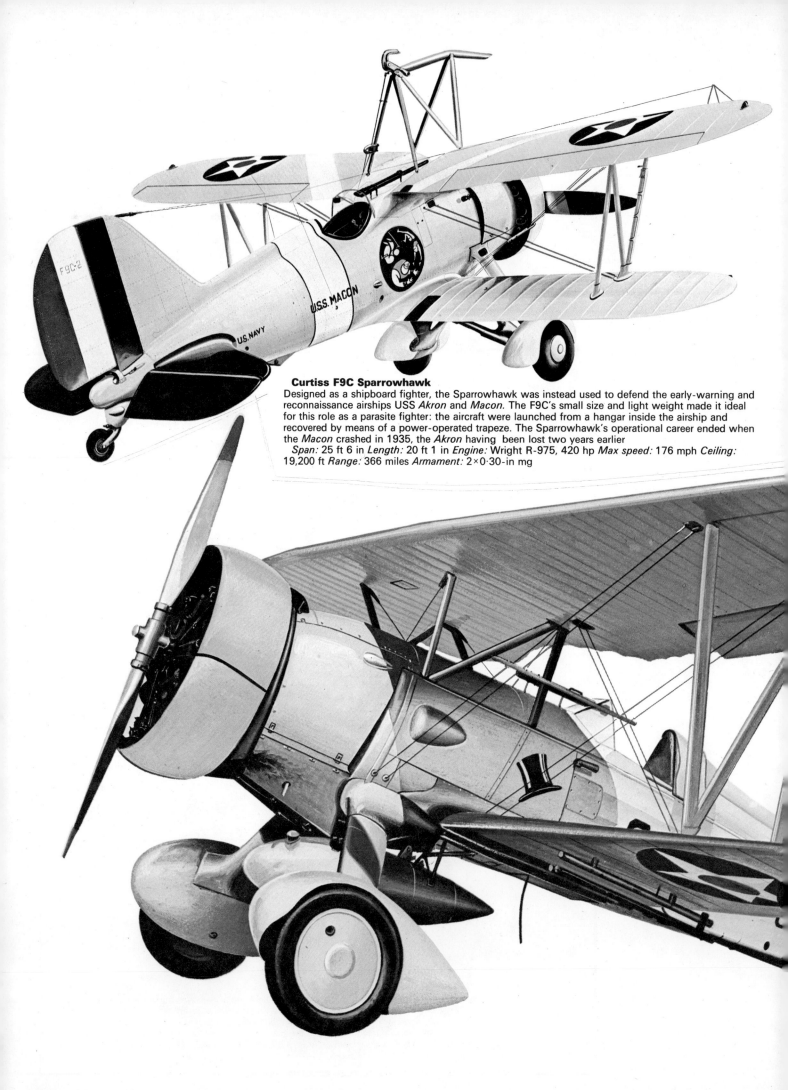

Curtiss F9C Sparrowhawk
Designed as a shipboard fighter, the Sparrowhawk was instead used to defend the early-warning and reconnaissance airships USS *Akron* and *Macon*. The F9C's small size and light weight made it ideal for this role as a parasite fighter: the aircraft were launched from a hangar inside the airship and recovered by means of a power-operated trapeze. The Sparrowhawk's operational career ended when the *Macon* crashed in 1935, the *Akron* having been lost two years earlier
Span: 25 ft 6 in *Length:* 20 ft 1 in *Engine:* Wright R-975, 420 hp *Max speed:* 176 mph *Ceiling:* 19,200 ft *Range:* 366 miles *Armament:* 2×0·30-in mg

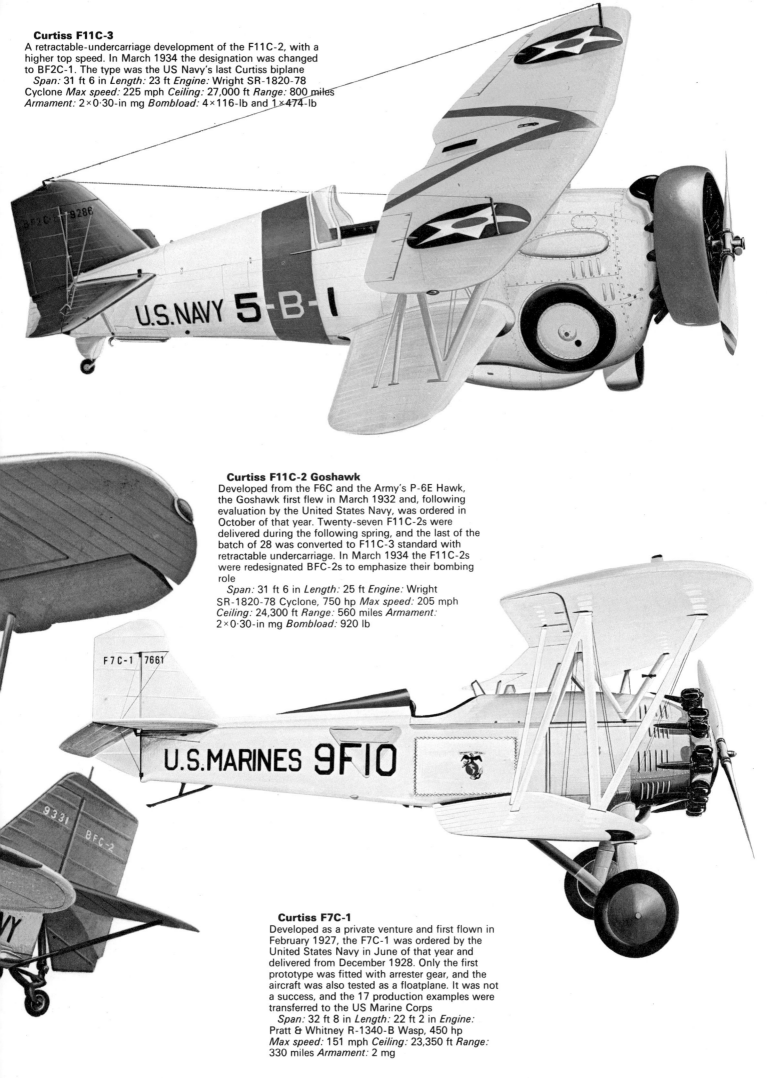

Curtiss F11C-3

A retractable-undercarriage development of the F11C-2, with a higher top speed. In March 1934 the designation was changed to BF2C-1. The type was the US Navy's last Curtiss biplane

Span: 31 ft 6 in *Length:* 23 ft *Engine:* Wright SR-1820-78 Cyclone *Max speed:* 225 mph *Ceiling:* 27,000 ft *Range:* 800 miles *Armament:* 2×0·30-in mg *Bombload:* 4×116-lb and 1×474-lb

Curtiss F11C-2 Goshawk

Developed from the F6C and the Army's P-6E Hawk, the Goshawk first flew in March 1932 and, following evaluation by the United States Navy, was ordered in October of that year. Twenty-seven F11C-2s were delivered during the following spring, and the last of the batch of 28 was converted to F11C-3 standard with retractable undercarriage. In March 1934 the F11C-2s were redesignated BFC-2s to emphasize their bombing role

Span: 31 ft 6 in *Length:* 25 ft *Engine:* Wright SR-1820-78 Cyclone, 750 hp *Max speed:* 205 mph *Ceiling:* 24,300 ft *Range:* 560 miles *Armament:* 2×0·30-in mg *Bombload:* 920 lb

Curtiss F7C-1

Developed as a private venture and first flown in February 1927, the F7C-1 was ordered by the United States Navy in June of that year and delivered from December 1928. Only the first prototype was fitted with arrester gear, and the aircraft was also tested as a floatplane. It was not a success, and the 17 production examples were transferred to the US Marine Corps

Span: 32 ft 8 in *Length:* 22 ft 2 in *Engine:* Pratt & Whitney R-1340-B Wasp, 450 hp *Max speed:* 151 mph *Ceiling:* 23,350 ft *Range:* 330 miles *Armament:* 2 mg

27

made to include two-place fighters in the inventory of carrier aircraft. In theory, the purpose was to increase the range of these fighting aircraft and to do so would require an additional crew member to relieve the pilot, to navigate, and to communicate. The US Navy chose to adapt the airframe of the well-tested Curtiss Falcon then in service with the Army Air Service. The major change for naval use was the installation of the well-tried, almost standardized Pratt & Whitney R-1340 Wasp engine. The distinctive swept-back upper wing gave the Falcons a rakish look that seemed to inspire diving. The resulting F8C-1s were delivered to the Marines in 1928 and assigned to Nicaragua and China. During this assignment they were called upon to serve in a variety of missions in an all-purpose role of fighter, dive bomber, air evacuation and observation.

During their tour of Nicaragua, the first dive bombing experiments were carried out. To take full advantage of the dive bombing ability later versions were modified in many details to improve this capability, including provisions for carrying a 500-lb bomb under the fuselage or two 116-lb bombs under each wing. These F8C-4s were given the name Helldiver, a name that was to remain in use far beyond the F8Cs. It was still appropriate and used with the SB2Cs of the Second World War.

French Carrier
With the completion of the *Béarn* in 1926, the French modified existing aircraft types for carrier duty. Modification consisted of

built carrier fighters to be accepted. In appearance, it bore a strong resemblance to the Gloster Grebe which had been a 1924-25 fighter in the Royal Air Force. This was replaced in the mid-thirties by the Nakajima Type 90s which bore more than a passing resemblance to the Curtiss Hawk series. 100 of these were built.

Japan was moving ahead with its programme of catching up with the other major powers in the field of aircraft design and construction. It was approaching independence in both aircraft and engine design, though the engines that powered these two aircraft were derived from foreign designs. In the Nakajima Kotobuki engine, design features were to be found which were directly traceable to the British Bristol Jupiter air-cooled radial.

Following the Wibault 74/75 in service aboard the *Béarn* in 1933 were a token number of three Morane-Saulnier 226s and a Morane-Saulnier 226 *bis*, equipped with folding wings. The interesting thing about these fighters selected for service aboard the French carrier was that they were all high-wing parasol monoplanes in contrast to the biplane fighters in service with the British, American and Japanese services. The introduction of a monoplane fighter as early as 1927 was revolutionary, and the fact that it was a parasol configuration showed that there were several design options to achieve the highly desirable line of vision forward and downward for deck landing operations.

The third fighter-type selected by the French Navy, to replace the ancient Wibault

Morane-Saulnier MS 225
Twelve MS 225 parasol monoplanes were delivered to the French Navy in 1933, flying from the shore station at Hyères. The success of the landplane inspired the MS 226, the 225 with tailwheel and arrester gear for duties aboard the *Béarn*. The 226 *bis* was an experimental version with folding wings
Span: 34 ft 7·75 in *Length:* 23 ft 9·25 in *Engine:* Gnôme-Rhône 9Kbrs, 500 hp *Max speed:* 207 mph at 13,125 ft *Ceiling:* 34,500 ft *Range:* 590 miles

Wibault 74
The exceptionally strong series of Wibault 7 fighters, the prototype of which first flew in 1924, carried the comparatively heavy armament for their day of four machine-guns. The Wibault 74 and 75 were the naval versions with arrester gear and served aboard the *Béarn* until 1934
Span: 36 ft 0·75 in *Length:* 24 ft 11·25 in *Engine:* Gnôme-Rhône Jupiter 9 Ady, 480 hp *Max speed:* 137 mph *Ceiling:* 26,900 ft *Range:* 373 miles

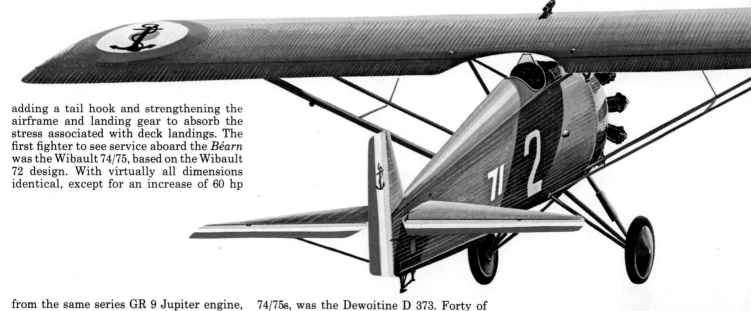

adding a tail hook and strengthening the airframe and landing gear to absorb the stress associated with deck landings. The first fighter to see service aboard the *Béarn* was the Wibault 74/75, based on the Wibault 72 design. With virtually all dimensions identical, except for an increase of 60 hp

from the same series GR 9 Jupiter engine, the naval version suffered performance-wise, a good example of the penalty borne by naval aircraft.

Model 72
| 3350 lb | 156 mph | 27,900 ft | 420 hp |
(GR9 Ac Jupiter)

Model 74/75
| 3416 lb | 137 mph | 26,900 ft | 480 hp |
(GR9 Ady Jupiter)

In 1930, Japan emerged with the first of its home-designed fighters, though they were based on the designs of British and US manufacturers. In 1927, a single-seat Nakajima biplane was one of the first Japanese-

74/75s, was the Dewoitine D 373. Forty of these carrier versions of the D 371 were ordered. Again, a high-wing parasol was selected for the conversion process. In this case the landing hook and flaps were fitted. As in the previous case, a second version was included in the conversion and was designated D 376. In this version the engineering was carried one step further to include provision for folding the wing for stowage aboard ship. In this case the performance penalty was one of additional weight which reduced the service ceiling by 3300 ft and the range slightly. The D 373s served until after the outbreak of war, but were withdrawn from service due to a high incidence of engine failure involving the crankshaft.

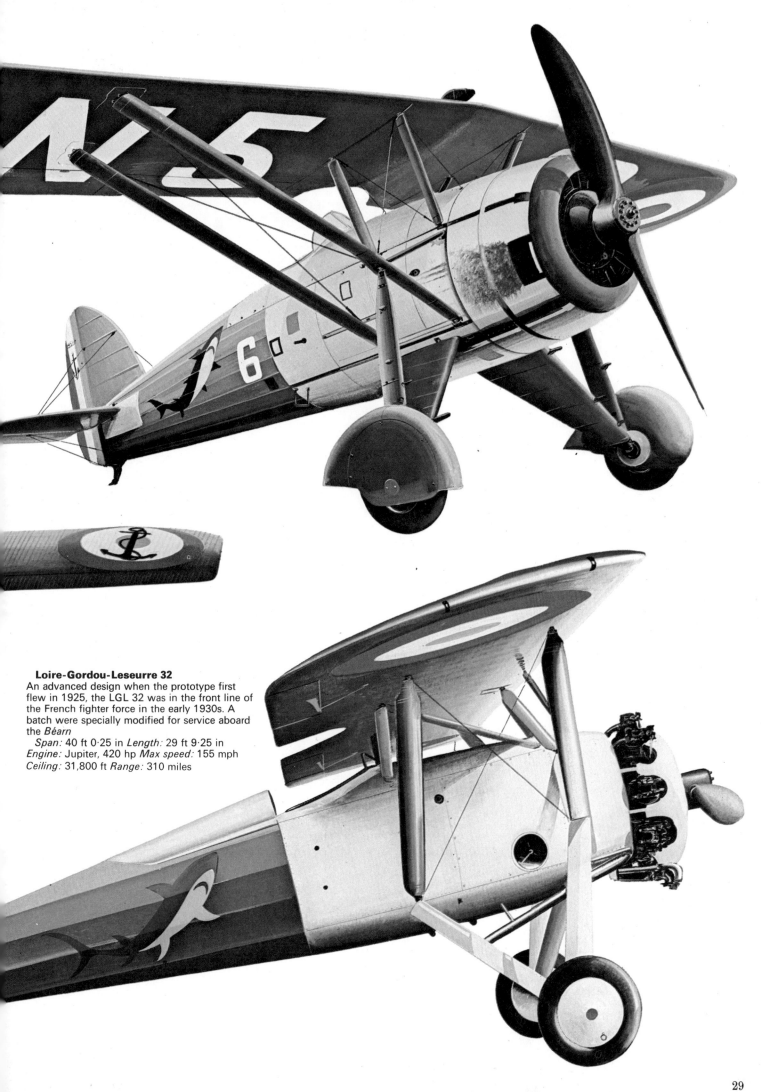

Loire-Gordou-Leseurre 32
An advanced design when the prototype first
flew in 1925, the LGL 32 was in the front line of
the French fighter force in the early 1930s. A
batch were specially modified for service aboard
the *Béarn*
Span: 40 ft 0·25 in *Length:* 29 ft 9·25 in
Engine: Jupiter, 420 hp *Max speed:* 155 mph
Ceiling: 31,800 ft *Range:* 310 miles

Grumman FF-1
The FF-1 was the first US Navy fighter with a retractable undercarriage and, though itself a two-seater, was faster than any of its single-seat contemporaries. The US Navy bought 27, a number of which were fitted with dual controls for training. These were designated FF-2. The type was also built in Canada, and operated by the Royal Canadian Air Force as the Goblin I
Span: 34 ft 6 in *Length:* 24 ft 6 in *Engine:* Wright R-1820-78, 775 hp *Max speed:* 207 mph *Ceiling:* 21,100 ft *Range:* 920 miles *Armament:* 2 mg

In 1932, the Hawker Nimrod replaced the much-loved Fairey Flycatchers after a decade of faithful service. The Nimrod was the naval version of the Hawker Fury which was highly regarded by the RAF. This was the era of steel and duraluminium construction with fabric cover still in vogue. Wood and glue fastening were rapidly disappearing from aircraft construction and anodizing of aluminium structures was becoming the standard practice for the preservation of airframes.

The Nimrod and the similar Osprey were favourites on the British carriers. They had low wing-loading, a good power-to-weight ratio, good aerobatic handling and formation flying with them was a pleasure. One might reflect on the many formation photographs taken during the mid-1930s and recall how many were photos of the Nimrod or the Osprey in naval service or their counterparts, the Fury or the Hart, in RAF service. It was a pleasure to fly them in formation, for it was effortless.

During this era, cruises about the Mediterranean, down the Red Sea, and to the Far East were made aboard the *Eagle* or *Hermes,* the two carriers that alternated duty in the Far East.

Ospreys Accompany Nimrods
The Hawker Osprey was the two-place carrier fighter in the Royal Navy, very similar to the Curtiss F8Cs in the US Navy. The Ospreys, while designated as fighters, were in fact built to accompany each flight of Nimrods to provide a navigator for extended overwater flights. In practical fact they were not fast enough to keep up with the Nimrods and therefore saw limited service in this capacity. They were all equipped with float fittings and often operated with floats installed for patrolling rivers and bays of the Far East which were then under the protection of the Royal Navy.

The Nimrod was powered by the Rolls-Royce Kestrel II developing 590 hp and the Osprey by the 640-hp Rolls-Royce Kestrel V. Even with this power difference, the Osprey was so badly outclassed by the Nimrod that the pairing of these two types for navigation or other purposes was not considered

Hawker Osprey
A naval variation of the long-lived Hawker Hart day bomber, the Osprey fleet reconnaissance-fighter served with the FAA from November 1932 until the outbreak of war
Span: 37 ft 3 in *Length:* 29 ft 1 in *Engine:* Rolls-Royce Kestrel V, 640 hp *Max speed:* 176 mph at 14,000 ft *Ceiling:* 24,500 ft *Endurance:* 3·3 hrs *Armament:* Vickers Mk IIIN mg, Lewis mg

prudent. Like the Flycatcher, the Nimrod and Ospreys enjoyed a long, happy service life with the Fleet Air Arm. They were replaced by the Blackburn Skua in 1939. Some were retained until 1941, as target tugs.

Curtiss F11C series. Though these planes were some of the most attractive types used by the US Navy, they did not enjoy a long service life. In fact these had an experimental 'air' about them for they went through a number of modifications and designation changes with bewildering speed. Deliveries of the F11C-2s began in February 1933. By March 1934, they had been redesignated BFC-2s to indicate that they had become fighter-bombers. By changes in engines and finally a redesign of the landing gear to a retractable type, and a partial enclosure of the cockpit, the plane was designated an F11C-3 and subsequently a BF2C-1. It is interesting to note that the cleaning-up aerodynamically, particularly the landing gear, resulted in an increase in speed from 205 mph (BFC-2) to 225 mph (BF2C-1).

Hawker Nimrod
A strengthened version of the Hawker Fury interceptor, the Nimrod carried more fuel and had an increased wing area. It was supplied in both float and wheel versions to the FAA as a replacement for the Flycatcher
Span: 33 ft 6·5 in *Length:* 26 ft 11·75 in *Engine:* Rolls-Royce Kestrel IIS, 590 hp *Max speed:* 205 mph at 13,000 ft *Ceiling:* 26,900 ft *Range:* 305 miles *Armament:* 2 Vickers Mk III mg

Nakajima A2N
Also known as the Type 90, this highly manoeuvrable single-seat carrier-based fighter was popular with pilots and ground crew alike. It entered production in 1931 to replace the A1N and was regarded as a better dogfighter than its eventual successor, the A4N. One hundred were built
Span: 30 ft 10 in *Length:* 21 ft 7 in *Engine:* Nakajima-built Bristol Jupiter VI, 450 hp *Max speed:* 200 mph *Ceiling:* 32,000 ft *Range:* 400 miles *Armament:* 2 mg

About this same period (1931), Grumman Aircraft Engineering Corporation was stepping into the aircraft building field. Prior to this it had been building floats for conversion of landplanes to seaplanes. Its first design was in answer to a proposal for the construction of a two-place fighter. One of the features of this first effort, to be designated the FF-1, was the wheel retraction system.

This retraction system, which was similar to that used on the Curtiss BF2C-2 with beneficial results, was an adaptation of the retraction system used on the Loening amphibians. While the down position placed the wheels fairly close to the sides of the fuselage, requiring some care on the part of the pilots when landing and during ground operation, the wheels, when retracted, fitted snugly into pockets in the sides of the for-

ward fuselage. The fuselage, of course, had been bellied down to permit this geometry and stowing. The result was a portly but attractive barrel-shaped fuselage which became a Grumman design feature for years.

The Grumman FF-1 proved itself to be a remarkable aircraft, for it was a two-place biplane fighter capable of out-flying its single-place contemporaries. Though it did accomplish this unusual feat it did not lead to large orders, for this period was the aftermath of the Depression in the US and large orders were out of the question.

Japanese Progress
The 27 FF-1s that were ordered did give naval pilots a taste of what was to come. They were modified to dual controls and served as training and 'check-out' planes for the single-place Grumman F2Fs and F3Fs. As a matter of interest, a single example of the FF-1 survives, completely restored in the US Naval Aviation Museum.

In 1934, Japan was rapidly closing the gap between its native-designed aircraft and those of the other naval powers, principally the US and Britain. The Japanese were still observing the products of the two other nations and, on occasion, making purchases of aircraft as a means of checking on their own progress and also with a view to checking for new design features. While this activity was progressing, they proceeded to build a replacement for the Type 90 carrier fighter. This new plane, the Nakajima A4N1 Type 95, filled the equipment progression gap.

The Type 95 displayed excellent manoeuvrability and was ordered in large quantities, 300 being built. It was to be the last of the biplane fighters in the Japanese Navy and, because of its very excellent manoeuvring ability, provided the comparison against which the next generation of monoplane fighters was judged. The Japanese placed great store on the ability

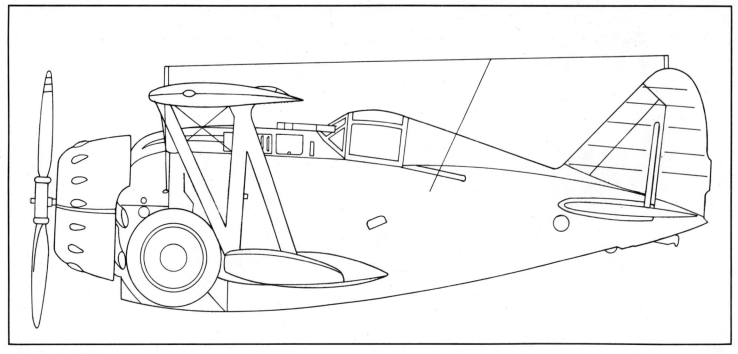

Grumman F2F-1

A single-seat fighter based on the FF-1 and its SF-1 derivative, the F2F retained the same general layout as its predecessors. The US Navy ordered 55, which were delivered from 1935 to equip the carriers *Lexington* and *Ranger*. They served until 1941, ending their life as gunnery trainers. The F2F-1 was developed into the F3F-1, with increased wingspan and a longer fuselage
Span: 28 ft 6 in *Length:* 21 ft 5 in *Engine:* Pratt & Whitney R-1535-72, 700 hp *Max speed:* 231 mph *Ceiling:* 27,100 ft *Range:* 985 miles *Armament:* 2×0·30-in mg *Bombload:* 225 lb

Grumman F3F-1

Developed from the F2F-1, with fuselage and wings lengthened to improve manoeuvrability, the prototype F3F-1 was ordered in October 1934. This aircraft crashed, but a second prototype was successful and 54 production models were delivered in 1936. This single-seat fighter, along with the F3F-2 and F3F-3 developed from it, remained in front-line service until the spring of 1941
Span: 32 ft *Length:* 23 ft 3 in *Engine:* Pratt & Whitney R-1535-84, 700 hp *Max speed:* 231 mph *Ceiling:* 28,500 ft *Range:* 880 miles *Armament:* 0·50-in Browning, 0·30-in Browning mg

of their fighters to execute manoeuvres with great agility. To a degree, it was their undoing, for they sacrificed other important factors, such as armour and airframe strength, to achieve this manoeuvrability.

The fourth generation of carrier fighter aircraft included the last of the biplane fighters and the first of the low-wing monoplane fighters. The Gloster Sea Gladiator was to be the last of the British biplane fighters and was a direct conversion of the RAF Gladiator. It provided a badly needed replacement for the Hawker Nimrod until the Blackburn Skua monoplane was ready for service. They were handsome, agile machines, but no match for the Messer-

schmitt Bf 109s which they were to encounter off Norway. Where they did not encounter such opposition, they were able to provide fighter cover for spotting aircraft in the Mediterranean and at least provide a morale booster for Malta during the crisis days of 1941.

The final naval biplane fighters were the Grumman F2F and F3F aircraft. These rotund, pugnacious little planes were of all-metal structure with fabric-covered wings and control surfaces. The semi-monocoque metal fuselage snuggled in behind the big 700-hp Pratt & Whitney R-1535 Wasp (F2F) or the even larger 950-hp Wright Cyclone R-1820 engines (F3F-2).

Though the total numbers produced of each type was substantial (F2F – 56 built, F3F – 164 built), their first-line life was short.

The most advanced aircraft design of this generation was the Mitsubishi A5M Claude. The Japanese had caught up, in fact had passed, their rivals in the development of carrier-based fighters. They began flight tests on the A5M in February 1935 and eventually built 1000 aircraft of this type. As if in anticipation of the events to come, these A5M Claude fighters saw service in the Sino-Japanese war in 1937-41. Design-wise, it was a large step forward, bridging the gap between the fabric-covered biplanes and the Mitsubishi A6M Zero.

Dive/Attack Bombers
THREAT FROM ABOVE

The Vought SB2U Vindicator scout bomber, deliveries of which began at the end of 1937

While a form of dive-bombing or glide-bombing is reported to have been used during the First World War, the beginning of serious development of the technique is generally credited to a section of US Marine Corps pilots flying Curtiss OC-1s in Nicaragua in 1928. When a small group of Marines were isolated and surrounded by a bandit group, the main body of Marines, by signal panels, directed the Marine aviators operating with the expeditionary force to bomb the insurgents. Close proximity of the two opposing forces made precision attacks necessary. Because of this the bombing took the form of near-vertical dives to place the bombs on the enemy strong points without endangering the Marine company.

At that date the OC (for Observation Curtiss) was called a Curtiss Falcon, for they were Navy modifications of the Army's Falcon. The main change was from a water-cooled engine to the air-cooled Pratt & Whitney R-1340 Wasp. These first OC-1s were not equipped for carrier operation. They were purchased as F8C-1 two-place fighters but were almost immediately re-designated OC-1s. With the introduction of the second version, the F8C-4 (O2C-1), the name Helldiver came into use, as the type was built to make dive-bombing its principal function. The resulting F8C-4 was capable of carrying a single 500-lb bomb under the fuselage or four 116-lb bombs in racks under the wings.

Indicating an early appreciation of the potential of dive-bombing as a method of ordnance delivery, the Japanese produced a two-place biplane dive-bomber for carrier use. The Nakajima N-35 Tokubaku powered by a 650-hp Lorraine engine was comparable in speed and general structural details to the state of the art in the US aircraft

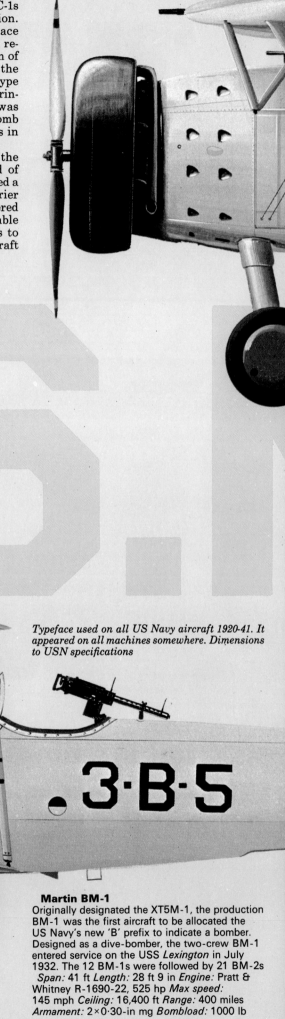

Typeface used on all US Navy aircraft 1920-41. It appeared on all machines somewhere. Dimensions to USN specifications

Martin BM-1
Originally designated the XT5M-1, the production BM-1 was the first aircraft to be allocated the US Navy's new 'B' prefix to indicate a bomber. Designed as a dive-bomber, the two-crew BM-1 entered service on the USS *Lexington* in July 1932. The 12 BM-1s were followed by 21 BM-2s
Span: 41 ft *Length:* 28 ft 9 in *Engine:* Pratt & Whitney R-1690-22, 525 hp *Max speed:* 145 mph *Ceiling:* 16,400 ft *Range:* 400 miles *Armament:* 2×0·30-in mg *Bombload:* 1000 lb

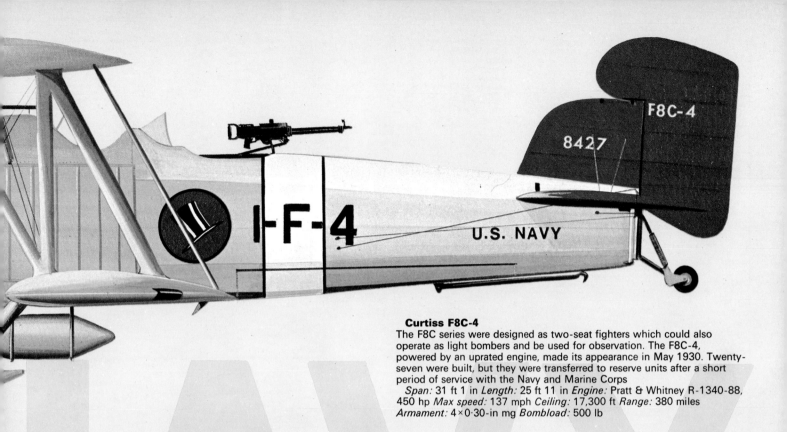

Curtiss F8C-4

The F8C series were designed as two-seat fighters which could also operate as light bombers and be used for observation. The F8C-4, powered by an uprated engine, made its appearance in May 1930. Twenty-seven were built, but they were transferred to reserve units after a short period of service with the Navy and Marine Corps

Span: 31 ft 1 in *Length:* 25 ft 11 in *Engine:* Pratt & Whitney R-1340-88, 450 hp *Max speed:* 137 mph *Ceiling:* 17,300 ft *Range:* 380 miles *Armament:* 4 × 0·30-in mg *Bombload:* 500 lb

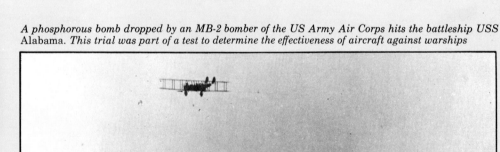

A phosphorous bomb dropped by an MB-2 bomber of the US Army Air Corps hits the battleship USS Alabama. *This trial was part of a test to determine the effectiveness of aircraft against warships*

The Curtiss BF2C-1, formerly designated F11C-3, featured a retractable undercarriage and was fitted with a new engine, raising its speed by 20 mph over the earlier BFC-2 fighter

industry. It was a 7-Shi development (1931) and was equivalent to the Curtiss F8C (O2C) Helldiver.

The same year, 1931, the US Navy was ordering a dive-bomber/torpedo-bomber, the Martin XT5M, and the Naval Aircraft Factory XT2N-1 two-place, dual purpose aircraft. The principal requirement for these aircraft was that they could pull out of a terminal-velocity dive with a 1000-lb bomb or torpedo attached. Bomb shackle hang-ups were not unheard of in those days. Deliveries of the first 12, designated BM-1s, began in September, 1931. Though the BM-1s and subsequently 16 BM-2s were designed primarily as dive-bombers, they were assigned initially to torpedo duties with VT-1S aboard the *Lexington*, and later when VT-1S was redesignated VB-1B in 1934 a second unit, VB-3B, used the Martins aboard the USS *Langley*. They were withdrawn from carrier duty in 1937, but continued to serve on utility duties until 1940.

Towards the end of the third generation of carrier aircraft, or the beginning of the fourth, depending on how you choose to break the periods, dive-bombing aircraft became popular in both the US and Japan. In fact, several feature films were produced with the dive-bomber as the main theme of the story. However, while they were a good public relations medium for the US Navy,

the films also resulted in a number of misconceptions about the technique, spectacular as it appeared in the films.

At the beginning of 1933 a new and attractive type of carrier fighter-bomber was delivered to the Navy—the Curtiss F11C-2. It was a single-place biplane with very attractive lines. Initially it had a neatly faired, single strut, fixed landing gear, but as the type progressed the landing gear became retractable with the wheels folding flush into the lower sides of the fuselage which had been bellied downward, guppy fashion, to accommodate the retraction mechanism and the fairings for the wheels when retracted.

Bombing Technique

Shortly after delivery in 1933, the 28 F11C-2s were redesignated BFC-2s. They were flown by the US Navy's famed High Hot Squadron VF-1B aboard the *Saratoga*. They remained in service until early 1938. Within the Navy Hawk series they were known as Goshawks and among the export models, basically the same aircraft, there were Turkey Hawks, etc. A pair of these Hawks was purchased by Ernst Udet in 1934 to demonstrate the technique of dive-bombing in Germany. The results of those demonstrations are well-known to the people of Europe who survived the opening days of

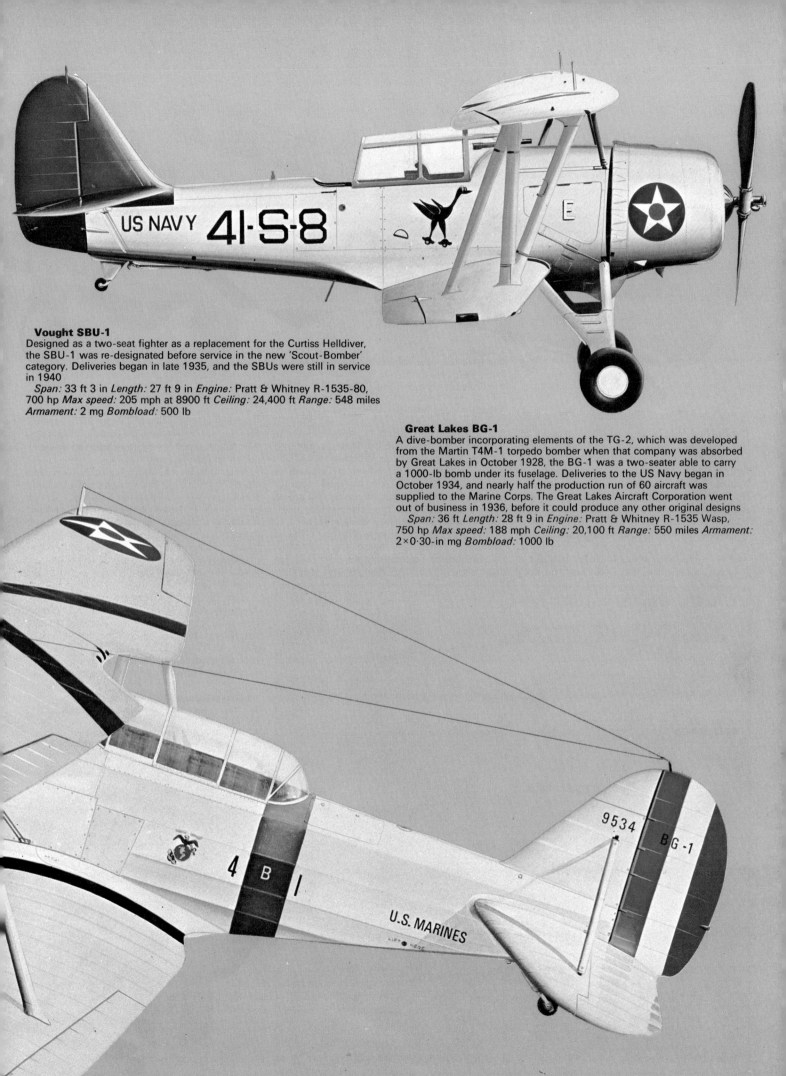

Vought SBU-1
Designed as a two-seat fighter as a replacement for the Curtiss Helldiver, the SBU-1 was re-designated before service in the new 'Scout-Bomber' category. Deliveries began in late 1935, and the SBUs were still in service in 1940
Span: 33 ft 3 in *Length:* 27 ft 9 in *Engine:* Pratt & Whitney R-1535-80, 700 hp *Max speed:* 205 mph at 8900 ft *Ceiling:* 24,400 ft *Range:* 548 miles *Armament:* 2 mg *Bombload:* 500 lb

Great Lakes BG-1
A dive-bomber incorporating elements of the TG-2, which was developed from the Martin T4M-1 torpedo bomber when that company was absorbed by Great Lakes in October 1928, the BG-1 was a two-seater able to carry a 1000-lb bomb under its fuselage. Deliveries to the US Navy began in October 1934, and nearly half the production run of 60 aircraft was supplied to the Marine Corps. The Great Lakes Aircraft Corporation went out of business in 1936, before it could produce any other original designs
Span: 36 ft *Length:* 28 ft 9 in *Engine:* Pratt & Whitney R-1535 Wasp, 750 hp *Max speed:* 188 mph *Ceiling:* 20,100 ft *Range:* 550 miles *Armament:* 2×0·30-in mg *Bombload:* 1000 lb

Northrop BT-1
The BT-1 first flew in 1935 incorporating Northrop's experience in attack bombers for the US Army. When Northrop in turn was taken over by Douglas the technology of this carrier-based scout/dive-bomber was incorporated in the SBD Dauntless
Span: 41 ft 6 in *Length:* 31 ft 8 in *Engine:* Pratt & Whitney R-1535, 825 hp *Max speed:* 222 mph *Ceiling:* 25,300 ft *Range:* 1150 miles

the Second World War and the attacks of the Luftwaffe. They were probably the first aircraft to be specifically designated as fighter-bombers and capable of carrying a bomb or bombs of sufficient size to have more than nuisance value in a tactical situation.

A contemporary of the Curtiss fighter-bombers was another two-place dive-bomber, the Great Lakes BG-1. It was an attractive plane, as large biplanes go, with a good profile and tapered wing planform. In ability, it was a substantial advance over the F8C

(O2C) Helldiver which it replaced at the beginning of 1934. The BG-1s were powered by the 750-hp Pratt & Whitney R-1535-82 engine which made it possible for them to carry a 1000-lb bomb, twice the load capacity of the F8Cs, for a range of nearly 550 miles. They were to remain in active service until 1938 at which time they were relegated to utility and training duties. Of the 60 BG-1s produced about half were assigned to a single carrier squadron, VB-3B/VB-4, for duty aboard the USS *Ranger* and the USS

Saratoga. They were the first of the two-place dive-bombers to incorporate enclosed cockpits for the crew.

Very similar to, though slightly smaller than the BG-1, was the Vought SBU-1 which was slightly faster than the BG-1 but carried only a 500-lb bomb similar to the earlier Helldivers. Range was equal to the BG-1 but the service ceiling was better than the Great Lakes. In comparison, the Great Lakes plane was a better performer with its 1000-lb load. It remained in service until the early 1940s.

Also in the 1933-34 period there was the Japanese Aichi D1A1, Type 94 dive-bomber. This was derived from the Heinkel He 50 single-seat biplane. The successor to this plane, the Type 96 or D1A2 Susie, built in 1936 was quite successful and was built in very large numbers of 428, at a time when

Loire-Nieuport 40/41
The LN 41 dive-bomber, developed from the LN 40 prototype, entered service in 1940 and was immediately thrown into action against invading German forces. Heavy losses were sustained, because the crews had not had sufficient time for training, but earlier trials had shown the aircraft to have a performance similar to that of the Ju 87
Span: 45 ft 11 in *Length:* 32 ft *Engine:* Hispano 12 Xcrs, 690 hp *Max speed:* 162 mph *Ceiling:* 31,200 ft *Range:* 745 miles

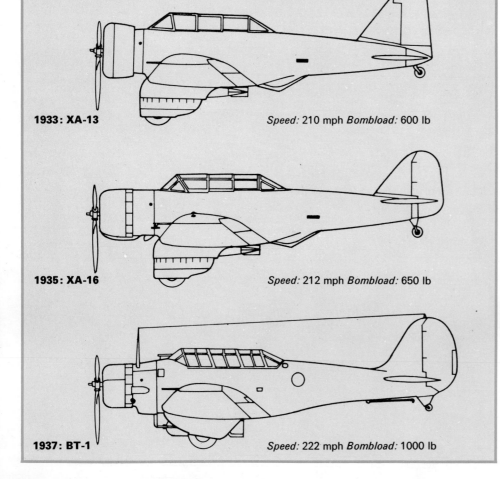

Northrop Navy Dive-Bomber Development

1933: XA-13 *Speed:* 210 mph *Bombload:* 600 lb

1935: XA-16 *Speed:* 212 mph *Bombload:* 650 lb

1937: BT-1 *Speed:* 222 mph *Bombload:* 1000 lb

the US was only ordering groups of 25 to 40 planes at a time. This gives some indication of the serious interest the Japanese Navy was taking in the dive-bombing tactic.

In 1937 two totally different aircraft, the biplane Curtiss SBC Helldiver and the monoplane Vought SB2U Vindicator, were received by the US Navy. The SBC clung to the biplane configuration, even though it

was to be the last biplane combat aircraft produced in the US. The SBC began as a parasol monoplane, the XF12C. Possibly inspired by the Morane-Saulnier 226 the XF12C-1 had many things in common with the Morane including the folding wing of the 226 *bis*. They were contemporaries and both probably were exploring the parasol monoplane configuration to improve the pilot visibility for carrier operations. Looking back, we can see some of the ungainly fuselage configurations—the result of trying to improve or at least maintain the proper degree of visibility over the nose or alongside the nose of the radial engine.

Biplane Comeback

Unlike the Morane, the XF12C-1 was a two-place fighter and the end of the two-place fighter was already in sight. During the testing programme it crashed. It was rebuilt as a scout aircraft, the XS4C-1, at the end of 1933. A second crash spelled the end of the parasol-wing configuration and when the plane was replaced, it was a totally new design, company model 77, US Naval designation XSBC-2. This time they reverted to the proven biplane configuration and completely redesigned the fuselage as well as incorporating a turtle deck of metal rather than the projecting greenhouse canopy of the XF12C-1. In 1936 the original Wright R-1510 was replaced by the Pratt & Whitney R-1535 Twin Wasp and the designation changed to SBC-3. The final configuration was the SBC-4, a few of which were delivered to the *Lexington* and about 15 to the US Marine Corps, but the majority were relegated to reserve squadrons.

Because of a desperate need for aircraft for the *Béarn*, the French were permitted to order 90 SBC-4s but only 44 were aboard when the *Béarn* sailed in June, 1940. Enroute across the Atlantic, the *Béarn* stopped

Vought SB2U Vindicators were the first low-wing monoplane dive-bombers to see service with the US Navy

at Martinique where it remained for the duration. The last photos of these SBC-4s indicated that they were last seen with tattered fabric rotting in a field in Martinique. The British took over the other French aircraft purchase contracts and in doing so, acquired five of the Helldivers which were rechristened Clevelands. Fortunately they never saw combat for they were no match for the fighters frequenting the skies of Europe at this time.

In April 1936, a single prototype Brewster SBA powered by a Wright R-1820-4 engine was produced. Eventually the Naval Aircraft Factory built 30 of these under the designation SBN-1s. Like the Brewster F2A fighters their landing gear did not stand up well to carrier landings and they were used as trainers aboard the USS *Hornet*. They were the first dive-bombers to carry their ordnance, a 500-lb bomb, internally. The successor to the SBA/SBN was the Brewster

Bermuda, known in the US Navy as the SB2A. In July 1940, the British Purchasing Commission ordered 750 of these aircraft and the Dutch Army ordered an additional 162 for the Royal Netherlands East Indies. In 1943 the US Navy purchased 80 SB2A-2s, and in 1944 the US Navy accepted 60 of the SB2A-3 variation—the only one to be equipped with arrester hooks and folding wings for use aboard carriers. With the fall of the Dutch East Indies, their 162 aircraft were acquired by the US Marine Corps to be used as trainers. The only distinctive feature about the SB2As was their ability to carry a bomb load of 1000 lb internally, twice that of their predecessor. They never were used in combat.

At the end of 1937 the US Navy began accepting the Vought SB2U-1s, a low-wing two-place dive-bomber and the first of the low-wing monoplane dive-bombers to actually see combat service. While the transition to monoplane configuration had been made with this aircraft, it was still of composite construction with substantial areas covered with fabric. It also had the distinction of being the first carrier based aircraft to have hydraulically operated wingfolding for stowage aboard ship. At the beginning of the Second World War, SB2Us were serving aboard the USS *Lexington*, USS *Saratoga*,

USS *Ranger*, and USS *Wasp*. They did see combat service in the early stages of the Second World War—flown by Marine pilots in 1942 and at the Battle of Midway.

Torpedo Bombers
STRIKE FROM THE SURFACE

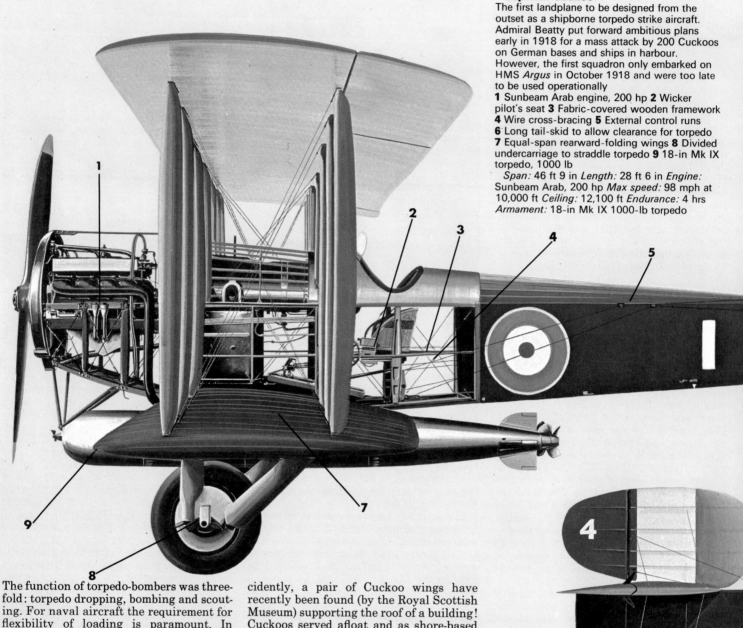

Sopwith Cuckoo
The first landplane to be designed from the outset as a shipborne torpedo strike aircraft. Admiral Beatty put forward ambitious plans early in 1918 for a mass attack by 200 Cuckoos on German bases and ships in harbour. However, the first squadron only embarked on HMS *Argus* in October 1918 and were too late to be used operationally
1 Sunbeam Arab engine, 200 hp **2** Wicker pilot's seat **3** Fabric-covered wooden framework **4** Wire cross-bracing **5** External control runs **6** Long tail-skid to allow clearance for torpedo **7** Equal-span rearward-folding wings **8** Divided undercarriage to straddle torpedo **9** 18-in Mk IX torpedo, 1000 lb
Span: 46 ft 9 in *Length:* 28 ft 6 in *Engine:* Sunbeam Arab, 200 hp *Max speed:* 98 mph at 10,000 ft *Ceiling:* 12,100 ft *Endurance:* 4 hrs *Armament:* 18-in Mk IX 1000-lb torpedo

The function of torpedo-bombers was threefold: torpedo dropping, bombing and scouting. For naval aircraft the requirement for flexibility of loading is paramount. In almost all cases provision must be made for substituting fuel for ordnance load to alter the function of the aircraft from attack to scouting.

The Sopwith/Blackburn Cuckoo was the pioneer torpedo-bomber finally introduced in mid-1918. When Admiral Beatty heard of this type of plane, he asked for 200 to be produced as soon as possible. Until this time the Grand Fleet had not shown much interest in torpedo planes. However, the Germans were known to have seaplane torpedo planes ready at North Sea bases and the British fleet did not want to be short-handed with weapons in case the German High Seas Fleet decided to make a break for open water beyond the North Sea.

Though 350 were ordered, less than 100 were delivered by the time of the Armistice. Their first use was at the Torpedo Aeroplane School at East Fortune where, in-

cidentally, a pair of Cuckoo wings have recently been found (by the Royal Scottish Museum) supporting the roof of a building! Cuckoos served afloat and as shore-based aircraft until early 1923. By this time they had been embarked on the carriers in commission during this period, *Argus*, *Eagle* and *Furious*. As in the case of their contemporaries, they were of wooden structure and fabric covered. Their powerplants were either the 200-hp Sunbeam Arab or, in the case of the Cuckoo Mk II, the Wolseley Viper engine. Their speed was in keeping with their times, slightly over 100 mph.

The 18-in torpedo for which the Cuckoo was designed as a carrier was found to be inadequate for the job and an earlier Mk with greater explosive charge was proposed as a replacement. To carry this heavier torpedo, contracts were negotiated for the purchase of a Cuckoo replacement. As a result the Blackburn Blackbird was designed. It was not an attractive aircraft by any standards, but it was the first of a long line of Blackburn aircraft designed as

torpedo aircraft and adopted as standard by the RAF. Being a contemporary or follow-on to the Cuckoo, it suffered from many of the disadvantages of the times, not the least of which were a clear-cut idea of what was wanted and how to design an aircraft for a carrier whose design was still experimental, especially the arrester system.

The Blackburd was ungainly, an ugly box with wings and a landing gear that could drop free after takeoff. The wheels, mounted on a solid axle, had to be dropped to permit launching a torpedo. After dropping the

Short seaplane drops its torpedo. The type made history in 1915 when a Short Type 184 from HMS Ben-my-Chree *became the first aircraft in the world to sink an enemy ship—a Turkish steamer— by means of a torpedo*

gear and launching its torpedo, the aircraft was landed aboard the carrier on a pair of skids which were very similar to those used on the contemporary Sopwith Pups and 1½ Strutters but adapted to the greater weight of the Blackburd.

The Germans had no carrier at this time and relied on float seaplanes for torpedo dropping, as did the US Navy. The Curtiss R-6Ls which were Liberty-powered float planes were modified to carry torpedoes after the war. The R-4 and R-6 series were generally referred to as scaled up JN-4 Jennies all of which had been designed as

Blackburn Blackburd

The first Blackburn aircraft designed specifically for torpedo-carrying, the Blackburd was intended for rapid and easy production. The wheels used for take-off had to be jettisoned before the torpedo could be released, leaving skids available for landing

Span: 52 ft 6 in *Length:* 36 ft 3 in *Engine:* Rolls-Royce Eagle VIII, 350 hp *Max speed:* 95 mph *Ceiling:* 12,000 ft *Endurance:* 3 hrs (with torpedo) *Bombload:* 1×1400 lb Mk VIII torpedo

Blackburn Ripon
The FAA's standard carrier-borne torpedo bomber in the early 1930s.
Although the prototype first flew in 1928, the type soldiered on
re-engined with a Pegasus radial as the Blackburn Baffin
Span: 44 ft 10 in *Length:* 36 ft 9 in *Engine:* Napier Lion XIA, 500 hp
Max speed: 116 mph at sea level *Ceiling:* 13,000 ft

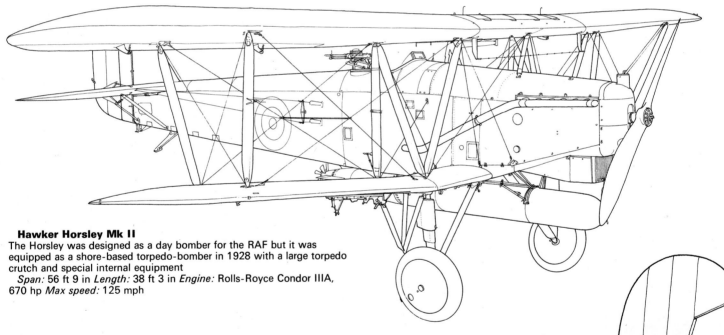

Hawker Horsley Mk II
The Horsley was designed as a day bomber for the RAF but it was
equipped as a shore-based torpedo-bomber in 1928 with a large torpedo
crutch and special internal equipment
Span: 56 ft 9 in *Length:* 38 ft 3 in *Engine:* Rolls-Royce Condor IIIA,
670 hp *Max speed:* 125 mph

trainers and observation aircraft. Originally powered by the Curtiss V-2 engines, the modification to the Liberty engine nearly doubled its power and made possible the carrying of the torpedoes.

In this same category of float plane torpedo-carriers was the Short 320 which was the largest float plane to enter service during the First World War. Though 110 aircraft of this type had been received by the end of the war, they were dropped in favour of the carrier-borne Cuckoos. Their performance was less than impressive though their 75-ft wingspan would not fail to catch one's eye for they were the same size as the Curtiss H-4 Small America flying boats undergoing trials at Felixstowe.

Second generation torpedo bombers included the Levasseur PL2A2 which was readied for the French carrier *Béarn*. The aircraft was flying in a squadron unit in

1923, fully three years before the *Béarn* was ready for service. Problems with the Renault 580-hp engine resulted in these planes being used for trainers rather than remaining aboard the carrier as operational squadron aircraft. In 1926 a new design was begun to replace the PL2s. The new model, the PL7, made its first flight in 1928, but details of the production model were not finalized until 1931. After experiencing structural failure in 1931, they were grounded until 1932. They were finally reinstated, serving until the beginning of the Second World War in 1939, as no replacement had been ordered.

In 1921 an improvement was made in the form of the torpedo plane. The fabric-covered box frame was still the basic form but a number of improvements were made, the most obvious being the landing gear. Instead of the droppable wheel and axle of

the Blackburd, the landing gear of the Blackburn Dart was split to enable the torpedo to be loaded and dropped without first dropping the wheels. Though it was an improvement, the landing gear of the Dart was still an ungainly bridge-like structure with wheels attached to the outboard ends. The upper cowling between the pilot and the 450-hp Napier Lion engine sloped

The Levasseur PL7 was the last French carrier-based torpedo bomber. After being withdrawn from service because of structural failures the type was redeployed and remained operational until 1939

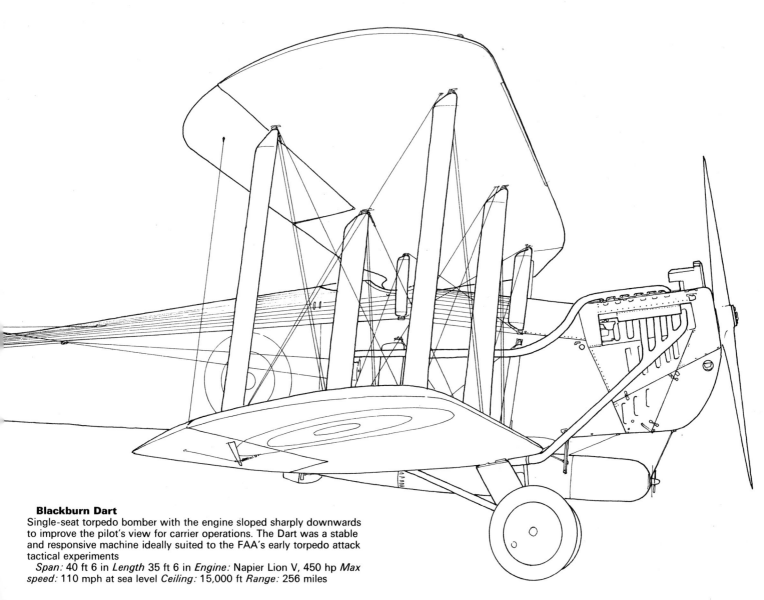

Blackburn Dart
Single-seat torpedo bomber with the engine sloped sharply downwards to improve the pilot's view for carrier operations. The Dart was a stable and responsive machine ideally suited to the FAA's early torpedo attack tactical experiments
   Span: 40 ft 6 in *Length* 35 ft 6 in *Engine:* Napier Lion V, 450 hp *Max speed:* 110 mph at sea level *Ceiling:* 15,000 ft *Range:* 256 miles

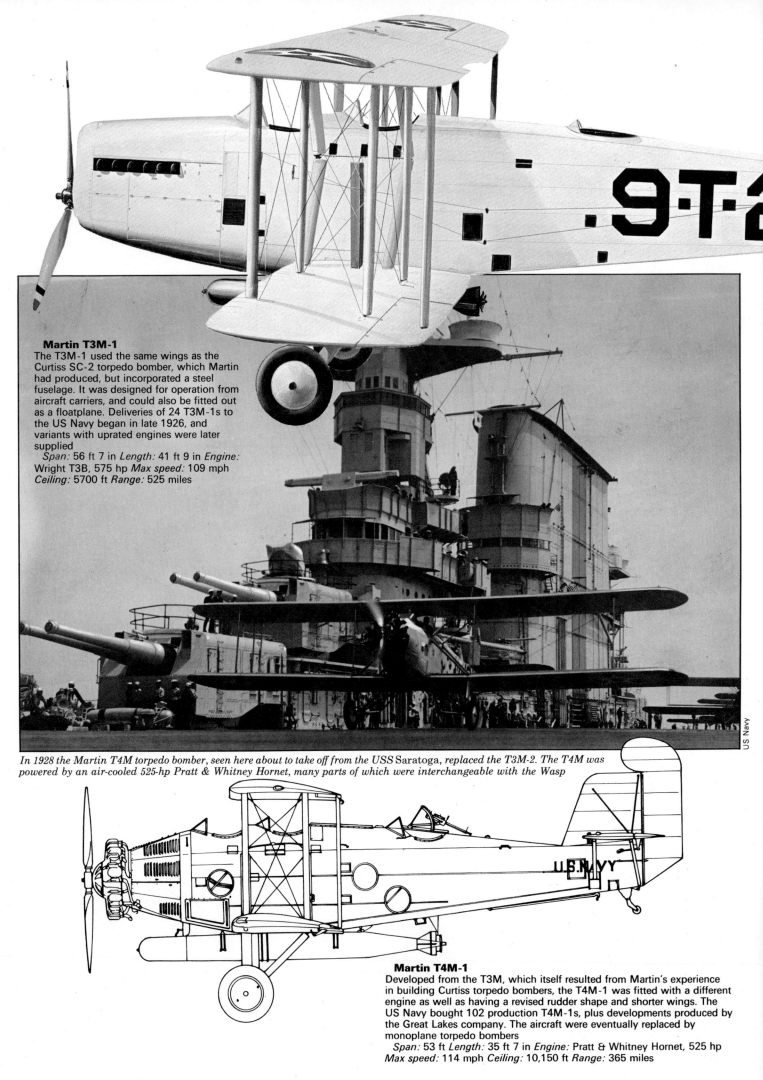

Martin T3M-1

The T3M-1 used the same wings as the Curtiss SC-2 torpedo bomber, which Martin had produced, but incorporated a steel fuselage. It was designed for operation from aircraft carriers, and could also be fitted out as a floatplane. Deliveries of 24 T3M-1s to the US Navy began in late 1926, and variants with uprated engines were later supplied

Span: 56 ft 7 in *Length:* 41 ft 9 in *Engine:* Wright T3B, 575 hp *Max speed:* 109 mph *Ceiling:* 5700 ft *Range:* 525 miles

In 1928 the Martin T4M torpedo bomber, seen here about to take off from the USS Saratoga, replaced the T3M-2. The T4M was powered by an air-cooled 525-hp Pratt & Whitney Hornet, many parts of which were interchangeable with the Wasp

US Navy

Martin T4M-1

Developed from the T3M, which itself resulted from Martin's experience in building Curtiss torpedo bombers, the T4M-1 was fitted with a different engine as well as having a revised rudder shape and shorter wings. The US Navy bought 102 production T4M-1s, plus developments produced by the Great Lakes company. The aircraft were eventually replaced by monoplane torpedo bombers

Span: 53 ft *Length:* 35 ft 7 in *Engine:* Pratt & Whitney Hornet, 525 hp *Max speed:* 114 mph *Ceiling:* 10,150 ft *Range:* 365 miles

abruptly downward and to the sides to preserve the possible view forward for the approach and landing of this massive box-like structure with wings. For its time, it was produced in large numbers (117) and entered service in 1923. What it lacked in performance, it made up in ease of handling. It did its job well and was used in the many exercises that were necessary to mate the aircraft and ship. A tribute to its ease of handling is the fact that the Dart was the first plane to make a night landing aboard a carrier.

As originally produced it was a single-place aircraft but a twin float version was created and fitted with a second cockpit, for there was ample room for at *least* one additional crew member in the cavernous fuselage. Further testimony to the acceptability of the Dart was the fact that production did not cease until 1927, four years

The Blackburn Shark torpedo bomber and reconnaissance aircraft combined experience gained with the Dart, Ripon and Baffin. It entered service in 1935 and was eventually replaced by the Swordfish

John Batchelor

Blackburn Shark
Designed to operate both from land and as a seaplane, the Shark was a two/three-seat torpedo bomber and reconnaissance aircraft which entered service with the Fleet Air Arm in 1935. The 16 Mk Is were followed by 126 Mk IIs and 95 Mk IIIs, the type eventually being replaced as a front-line aircraft by the Swordfish in 1938
Span: 46 ft *Length:* 35 ft 2 in *Engine:* Armstrong Siddeley Tiger VIc, 700 hp *Max speed:* 152 mph *Ceiling:* 16,400 ft *Range:* 625 miles *Armament:* 1 Vickers mg, 1 Vickers-Berthier mg *Bombload:* torpedo or 1500 lb

after entering service, and reserve units continued to operate them as late as 1935. They were of wood and fabric construction with large two-bay constant chord biplane wings. Ailerons were fitted to both upper and lower wings and automatic slots were fitted to the upper wings in line with the ailerons. These features undoubtedly contributed to their controllability and long active service.

The Dart, when it was phased out, was followed by another Blackburn torpedo plane, the Ripon, which became the standard torpedo plane of the Fleet Air Arm late in 1929. There was a strong family

resemblance though the fuselage took on more attractive lines and the landing gear improved visibly from that of the Blackburd and Dart. The angle of the cowling was retained for operational reasons and the power was increased by the installation of the 570-hp Napier Lion XIA. It was intended

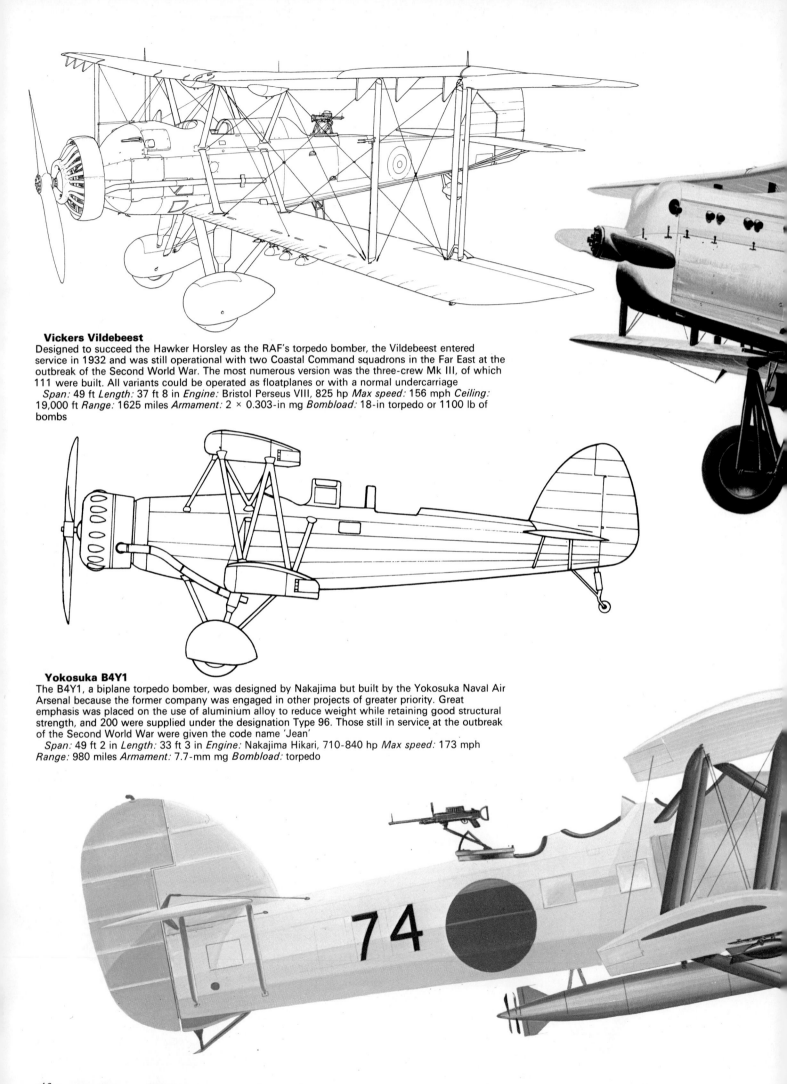

Vickers Vildebeest

Designed to succeed the Hawker Horsley as the RAF's torpedo bomber, the Vildebeest entered service in 1932 and was still operational with two Coastal Command squadrons in the Far East at the outbreak of the Second World War. The most numerous version was the three-crew Mk III, of which 111 were built. All variants could be operated as floatplanes or with a normal undercarriage

Span: 49 ft *Length:* 37 ft 8 in *Engine:* Bristol Perseus VIII, 825 hp *Max speed:* 156 mph *Ceiling:* 19,000 ft *Range:* 1625 miles *Armament:* 2 × 0.303-in mg *Bombload:* 18-in torpedo or 1100 lb of bombs

Yokosuka B4Y1

The B4Y1, a biplane torpedo bomber, was designed by Nakajima but built by the Yokosuka Naval Air Arsenal because the former company was engaged in other projects of greater priority. Great emphasis was placed on the use of aluminium alloy to reduce weight while retaining good structural strength, and 200 were supplied under the designation Type 96. Those still in service at the outbreak of the Second World War were given the code name 'Jean'

Span: 49 ft 2 in *Length:* 33 ft 3 in *Engine:* Nakajima Hikari, 710-840 hp *Max speed:* 173 mph *Range:* 980 miles *Armament:* 7.7-mm mg *Bombload:* torpedo

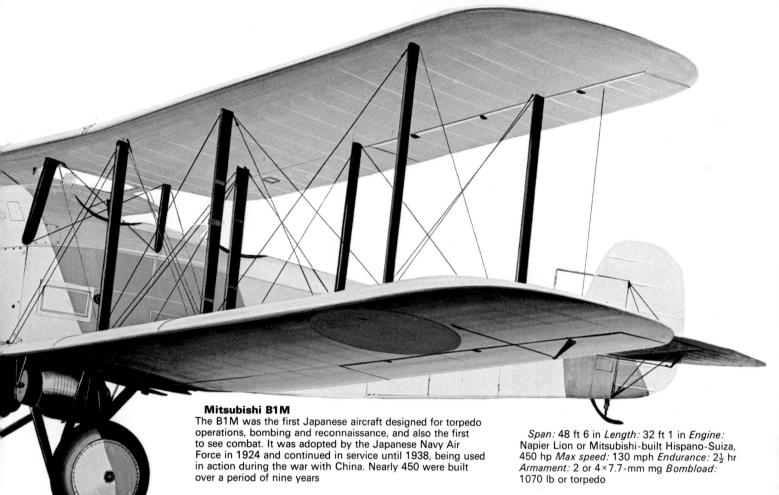

Mitsubishi B1M

The B1M was the first Japanese aircraft designed for torpedo operations, bombing and reconnaissance, and also the first to see combat. It was adopted by the Japanese Navy Air Force in 1924 and continued in service until 1938, being used in action during the war with China. Nearly 450 were built over a period of nine years

Span: 48 ft 6 in *Length:* 32 ft 1 in *Engine:* Napier Lion or Mitsubishi-built Hispano-Suiza, 450 hp *Max speed:* 130 mph *Endurance:* $2\frac{1}{2}$ hr *Armament:* 2 or 4×7.7-mm mg *Bombload:* 1070 lb or torpedo

to be used, from the outset, as a dual purpose aircraft for torpedo work and long-range reconnaissance. For reconnaissance work it had a range of over 1000 miles (14 hours) and in the torpedo configuration its range was 815 miles, almost double that of its predecessor. To cope with the navigation, it was designed to carry a crew of two.

The Ripons merged with the Baffins that succeeded them. The Baffins were, in fact, originally called Ripon Vs in their proto-type stage and as the Baffins came into service 68 surviving Ripons were converted to Baffin configuration. This change from Ripon to Baffin consisted mainly of changing engines from the water-cooled Napier Lion to the air-cooled Bristol Pegasus, cleaning up the landing gear details and increasing the length by about 2 ft—all very trivial. The results were interesting though, for with a slight reduction in available power and the substitution of the air-cooled engine, the airspeed actually increased by 10 mph.

In America, Martin T3M-1 and T3M-2s were produced in substantial numbers in 1926 and 1927, powered by the Wright and Packard engines. They carried equipment that gradual experience indicated was necessary. In September 1928, the first torpedo planes to go aboard a US carrier were the Martin T3M-2s, employed aboard the USS *Lexington*. These aircraft also had the distinction of being the last of the water-cooled engine torpedo planes in the US Navy. They were replaced in 1928 by the Martin T4M-1 powered by the Pratt & Whitney Hornet air-cooled engine which produced 525 hp. One of the most important features of this new engine was that many

parts were interchangeable with the Pratt & Whitney Wasp engines, already in extensive service use. This unique feature reduced the spare parts stocked aboard ship, a very important feature where space and weight, not to forget cost, are important. Almost identical to the T4M-1s were the Great Lakes TG-1s and TG-2s. These designations resulted when the Detroit Aircraft Company purchased the Cleveland plant of the Martin Company when Martin moved to Baltimore.

The fourth generation of torpedo bombers consisted of the Blackburn Shark, the Fairey Swordfish and the Douglas SBD.

Continuing its hold on the torpedo-plane market, Blackburn had in-hand a replacement for its own Baffin. During 1934-35 tests were underway on the Blackburn Shark. It still retained that all-important high position for the pilot for good visibility, but aside from that and the basic geometry of the machine, it was a rather drastic technological change from its predecessors.

Aside from this one peculiarity, the Shark had a well constructed, robust appearance which included a cowled air-cooled Armstrong-Siddeley Tiger VI engine of 760 hp. In addition to being a torpedo plane, it became a spotter-reconnaissance plane with provision for a third crew member. However, refinement in structure and powerplant performance of the Shark over its predecessors was not sufficient to give it more than passing notice in the progression of torpedo planes, for its successor was the Fairey Swordfish. The Swordfish's long career in the Second World War puts the biplane torpedo-bomber with the Avengers and Barracudas covered in that section.

Mitsubishi B2M

Built for the Japanese Navy as a replacement for the B1M, the B2M was a disappointment in service and never really replaced the earlier machine. It was in service from 1932 to 1937 and saw limited service during the Sino-Japanese war

Span: 49 ft 11 in *Length:* 33 ft 8 in *Engine:* Mitsubishi-built Hispano-Suiza, 600 hp *Max speed:* 132 mph *Ceiling:* 14,300 ft *Range:* 1100 miles *Armament:* 2×7.7-mm mg *Bombload:* 1764 lb torpedo

SERVICING THE FLEET

Imperial War Museum

Sqn Cdr Bigsworth and the Avro 504B he used to attack Zeppelin LZ39 over Ostend on May 17, 1915. The Avro 504 was the Royal Navy's best combat aircraft in 1914 serving as bomber, fighter and reconnaissance aircraft but was soon relegated to secondary roles becoming an outstanding basic trainer

Westland Walrus

Designed as a shipboard utility aircraft the Walrus used surplus D.H.9 wings and was characterised by humps and bulges for its special equipment. The undercarriage was equipped with complex arresting gear and flotation bags
Span: 46 ft 2 in *Length:* 30 ft *Engine:* Napier Lion II, 450 hp *Max speed:* 110 mph

Aeromarine 39B

The USN's first shipboard trainer, first flown in 1917. In October 1922 Cdr G deC Chevalier USN made the first landing on the USS *Langley* in an Aeromarine 39B
Span: 47 ft *Length:* 30 ft 4.25 in *Engine:* Curtiss OXX6, 100 hp *Max speed:* 73 mph at sea level *Ceiling:* 5000 ft *Range:* 273 miles

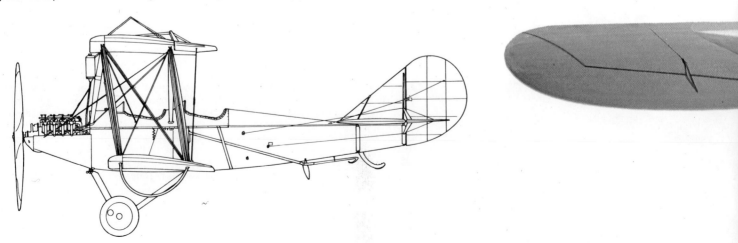

Though few in numbers, the variety of aircraft that came within this category covers the entire span of carrier aviation operations. From the very beginning, the aircraft that were first experimentally operated from carriers were trainers or multi-purpose aircraft. Probably best known of these is the Avro 504, which because of its docile flying characteristics and its period of operation, was used in almost every category including bombing and as an anti-Zeppelin fighter.

Though not operated from a carrier at that time, 504s were used in the historic RNAS raid of November 21, 1914, on the Zeppelin sheds at Friedrichshafen on Lake Constance. Three 504s, each armed with four 20-lb bombs, attacked from an altitude of 700 ft and succeeded in exploding a gas works with spectacular results and also severely damaged one Zeppelin. Later, on May 16-17, two RNAS Avros intercepted two Zeppelins in the vicinity of Ostend. Though the Zeppelins were damaged by the Avros' 20-lb bombs they escaped complete destruction.

The Avros were included in the aircraft types making the carrier landings and take-offs in the 1915-1917 period, and one of the first aircraft to be launched by catapult was an Avro 504H, piloted by Flight Commander R E Penny in 1917.

The 504s' extensive use as trainers is well known and, in this configuration were the first aircraft to be selected by the Japanese Navy when they began their carrier operations. Their simple wood and fabric airframe and generous wing area encouraged the use of these Avros whenever a new development was attempted. Their rotary engines made them the logical transition trainers for pilots training to fly the Parnall Panther, which was to be one of the first British aircraft to be designed from the outset for carrier operation.

Hump-Backed

The Panther was a two-place spotter/reconnaissance machine, but was not fitted with dual controls. It has a hump-backed fuselage, appearing to have the crew cockpits mounted on top of a Nieuport fuselage. The pilot was afforded a good view for carrier landings by being perched on top of and slightly to the rear of the 230-hp Bentley BR2 rotary engine. The Panther was equipped with all the accoutrements of the early carrier aircraft including flotation bags, hydrofoil fitted to the landing gear and axle hooks to engage the landing wires then in use aboard the *Argus* and *Hermes*.

Additionally, the Panther was unique in that it could be folded for stowage aboard ship. The unusual aspect of this folding was that the fuselage was folded rather than the wings, as became standardized at a later date. The fold point was immediately behind the observer's cockpit and required an indentation in the curved starboard side of the fuselage at the hinge line, a concession to reducing the complexity of folding the fuselage. The wing span was 29 ft 6 in, keeping it marginally under the 30-ft limit of the aircraft lift aboard the carriers. Since Panthers were not intended for combat, their only armament was a single ·303 Lewis gun mounted for defence purposes in the rear observer's cockpit. Their airframe was constructed of wood with fabric covering.

Loening M-8-0
In 1918 the Loening company was asked to develop a two-seat fighter for the US Navy able to outperform the British Bristol Fighter. The result was the monoplane M-8-0 but the 46 production models delivered saw shipboard service as observation aircraft
Span: 32 ft 9 in *Length:* 24 ft *Engine:* Hispano-Suiza, 300 hp *Max speed:* 145 mph *Ceiling:* 22,000 ft *Armament:* 2 Lewis mg

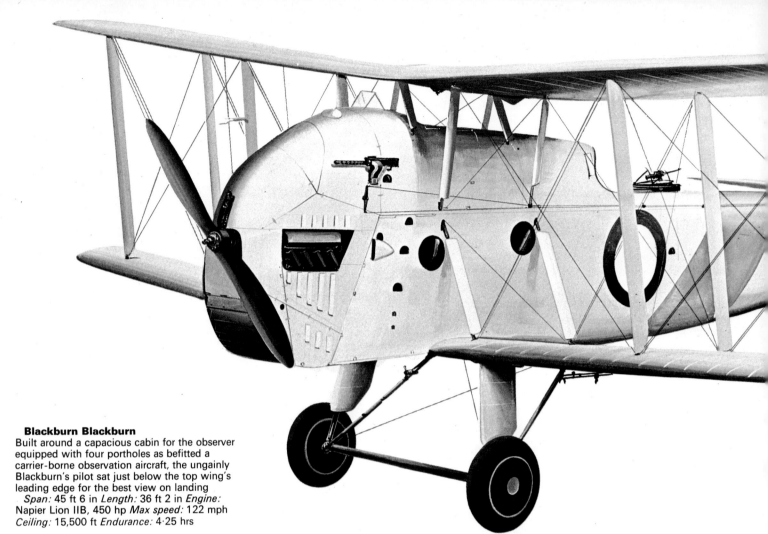

Blackburn Blackburn
Built around a capacious cabin for the observer equipped with four portholes as befitted a carrier-borne observation aircraft, the ungainly Blackburn's pilot sat just below the top wing's leading edge for the best view on landing
Span: 45 ft 6 in *Length:* 36 ft 2 in *Engine:* Napier Lion IIB, 450 hp *Max speed:* 122 mph *Ceiling:* 15,500 ft *Endurance:* 4·25 hrs

Despite this construction and the idiosyncrasies of their rotary engines, they remained in service until 1926. In 1919, 12 Panthers were sold to the Japanese Navy as trainers for reconnaissance pilots.

The first aircraft actually designed for spotter/reconnaissance duties after the Armistice was the Westland Walrus. Its service life was overlapped by the Panther just described. The Walrus was the result of an economy drive that usually follows a major military effort. The de Havilland D.H.9As were redesigned into a configuration suitable for carrier deck operation. The resulting aircraft was surely one of the most unattractive of all times. There really was no redeeming feature to this aircraft other than the modest out-of-pocket initial cost. To make this conversion the D.H.9A was the point of departure, to which was added space for a third crew member, flotation gear, detachable wings and special landing gear fixtures to grasp the longitudinal deck cables in a manner similar to cable car grippers. These served as brakes for landing, since wheel brakes were not in use at this date. With a humped turtle deck aft of the rear cockpit, a pannier bulge beneath the fuselage for the observer, flotation bags extending from under the lower wings forward to the front of the engine and a radiator suspended beneath, the Walrus can only be described as a flying apparition. In 1925 the 36 Walruses were phased out of service to be replaced by Blackburn Blackburds and Avro Bisons, both designed for the same duty, spotter/reconnaissance.

As for the Avro Bison, there was some merit in this choice of name for, in profile and general overall ugliness, it could be compared with its namesake, the bison, a massive beast, native to the Plains states of

North America. The Bison was a slab-sided, hump-backed monstrosity whose one good feature appears to have been a very substantial 'picture window' for the observer on both sides of the fuselage just forward of the rear cockpit. Its wing span of 46 ft made it necessary to find a means for folding it. As it developed, the wing panels, completely rigged, were folded backward to rest between the wing stub and the horizontal stabilizer. Performance was less than spectacular. Since it was intended for spotting and reconnaissance this was no great failing though its range of 360 miles would not qualify it for any accolades.

Designed for Comfort
The Bison's successor, the Blackburn Blackburn, was slightly improved in performance with a range of about 440 miles. Along with the Bison and the Walrus, the Blackburn was designed with the comfort of the navigator/observer in mind and with little regard for aesthetics or aerodynamic streamlining. The pilot was 'mounted' directly above the rear of the Napier Lion engine, in what appears to be an appendage to the forward fuselage which extended to a notched break in the fuselage at the trailing edge of the lower wing. To the rear of this notch, a gunner's cockpit was installed with a Scarff ring mount. To the rear of the engine, directly under the pilot, and back to the trailing edge of the wing was the compartment for the navigator/observer. From the dimensions of the fuselage, in the area described, this crew member had an accommodation not unlike an 'efficiency apartment' complete with two porthole windows on each side to maintain the nautical flavour. These were the ugly sisters of the Blackburn Dart torpedo-bomber

which is to say they were really unattractive, for the Dart was not a thing of beauty. The total Mk I and Mk II Blackburns amounted to 62 aircraft constructed and operated from 1922 until they were declared obsolete in 1935.

A side-by-side seat trainer variant of the Blackburn known as the Blackburn Bull carried the design to absurd lengths. The drag was so high as to make its operation from existing land bases extremely risky, without adding the danger, if not the impossibility, of operating from a carrier. Only two aircraft of this type were built.

The second generation carrier aircraft had the benefit of technical improvements in a number of details but the aircraft in carrier service were still left-overs from First World War designs. As such, they were still of the wood and fabric structure characteristic of the period of their design but modified by the addition of a tail hook and the axle hooks that were then in favour.

The two aircraft trainer/utility types that figured prominently in early US carrier operation were the Aeromarine 39B and the Vought VE-7. The VE-7SF, piloted by Lt VC Griffin, made the first takeoff from the carrier USS *Langley* on October 17, 1922, and on October 26, 1922, Lt Cdr Godfrey de Chevalier landed an Aeromarine 39B aboard the USS *Langley* while underway.

The Fairey IIID was of later design but still of the wood and fabric construction as were the Aeromarine and Voughts. The IIIDs entered service in 1924 and continued service until 1930. They were developed from the IIIC which was well-proven, having been produced before the Armistice and used during the period following the war. The IIIDs were used extensively as carrier based landplanes from HMS *Argus* and also

Imperial War Museum

The 450 hp Napier engine had great difficulty pulling this float-equipped Blackburn Blackburn through the air so great was the 'built in headwind' from wires, struts and the ungainly fuselage

as floatplanes with HMS *Vindictive*. This dual capability was a standard feature of most naval aircraft of this period, including the Aeromarine 39 and Vought VE-7, mentioned previously.

The third generation was characterized by a shift to metal fuselage structures with wood wing structure still the standard. Notable among these aircraft was the

Fairey IIIF, a further refinement of the IIID, but really a complete redesign. The fuselage, of tubular steel construction, was refined aerodynamically as well. Possibly the best-known aircraft type between the wars, the IIIF served aboard every operating British carrier. During their operating life, from 1927 to 1940, over 350 of this aircraft were produced. During this extremely

lengthy period numerous structural changes took place, the most significant of which was the transition to all-metal primary structure. Also during their tenure, another technical detail was resolved.

During the early days of carrier operation, the deck wires were stretched longitudinally to the detriment of aircraft landing gears. Then, because of excessive damage to landing gears, landing wires were eliminated altogether, but as aircraft weight and speeds increased interest in arrester systems were renewed. A Fairey IIIF was used to experiment with the tail hooks used, with the transverse arrester wires similar to those still in use aboard carriers today. The IIIF could be mounted on twin floats to be used aboard battleships and were fitted to carry a light load of bombs, up to 500 lb, under the wings. In keeping with their limited combat capability, they carried only one forward firing Vickers machine-gun and one free-swivelling Lewis gun in the rear cockpit.

The Fairey Seal followed the IIIF and was

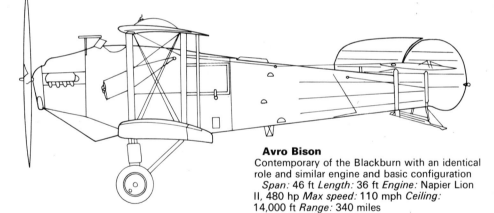

Avro Bison
Contemporary of the Blackburn with an identical role and similar engine and basic configuration
Span: 46 ft *Length:* 36 ft *Engine:* Napier Lion II, 480 hp *Max speed:* 110 mph *Ceiling:* 14,000 ft *Range:* 340 miles

Blackburn Shark comes in to land on HMS Courageous, *the handling crews already running to grab the plane as soon as it settles*

US Navy

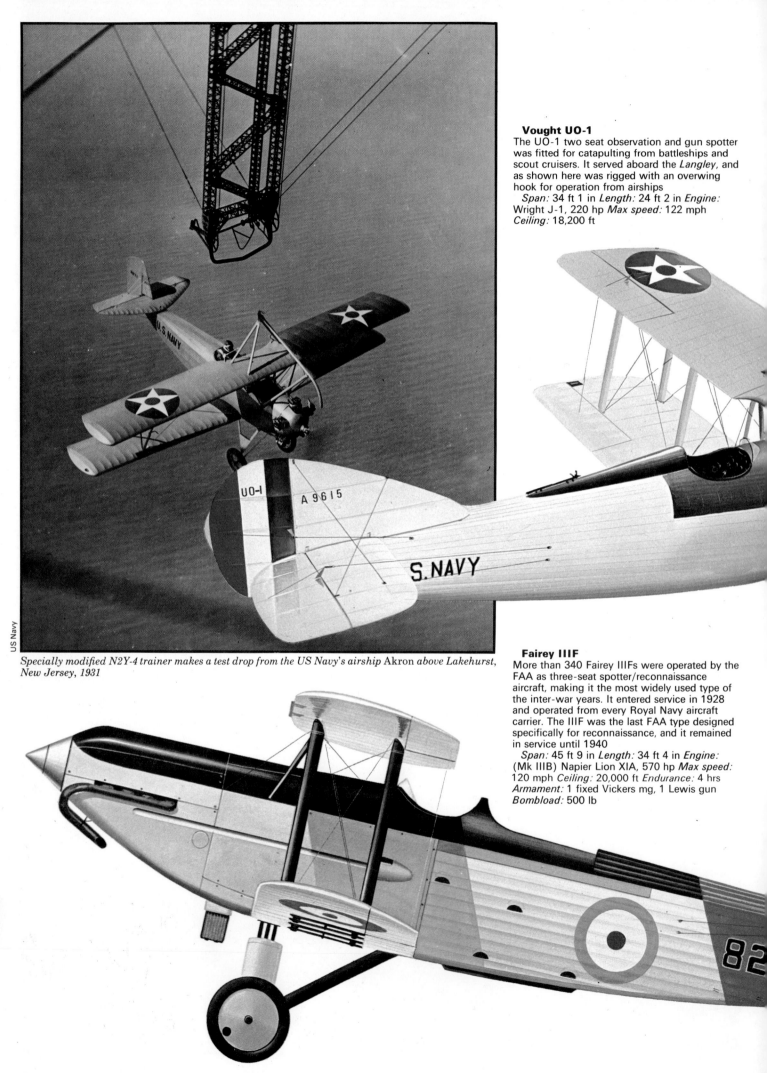

Vought UO-1

The UO-1 two seat observation and gun spotter was fitted for catapulting from battleships and scout cruisers. It served aboard the *Langley*, and as shown here was rigged with an overwing hook for operation from airships
Span: 34 ft 1 in *Length:* 24 ft 2 in *Engine:* Wright J-1, 220 hp *Max speed:* 122 mph *Ceiling:* 18,200 ft

Specially modified N2Y-4 trainer makes a test drop from the US Navy's airship Akron *above Lakehurst, New Jersey, 1931*

Fairey IIIF

More than 340 Fairey IIIFs were operated by the FAA as three-seat spotter/reconnaissance aircraft, making it the most widely used type of the inter-war years. It entered service in 1928 and operated from every Royal Navy aircraft carrier. The IIIF was the last FAA type designed specifically for reconnaissance, and it remained in service until 1940
Span: 45 ft 9 in *Length:* 34 ft 4 in *Engine:* (Mk IIIB) Napier Lion XIA, 570 hp *Max speed:* 120 mph *Ceiling:* 20,000 ft *Endurance:* 4 hrs *Armament:* 1 fixed Vickers mg, 1 Lewis gun *Bombload:* 500 lb

Vought O2U Corsair
Conceived as two seat fighter quickly convertible as a landplane or floatplane, the Corsair saw most service as an observation machine
Span: 34 ft 6 in *Length:* 24 ft 8 in *Engine:* Pratt & Whitney Wasp, 425 hp *Max speed:* 151 mph *Ceiling:* 22,100 ft
Range: 580 miles *Armament:* 2 Browning mg, 2 Lewis mg

An early experiment with parasite fighters involved the airship R23 and Sopwith Camels in the summer of 1918. The aircraft was attached to a horizontal surface under the airship's keel. The war ended before the proposal could proceed beyond the experimental stage

Imperial War Museum

Imperial War Museum

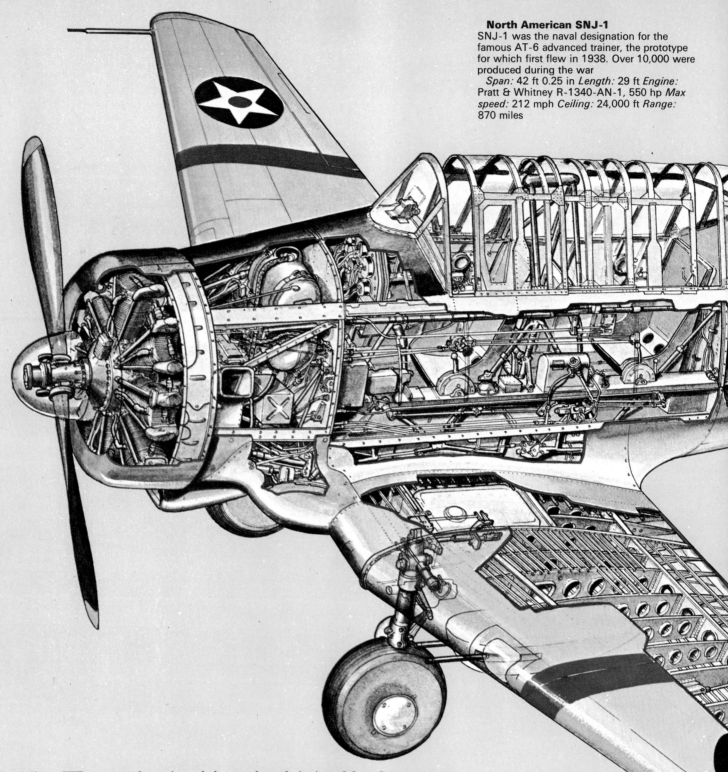

North American SNJ-1
SNJ-1 was the naval designation for the famous AT-6 advanced trainer, the prototype for which first flew in 1938. Over 10,000 were produced during the war
Span: 42 ft 0.25 in *Length:* 29 ft *Engine:* Pratt & Whitney R-1340-AN-1, 550 hp *Max speed:* 212 mph *Ceiling:* 24,000 ft *Range:* 870 miles

essentially a IIIF converted to air-cooled engine. The IIIF used the 570-hp Napier Lion engine and the Seal was powered by the 525-hp Armstrong-Siddeley Panther engine. In spite of the reduction of horsepower, the maximum speed actually increased from 120 mph for the IIIF to 138 mph for the Seal.

The concept of spotter/reconnaissance aircraft was running out of favour with their duties being added to new design requirements of other aircraft. As a result, some squadrons were re-equipped with Fairey Swordfish by 1938, the other squadrons converting to the Blackburn Sharks (torpedo planes) as early as 1935, the year that production of the Seals ended. As a part of their training programme, both construction-wise and operationally, a number of Seals were purchased by the Japanese Navy but these were about the last of the aircraft imports of any size, for they were about to

purchase their aircraft from Japanese manufacturers as a means of developing their own design and production capabilities.

The Vought O2U Corsair was the US contemporary of the Fairey IIIF and, like the IIIF, it was capable of operating from catapults or from carrier decks. A notable difference in operating philosophy between the British on one hand, and the American and Japanese on the other hand, concerned the floats. The British favoured two parallel and equal displacement floats while the US and the Japanese favoured a single main float with smaller outrigger wing-tip floats to maintain balance when at rest. The US technique dates back to the first naval aircraft and the decision by Glenn H Curtiss to use the single float. The single float prevented an imbalance should the float develop a leak for any reason. A single float might fill a compartment if damaged and prevent takeoff, but the landing or takeoff, if poss-

ible, would be in a balanced condition. Also, when taxiing at high speed, the single float offers less resistance, the wing floats are well clear of the water at planning speed, and balance is achieved somewhat like riding a bicycle. Additionally, waves striking twin floats unequally have a tendency to twist the floats and their fittings. The twin floats, however, generally speaking, are easier to train on and make for easier entry to and egress from the aircraft. Twin floats find their greatest use in civil aircraft.

The O2Us entered operational service in 1927 with 130 O2U-1s, plus two prototypes. They followed the pattern of their contemporaries: tandem two-place biplanes with a single .30 cal machine-gun firing

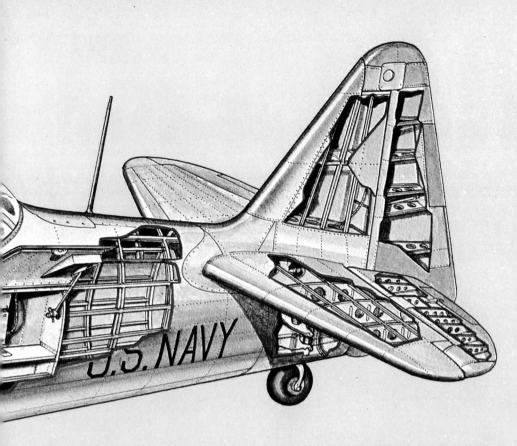

E Byrd as the detachment commander.

The Army used them for surveys and several famous flights, the most notable being the first South American Goodwill Flight in 1927. The importance of the flight was lost in the publicity resulting from the trans-atlantic attempts and their return to the US coincided with Lindberg's famous solo transatlantic flight in May 1927.

Various engine installations were used in the Loenings. The most interesting to Loening was the first inverted Liberty installation. Other than the Loenings, the only other widely used amphibians were the Supermarine Walrus and the Grumman JF-1 which, in general, resembled the Loening design formula.

The Walrus was of a flying boat configuration and was stressed for catapult launching which made it one of the most versatile spotter/reconnaissance aircraft to see naval service. Its versatility resulted in a very large production run of over 740 aircraft and a useful service from 1933 to 1944. This was a long period of service for an ungainly looking biplane in an era when transition to monoplanes was in progress. Like its equally improbable contemporary, the Fairey Swordfish, the Walrus was highly regarded by FAA crews.

Utility Amphibians

About the time the Walrus was entering service, on the other side of the Atlantic, Grumman Aircraft Engineering Company was testing a replacement for the Loening amphibians. The design concept for this aircraft followed that of the Loenings; a single central float joined to a fuselage that seated its crew in tandem, and had floats mounted at the outboard tips of its biplane wing. Their duties were utility and general communications, providing a link between ship and shore. The Grumman J2F Duck was built in small numbers until the expansion programme preceding the Second World War. At the end of 1940, Grumman received its last and largest order for 144 Ducks. As in the case of the TBFs, war was declared, and production was shifted to Columbia Aircraft Corp. from where 330 were ordered. Grumman production facilities were fully committed to the production of the F6F Hellcats.

The last of the Curtiss biplanes in naval service was the SOC Seagull which, like so many Scout/Observation/Reconnaissance/Spotter aircraft, was a jack of all trades. It was required to operate as a float plane from battleships and cruisers and be convertible to land operation and aboard carriers.

It is a fine point of distinction, but observation planes were attached to battleships and scouting planes were normally operated from cruisers. With the SOCs, the duties were combined. After 135 SOCs were delivered, the next 40 were land based with a single strut and fixed streamlined landing gear similar to that used on the F11Cs and the Army's P6E. On these latter two aircraft, the landing gear was an attractive appendage but on the SOC it resulted in an odd bird-legged appearance. Aircraft that were equipped for carrier operation were designated SOC-2A and SOC-3A. Though scheduled to be retired with the introduction of the SO3C Seagull, the SOCs were retained and used until the end of the Second World War when the SO3Cs failed to meet operational expectations and were retired.

forward. A pair of .30s were mounted on a Scarff ring in the rear cockpit. The O2Us were powered by a radial air-cooled Pratt & Whitney R1340-88, producing 450 hp. Speeds were improving and the Corsair showed its mettle by establishing a number of records for speed and weight carrying. As in the case of the Fairey IIIFs the landing gear still had a fixed solid axle. An innovation of the Vought planes was the 'cheek' fuel tanks which were mounted on the fuselage sides from the firewall back to the seat of the forward pilot's cockpit. They were faired to the contours of the fuselage.

The Japanese copied the Vought in almost every detail. In 1930, the Nakajima E4N2 and the E4N2-C (for carrier operation) reached operational status, the same year that the improved O3U-1 began to replace the O2Us. Other than rudder configuration there was little external difference between the Nakajima and the O3U-1. The E4N2 was followed by the E8N in 1933, which was an improved version and was an even closer match for the O3U series, even to engine power. The E8N1 and its variations were produced in quantity, totalling over 750 planes, and in a number of variations. Like its Vought counterpart, it was stressed for catapult launching and could be used on carriers as well. It was the standard Japanese reconnaissance aircraft until the introduction of the Nakajima C6N1 Myrt.

Among the more interesting carrier observation aircraft was the Loening OL-8A amphibian, 20 of which were built. A number of OL-8s were built but were not equipped for carrier operation. The first of this unique series of aircraft was built to match the performance of the de Havilland DH-4s which were still the standard Army aircraft at the time of their introduction. Grover C Loening anticipated difficulty in selling these to the military and, with this in mind, positioned the pilot and observer exactly as they were in the old DHs, figuring that if the crew felt at home with all their accustomed reference points, the chance for sale would be improved. As it turned out he was correct but the real breakthrough came when General Billy Mitchell had a forced landing in the Mississippi River while flying a DH on an inspection tour. After getting ashore, his first action was a phone call to the purchasing department which resulted in the purchase of five Loening amphibians. Additional small orders followed and the Navy purchased a number which were used by the McMillan Arctic expedition with Commander Richard

ARMAMENT

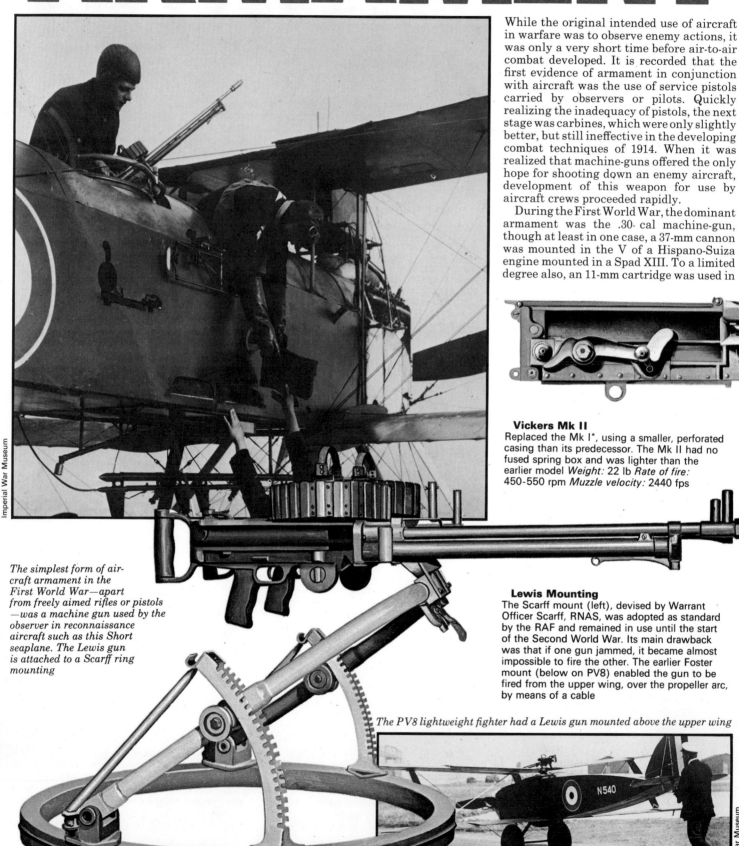

While the original intended use of aircraft in warfare was to observe enemy actions, it was only a very short time before air-to-air combat developed. It is recorded that the first evidence of armament in conjunction with aircraft was the use of service pistols carried by observers or pilots. Quickly realizing the inadequacy of pistols, the next stage was carbines, which were only slightly better, but still ineffective in the developing combat techniques of 1914. When it was realized that machine-guns offered the only hope for shooting down an enemy aircraft, development of this weapon for use by aircraft crews proceeded rapidly.

During the First World War, the dominant armament was the .30· cal machine-gun, though at least in one case, a 37-mm cannon was mounted in the V of a Hispano-Suiza engine mounted in a Spad XIII. To a limited degree also, an 11-mm cartridge was used in

Vickers Mk II
Replaced the Mk I*, using a smaller, perforated casing than its predecessor. The Mk II had no fused spring box and was lighter than the earlier model *Weight:* 22 lb *Rate of fire:* 450-550 rpm *Muzzle velocity:* 2440 fps

The simplest form of aircraft armament in the First World War—apart from freely aimed rifles or pistols—was a machine gun used by the observer in reconnaissance aircraft such as this Short seaplane. The Lewis gun is attached to a Scarff ring mounting

Lewis Mounting
The Scarff mount (left), devised by Warrant Officer Scarff, RNAS, was adopted as standard by the RAF and remained in use until the start of the Second World War. Its main drawback was that if one gun jammed, it became almost impossible to fire the other. The earlier Foster mount (below on PV8) enabled the gun to be fired from the upper wing, over the propeller arc, by means of a cable

The PV8 lightweight fighter had a Lewis gun mounted above the upper wing

Crashed Sopwith Pup reveals its Gnôme rotary engine and the Vickers .303 Mk 1* with ammunition panniers

aviation guns. Following the war, development of various aviation machine-guns and light cannon continued but, because of weight considerations, the cal 30 guns dominated the field. In many instances, new plane specifications stipulated the ability to mount one cal 30 (7·9 mm) and one cal 50 (12-13 mm) or two cal 30 guns.

Though development continued between the wars, it was not until stimulated by the preparation for war in the latter part of the 1930s that dedicated efforts were made to develop a suitable 20-mm aircraft cannon. During the evolutionary period of carrier aircraft, the 1920s and 1930s, the cal 30 guns were the mainstay of shipboard aircraft.

As the weight of the aircraft increased, with the addition of armour plate to protect the crew and vital parts of the aircraft, and with increased weight of projectiles, an increased rate of firing became necessary. The dual problems of slow rate of fire and magazines of limited capacity (as few as 60 rounds per gun) considerably dampened official and designers' enthusiasm for air-

An RNAS armourer works on the twin Lewis guns in the front cockpit of a Handley Page O/100 operated by No 14 (RNAS) squadron at Dunkirk on June 1, 1918. The bomber carried up to five Lewis guns

Vickers .303 Mk 1*
The first Allied gun able to be synchronised to fire through propeller blades, this was a Mk 1 Vickers modified for air cooling with louvres cut in the barrel casing and belt containers for the ammunition *Weight:* 38 lb *Rate of fire:* 450-550 rpm *Muzzle velocity:* 2440 fps

craft cannon. As a result, the compromise solution was the development of the ·5-in cal 50 (12·5 – 13 mm) size gun for use by most military services.

While not capable of the same range as the cannon, nor easily adaptable to the use of explosive type projectiles, they were a decided improvement over the cal 30 (·303 – 7·9 mm) guns whose rate of fire had been their greatest asset. As the rate of fire of the ·5-in machine-gun was increased, a cyclical rate acceptably close to that of the cal 30 guns resulted.

Representative Machine-Guns for Naval Aircraft

Name	Country of origin	Ammunition	Cooling	Rate of fire (rpm)	Muzzle velocity (fps)
Lewis Air Mk II	Britain	0.303-in	Air	500–600	2440
Vickers Mk I*	Britain	0.303-in	Air	450–550	2440
Vickers Mk II	Britain	0.303-in	Air	450–550	2440
Madsen 23-mm	Denmark	23-mm	Air	500	2920
Darne Model 29 Aircraft	France	7.5-mm rimless	Air	1200	2700
Lubbe Air	Germany	20-mm	Air	360	2650
Semag	Switzerland	20-mm	Air	350	
American Armament Corp Type M	US	37-mm	Air	125	1250
Browning aircraft mg M1919	US	0.30-in	Air	1100	2750
Marlin aircraft mg M1917	US	0.30-in	Air	850–1000	2750

The next plateau was the cannon in the 20—30-mm range, dictated by steadily increasing weight of aircraft and speed. Development of this armament category was slow and did not reach quantity use until the Second World War when the Japanese used the 20-mm cannon in their nimble Mitsubishi A6M Zeke naval fighters. Unfortunately, the muzzle velocity of these Japanese cannon left much room for development as their rate of fire was not in the spectacular class. As the war progressed, aircraft of the US and British navies standardized on the 20-mm cannon as the next advance in armament.

Enemy Target

At about the same time that the 20-mm cannon began to find favour as a weapon for attack-type aircraft, rockets were added to the stores to be carried by naval aircraft. Air-to-air and air-to-ground missiles began to take over the roles of the aircraft gun. Like the cannon, the rocket could be adapted to a multitude of warheads and fuses, including proximity fuses which explode the missile even without the necessity of a direct hit on the enemy target.

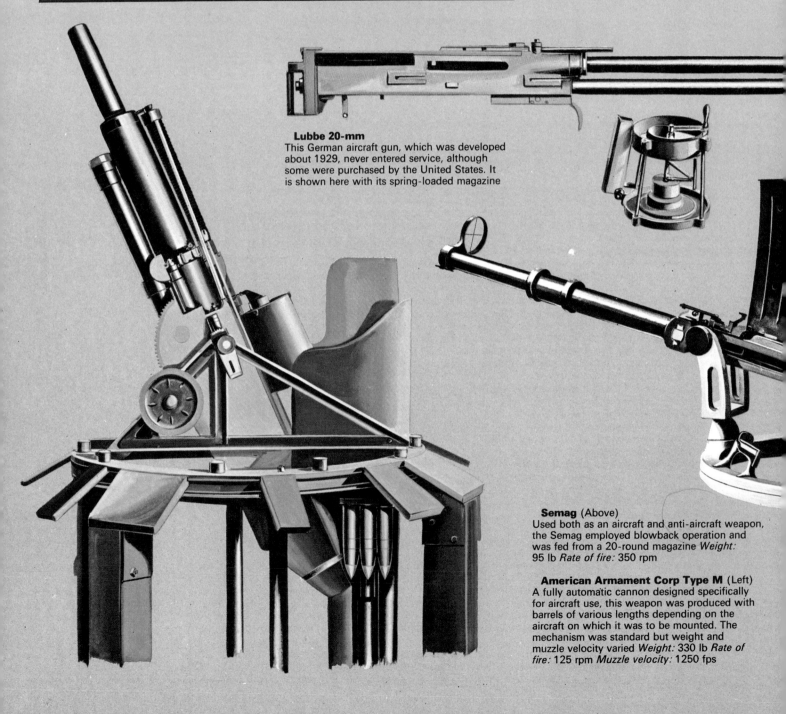

Lubbe 20-mm
This German aircraft gun, which was developed about 1929, never entered service, although some were purchased by the United States. It is shown here with its spring-loaded magazine

Semag (Above)
Used both as an aircraft and anti-aircraft weapon, the Semag employed blowback operation and was fed from a 20-round magazine *Weight:* 95 lb *Rate of fire:* 350 rpm

American Armament Corp Type M (Left)
A fully automatic cannon designed specifically for aircraft use, this weapon was produced with barrels of various lengths depending on the aircraft on which it was to be mounted. The mechanism was standard but weight and muzzle velocity varied *Weight:* 330 lb *Rate of fire:* 125 rpm *Muzzle velocity:* 1250 fps

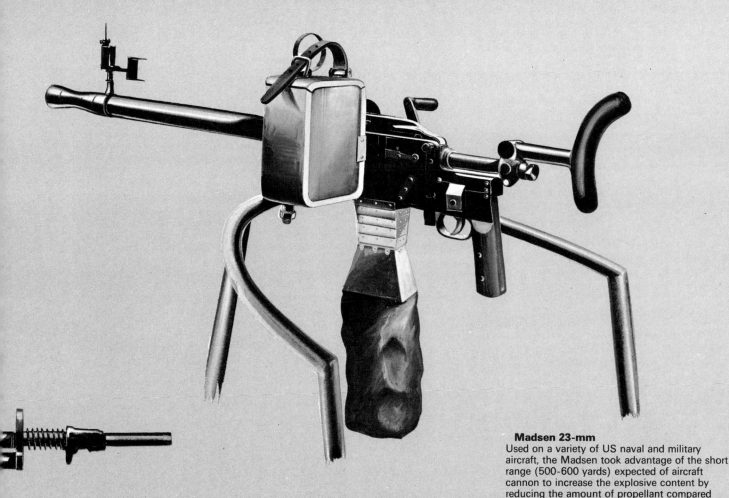

Madsen 23-mm
Used on a variety of US naval and military aircraft, the Madsen took advantage of the short range (500-600 yards) expected of aircraft cannon to increase the explosive content by reducing the amount of propellant compared with that necessary in naval guns *Weight:* 118 lb *Rate of fire:* 500 rpm *Muzzle velocity:* 2920 fps

SIGHTS

One of the least discussed equipment items for naval aircraft, and one of the most important, is its armament (gun) sight.

During the First World War, through the 1920s and, in many instances, into the Second World War period, a simple ring and post system was used. This consisted of a single post, sometimes with a small knob on top, and a second unit consisting of multiple concentric rings. In use, the pilot or gunner would manoeuvre his aircraft or flexible machine-gun, to bring the post, ring and target into alignment. The multiple rings

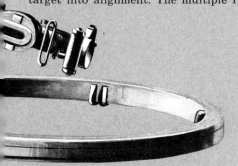

gave the pilot an opportunity to establish a rough estimate of lead or deflection.

A successor sight consisted of a telescope mounted on the cowling and through the windshield where it was adjusted for close proximity to the pilot's eye. Unfortunately, theoretical improvement was not matched by practical use. It was unusually restric-tive, requiring the pilot to concentrate his vision only on the eyepiece of the sight. In addition, the optics of the sight had a bad characteristic of fogging up, thus rendering it inoperable.

It became quite apparent that a sight was required which allowed greater eye freedom and retained the degree of accuracy made possible by the telescope. The answer was the reflector sight introduced at the beginning of the Second World War. This sight consisted of an angled piece of glass, mounted on the glare shield above the pilot's instruments. Beneath this angled glass was a projector which projected a reticle pattern onto this glass for the pilot to see. It was like a ring and post sight suspended in air and when it was superimposed on an enemy plane it ensured that the plane and guns were boresighted on the target.

Computing Gunsights
By joint efforts the British and US scientific teams co-operated to produce the Illuminated Sight Mark 8 which was used extensively throughout the Second World War for fixed guns. By a succession of modifications, the Mark 8 was steadily improved during this period. Paralleling the development of this sight was the Illuminated Sight Mark 9 for use with free guns as used in turrets.

Computing gunsights were considered as early as 1937, but it was not until the closing days of the Second World War that the British produced a sight which was further developed for production by the Bureau of Ordnance of the US Navy.

With the introduction of the Mark 18 sight for turrets, the expenditure of ammunition dropped substantially and hits increased. The success of this Mark 18 sight resulted in an intensive redesign of this sight for fixed installation in fighter aircraft. When completed, it was designated the Gun Sight Mark 21. This Navy-developed sight, based on a basic British design, became the standard for all Allied air services.

No less important than gun sights were bomb sights, though as it turned out, the Army was the principal beneficiary of a gyro stabilized sight which began its development by the US Navy shortly after the end of the First World War. This sight became the most talked about 'secret weapon' of the Second World War.

The first model Mark II was accepted in 1929 and a later development, the Mark 15, began tests in 1931. As it turned out the Mark 15 was unsuitable for low level bombing, which was more typically a navy tactic. To meet this requirement, a 'field modification' was made using an Illuminated Sight Mark 9 as the basis. For dive bombing, 'straight down', or nearly so, the normal gunsight served well with the pilot applying aiming factors based on his own experience. A gratifying number of hits were scored in this manner.

While torpedo sights were available at the beginning of the Second World War, their shortcomings caused the pilots of these torpedo-bombers to favour the use of the gunsight and personal experience to place the torpedo in the most advantageous position in relation to its target.

FLOTATION GEAR

Ditched Sopwith Pup with its flotation bags inflated gets a tow back to a North Sea shore station

The first case of a landing aboard a carrier as we know it today, was in 1917 aboard the British carrier HMS *Furious*. At the time, only the forward part of the ship was used as a 200-ft flight deck. On this rudimentary deck, Squadron Commander Dunning made the first landing. With the ship steaming into the wind, Dunning threaded his way round the bridge until he was over the landing area forward, at which time he throttled back his Sopwith Pup and settled toward the deck where a landing crew caught the plane as it was about to make contact and guided it safely down.

With this successful landing, Dunning was confident of an equally successful, un-assisted touchdown and directed that, on the second landing, the crew not assist until he was completely landed. Unfortunately, as he touched down for a second time, a tyre burst, causing his plane to swerve to one side and to plunge over the side of the

ship into the water, where Dunning was drowned before help could reach him. This freakish, tragic accident gave added incentive to the development of flotation equipment for aircraft and crew.

To save the aircraft after a ditching at sea, 'flotation gear' in the form of large air bags was installed in carrier-based aircraft. The size of the flotation bags depended on the type (size) of the aircraft involved.

The flotation bags themselves were constructed of multiple layers of rubberized fabric and were provided with fabric flaps for attaching them to the aircraft structure. The bags were stowed in containers built into the structure of the aircraft where they were faired in to prevent air drag. Installation was usually in the upper wing or in the sides of the forward fuselage, the location of the greatest concentration of weight.

Usually two bags were installed, but when the aircraft was unusually heavy, a

third bag was often installed and inflated inside the fuselage of the tail section. Location of bracing wires and the balance point of the aircraft were considered in determining the exact location of the bags. A release 'T' handle for simultaneous release of all bags was usually installed in the upper right side of the instrument panel or in the centre section of the upper wing, offset to the right side. A hand-operated air pump was also provided to top-off the flotation bags after inflation or to replace air lost as a result of a possible slow leak. The bags were capable of supporting a plane for about 10 hours in a relatively calm sea, but in a rough sea, rubbing against the fuselage or other structure could cause them to chafe and to lose pressure and, therefore, buoyancy.

With the beginning of the Second World War, all flotation gear was removed from US aircraft to increase payload and to sink the aircraft to avoid detection.

Inflatable Doughnut
Along with flotation bags for the aircraft, it was considered necessary to include personal flotation gear for the pilot and other crew members. This flotation gear consisted of an inflatable life raft and life preserver. The life raft consisted of an oval-shaped doughnut tube made of rubberized fabric and inflated by a CO_2 cartridge. These varied in size according to the crew complement for the plane. Later models of life rafts were made as a complete circle to reduce the risk of overturning. Life rafts were packaged in fabric carrying cases to prevent chafing or ripping. In addition, they were usually packed with survival gear and rations and installed in or near the cockpit.

Life rafts and life preservers were standard equipment during the Second World War, and were responsible for saving the lives of many air-crewmen during the Second World War. With the development of miniaturization, dehydration and special packing materials and techniques, it became possible to pack parachute seat cushions with relatively complete survival kits tailored for the geographic area of the earth over which the air operations were

Squadron Commander Dunning's fatal accident as his Pup goes over the side of HMS Furious *with a burst tyre. Flotation equipment could have saved his life and the tragedy spurred on development work*

Parnall Panther
Designed as a fleet reconnaissance aircraft specifically for use from carriers, the Panther's humpback cockpit gave the pilot an excellent view for deck landing. A hydrovane was fitted to prevent overturning in the event of a ditching and flotation bags were fitted to the top of the undercarriage.
Span: 26 ft 6 in *Length:* 24 ft 11 in *Engine:* Bentley BR 2, 230 hp
Max speed: 108 mph at 6500 ft *Ceiling:* 14,500 ft *Endurance:* 4.5 hrs
Armament: Lewis mg

taking place. In the case of carrier operations, these seat packs also included one-man life rafts, signal devices, dehydrated nourishing foods and first-aid materials.

The life preservers were initially kapok or cork filled; however, because of the bulk, these gave way to air-filled jacket-type 'Mae West' preservers that were worn at all times by carrier-based pilots.

The earliest form of inflatable life preserver dates back to November 14, 1910, when Eugene Ely made the first takeoff from aboard the USS *Birmingham*. As an added insurance Ely inflated two motor-cycle inner tubes and wrapped them around his neck and across his chest to form the earliest version of the Mae West.

During the final stages of the Second World War light-weight belt style preservers came into use. However, the standard aircraft life preserver has continued to be the horsecollar style.

POWERPLANTS

When the pilots of single-engine aircraft venture out over water beyond gliding distance back to a land mass, the psychological effect is equivalent to their engine switching to the 'automatic rough' operating condition. Whether this is literally correct or not, the response is normal for those pilots not accustomed to over-water flying.

Carrier-based pilots, whose daily operations are almost exclusively over water, understandably have a great interest in their engines and treat them with care and respect. In addition, powerplants that are adapted for naval use are designed, tested and maintained with maximum care. Reliability, durability and performance are the prime considerations in the selection of engines for carrier-based aircraft.

With these requirements in mind, it is interesting to note that the dominant engine type, during the years prior to the introduction of the turbine engine, has been the radial air-cooled engine. By type or numerical count, the liquid-cooled engine is in the minority. Though the liquid-cooled engine has undeniable qualities which merited its development, its use in carrier-based aircraft was not as extensive as its air-cooled counterpart. Plumbing, including the radiators, did not stand up well to the pounding which is normal in carrier operations.

The main reasons given for preference of the air-cooled engine in naval service were:
1. Generally, the air-cooled engine was lighter than the liquid-cooled engine of equivalent power. Radiators, plumbing and coolant liquids could add up to a 500-lb weight penalty per aircraft, a substantial amount when added to the weight of equipment such as tail hooks, beefed-up landing gear, etc.
2. The air-cooled engine was simple and easy to start with large tolerances between mov-

ing parts until operating temperatures were reached. Additionally, maintenance, installation and engine changing were simplified.
3. The air-cooled engine was less vulnerable in combat where the radiator and attendant plumbing were subject to battle damage and high stresses resulting from deck landing and handling.
4. There is limited space on a carrier. The more compactly-shaped radial engine and its lack of liquid-cooled system and attendant parts saved valuable space.

Performance Primary Requirement
In operation, carrier aircraft were brought in high above the fantail of the ship to insure that they clear it should the stern rise on the swell as the plane prepared to touch down. The plane was then dropped 15 to 20 ft in a semi-stalled condition to engage the tail hook with the arresting cable (pendant).

During the First World War and shortly thereafter, the primary requirement for aircraft engines was performance but, as carrier aviation developed, it became obvious that these jarring landings aboard carriers would soon put an end to the liquid-cooled engine as a naval powerplant.

A notable exception to this was the number of aircraft produced in the late 1930s and during the Second World War with liquid-cooled engines. It should be noted that a number were expediencies dictated by war-time production and modification of existing land-based planes to naval use. Examples included Hurricanes, Spitfires and even Mosquitoes in British service, and the planned use of the Bf 109 and Ju 87 for the German carrier *Graf Zeppelin*.

Following the First World War, the early days of carrier development, most aircraft were powered by the engines which were

war surplus or those which were under development during the closing stages of the war. This resulted in a number of powerplants which were unsuited for naval service. In the early 1920s, there were engines under development which held promise for naval use. The French were using the water-cooled Hispano-Suiza engines but soon made arrangements to build the British 400-hp Bristol Jupiter.

The British Air Ministry policy was definitely toward air-cooled engines to the extent, in some cases, of replacing water-cooled Rolls-Royce engines with air-cooled engines in existing airframes. The appearance of the aircraft suffered by the change, but the overall performance improved. The Japanese followed the practice of the British, generally, starting with the Nieuport Nighthawks powered by the Bentley 220 BR rotary engine. They became quite expert in handling this combination and landed aboard carriers with ease. These Nighthawks were re-engined with the 400-hp Bristol Jupiter.

In the US, a number of manufacturers attempted to meet naval requirements using liquid-cooled engines. Only Boeing and Curtiss enjoyed any real success, with aircraft powered by the Curtiss D-12 liquid-cooled engine. The Navy tested the TS, a single-seat shipboard fighter, in a number of configurations starting with the Wright-built, water-cooled Hispano-Suiza engine. Eventually, the TS (Curtiss F4C-1) was totally redesigned. The wings were redesigned using a new section and the Wright-Lawrence J-1 radial air-cooled engine was installed to bring it up to performance parity with contemporary British and Japanese naval fighters of 1923. The TS was overtaken by technical progress and was relegated to advance trainer status. In

British service, the Rolls-Royce Kestrel, Merlin and Griffon and the Napier Lion were the dominant liquid-cooled engines.

During the period 1923-25, the US Navy pinned its hopes on the air-cooled Wright P-1, followed by the R-1340 Wasp which was produced by the newly founded Pratt & Whitney company. The Wasp quickly dominated the field. During the 1930s, air-cooled engines powered the majority of carrier-based aircraft. The Bristol Pegasus, Perseus, Taurus, Hercules and Centaurus engines, the Armstrong-Siddeley Tiger, Jaguar and Puma engines in British naval service, and the Wright Cyclone, and Pratt & Whitney Wasp and Hornet series engines in the US were produced in the greatest numbers.

The Japanese initially relied on licence-built engines, primarily of French and British design, but by the mid-1930s were developing their own designs of air-cooled engines for naval use, which were comparable to any in service with the other naval (carrier) powers. Liquid-cooled engines were used in several early carrier aircraft designs and even as late as the Second World War, the very clean, high-performance Yokosuka D4Y *Suisei* dive-bomber was designed to be powered by the licence-built Daimler-Benz DB601 liquid-cooled Atsuta engine. Here again, maintenance problems plagued the engine from the beginning, though it was a well-proven engine in wide use in land-based planes. The aircraft was redesigned to install the Mitsubishi Kinsei 62 air-cooled radial engine. With few exceptions, Japanese carrier aircraft also used air-cooled engines.

Of passing interest was the design change in the British Bristol engines, beginning with the Taurus, to sleeve-valve rather than poppet-valve configuration.

As the Second World War approached, the engine production lines geared for all-out effort. Along with quantity production, a requirement for greater power was evident. To meet these requirements, twin-row, air-cooled radial engines were developed and produced. Power output in the 3000-hp range became the designers' goal. In the case of the Wright R-3350 and the Pratt & Whitney R-4360 (four row, air-cooled) the maximum output reached 3000 hp.

The Gnôme Monosoupape rotary, 80 hp model

Advantages: Good power-to-weight and size-to-power ratios and relative mechanical simplicity.

Disadvantages: Fine tolerances required in maintenance, tendency to shed cylinders and no proper throttle (the only way of controlling the engine was by cutting the ignition to a number of cylinders). Unlike more conventional engines, the rotary had a stationary crankshaft, around which rotated the cylinders and crankcase, with the propeller bolted to their front. The crankshaft itself (**1**) is bolted to the aeroplane's structure. Into the crankshaft are led three inlets (only two are visible) (**2**) for air, fuel and lubricant

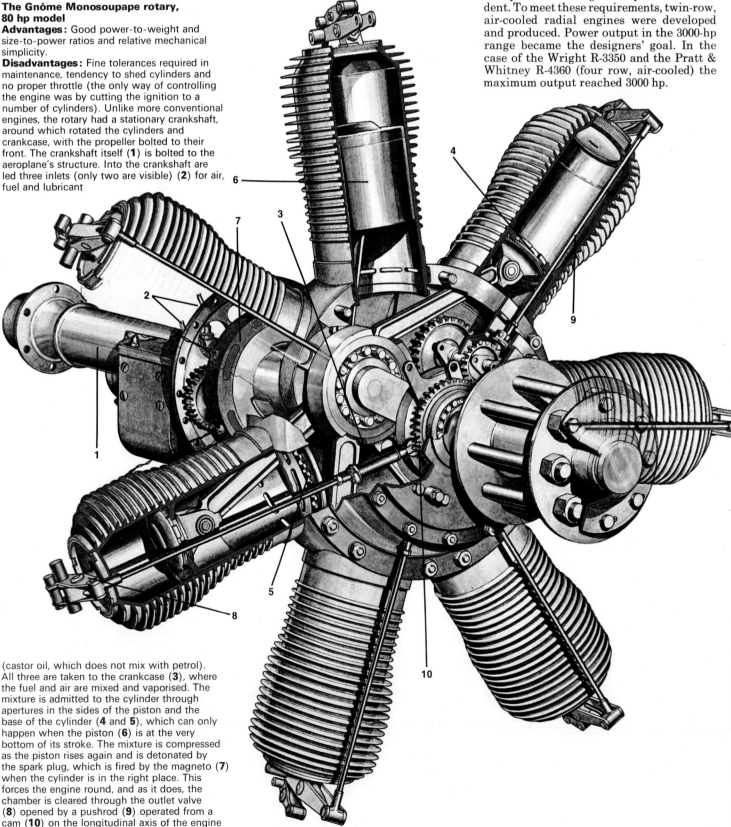

(castor oil, which does not mix with petrol). All three are taken to the crankcase (**3**), where the fuel and air are mixed and vaporised. The mixture is admitted to the cylinder through apertures in the sides of the piston and the base of the cylinder (**4** and **5**), which can only happen when the piston (**6**) is at the very bottom of its stroke. The mixture is compressed as the piston rises again and is detonated by the spark plug, which is fired by the magneto (**7**) when the cylinder is in the right place. This forces the engine round, and as it does, the chamber is cleared through the outlet valve (**8**) opened by a pushrod (**9**) operated from a cam (**10**) on the longitudinal axis of the engine

WING FOLDING

Beardmore WB III, an extensively redesigned Sopwith Pup with folding wings and retracting under-carriage. Modest production was undertaken and 18 were embarked aboard Furious.

Carrier-based aircraft necessarily have two options on wing design. They have wings of short span that fit within the limits imposed by the aircraft elevators of the carrier, or they have folding wings to permit stowage in the hangar decks, on the flight deck and again, most importantly, on the aircraft elevators that move the planes between these two decks.

Whatever the configuration, it should be remembered that folding wings and tail hooks are two of the several penalties and costs that a naval aircraft must bear over its land-based counterpart. The folding joint or joints must be designed so they will not exact any performance penalty on the operating crew. When in the flying position, the hinge must be at least as strong as an equivalent solid wing spar. To insure this strength, the spars must be reinforced and all control lines, fluid lines and electrical lines must pass through this fold point without, in any way, compromising the strength or reliability of the structure or function of the components.

Simplest Solution

Of the many variations of the folding wing principle, the overhead folding configuration, as used on the Vought F4U Corsair, Supermarine Seafire III, Hawker Sea Fury, Curtiss SB2C Helldiver, the Nakajima B5N1 Kate, B6N Jill, and the Aichi B7A2 Grace, offers the simplest solution geometrically speaking. One variant of the famed Mitsubishi A6M, the Model 21 Zeke, had, by all odds, the simplest folding wing. This consisted of manually folding the outboard one half meter of each wing tip upwards. Conversely, the low clearance aboard British carriers required a double fold in the wing of the Seafire III, with the main outboard wing panels folding upward and the tips, outboard of the aileron, folding downward.

The earliest form of wing folding, and one of the most difficult, was the rearward folding of the entire outboard bays of biplane wings. The geometry of this manoeuvre was a real design problem which involved rotating a completely rigged bay of a biplane, complete with flying wires, landing wires and drift wires and upper and lower wing panels, about a single vertical axis and stowing them in this assembled condition along each side of the fuselage, with trailing edges of the wing facing inward. Often the wing bays would rest on the horizontal stabilizer or special brackets which suspended the panels in that position, or with one panel above and one panel below the stabilizer.

The problems of handling these planes on the flight decks in even modest winds must have been quite impressive. Aircraft of this configuration were commonplace between 1920 and 1930, and the Fairey Swordfish and Albacores brought the type right up to the end of the Second World War, though by that time as types of aircraft they were long past their prime.

A third folding configuration involved a twist and a turn. From the flying position, the wing was twisted about its lateral axis and then, with the leading edge at the bottom point, in the case of the Grumman aircraft, the whole panel was rotated about a vertical axis toward the tail to lie parallel to the fuselage. The Fairey monoplane aircraft used a similar arrangement except that the trailing edge of the wing was rotated to the bottom position before the wing panel was rotated to the tail to lie parallel to the fuselage. The preference of the service for accessibility of armament while the wings were in the stowed position was a determining factor on which way the wing was to be stowed. The primary examples of each were the Grumman F4F Wildcat, F6F Hellcat, TBF Avenger, rotating the leading edge down and the Fairey Firefly, rotating the trailing edge downward.

Operating mechanisms varied with the manufacturer and model. Accumulated experience dictated operating systems all the way from full hydraulic operation, as used on the Vought SB2U Vindicator, to totally manual operation, as on such aircraft as the Mitsubishi A6M Model 21 previously mentioned. There were combinations of manual folding and hydraulic or mechanical safetying as well as hydraulic folding and manual or hydraulic safetying.

In all cases, deck crews were an essential part of the operation. In most cases, the price in weight and complexity dictated that human power was the primary operating medium, since crews were required during the action cycle at all times.

One monoplane folding system which was a design resurrection from the biplane era was the Fairey Barracuda torpedo-bomber which rotated the wing straight back, folding the wing of the plane about a vertical axis without any twist about the lateral axis.

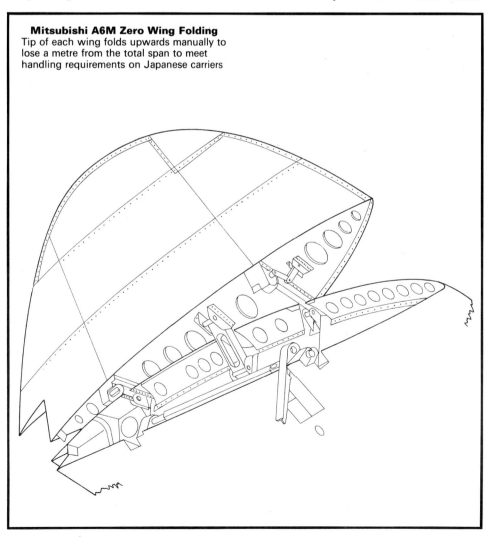

Mitsubishi A6M Zero Wing Folding
Tip of each wing folds upwards manually to lose a metre from the total span to meet handling requirements on Japanese carriers

THE CARRIER GROWS UP

1914

HMS Ark Royal, the first ship fully converted to an aircraft carrier, was completed in 1914 and began operations in the Dardanelles in February 1915. Her holds were converted into hangars and cranes were installed to handle her eight seaplanes. After only five months' service she was withdrawn from these duties

1917

The first true aircraft carrier was HMS Furious, converted from a light battle cruiser by building a slanted flight deck over the forecastle. The space underneath formed a hangar, and later a landing deck — which proved to be unusable — was added aft of the superstructure

1922

The US Navy's first aircraft carrier was the USS Langley, converted from a collier, which entered full-scale service in 1925 after three years of trials. She could carry up to 34 aircraft and was converted to a seaplane tender in 1937. The Langley was sunk in 1942

The first vessel to be completed as an aircraft carrier was HMS *Ark Royal* in 1914. A converted merchantman, she was fitted with a flying-off deck forward which was in fact never used in action. Instead she was operated as a seaplane carrier, deploying aircraft on fleet reconnaissance missions.

The next step towards the true aircraft carrier was HMS *Furious*, commissioned in 1917. She had started out as a light battle-cruiser before having a flying-off deck added over her forecastle and a hangar built underneath. The vessel was intended to operate Sopwith Pups and 1½-Strutters, which would be ditched after their mission. Trials were carried out in 1917 to see whether it was possible to land aircraft back on the flying-off deck, and Squadron Commander Dunning made a successful landing in a Sopwith Pup while the ship was steaming in Scapa Flow. On his second attempt, however, his aircraft ran off the side of the carrier and he was drowned. A landing deck was later added behind the superstructure, but air currents made operations too difficult and the futility of a hybrid vessel was eventually realized.

The United States Navy's first carrier was the converted collier USS *Langley*, which was commissioned in 1922. A continuous wooded flight deck was built above the hull, leaving space for aircraft storage —rather than a hangar—underneath. *Langley* was later converted to an aircraft tender, the forward 200 ft of deck being removed, and she was finally sunk in 1942.

HMS *Courageous* was the first carrier in which a really effective arrester gear was fitted. Wires connected to hydraulic cylinders were paid out gradually when engaged by a hook on the aircraft, giving smooth deceleration. This method of safely recovering aircraft, first installed in 1933, had endured to the present. *Courageous* was fitted with a 60-ft-long flying-off deck below the main flight deck, but this proved of little use in action because the vessel was sunk within a month of the outbreak of the Second World War when its Swordfishes failed to deter an attack by a German U-boat.

The US Navy's next two carriers were the more ambitious *Lexington* and *Saratoga*, converted from incomplete battle-cruisers. The massive funnel on the starboard side was a distinguishing feature.

The first US vessel designed from the outset as an aircraft carrier was the *Ranger*, commissioned in 1934. Although displacing only 14,500 tons, the *Ranger* could carry 75 aircraft because power, protection and

1928

US Navy

HMS Courageous *was fitted with a 60-ft flying-off deck in addition to the normal flight deck, allowing light fighters such as the Fairey Flycatcher to take off independently of other operations. The* Courageous *and her sister ships* Furious *and* Glorious *were all converted from cruisers*

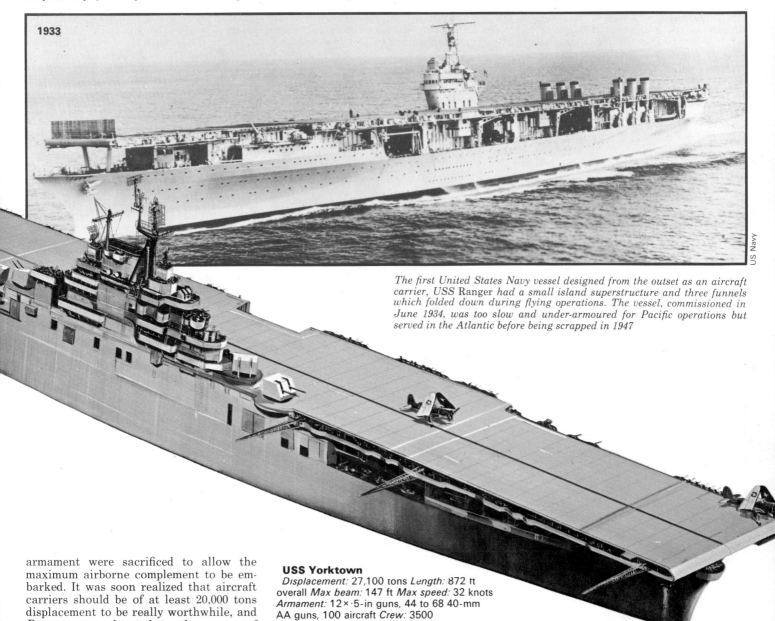

1933

US Navy

The first United States Navy vessel designed from the outset as an aircraft carrier, USS Ranger *had a small island superstructure and three funnels which folded down during flying operations. The vessel, commissioned in June 1934, was too slow and under-armoured for Pacific operations but served in the Atlantic before being scrapped in 1947*

armament were sacrificed to allow the maximum airborne complement to be embarked. It was soon realized that aircraft carriers should be of at least 20,000 tons displacement to be really worthwhile, and *Ranger* was relegated to the status of aircraft transport, then used for training, before being scrapped in 1947.

USS Yorktown
Displacement: 27,100 tons *Length:* 872 ft overall *Max beam:* 147 ft *Max speed:* 32 knots *Armament:* 12×·5-in guns, 44 to 68 40-mm AA guns, 100 aircraft *Crew:* 3500

EVE OF THE CARRIER'S WAR

With the Battle of the Coral Sea in May 1942, aircraft carriers came of age. The carrier was and still is the long arm of the navy and the aircraft of these carriers are the mailed fist to strike again and again at an enemy force whether it be on land or sea.

Until the Battle of the Coral Sea, the role of the carrier was that of a supporting force for the big ships of the navy – battleships, cruisers and heavy cruisers. When land armies move forward they take airstrips or create airstrips to bring their supporting air-power forward, shortening the round-trip time needed to rain blows on the enemy and to refuel, rearm and repair the aircraft involved. When a naval force moves forward, or in any direction in unison with the fleet or task force, the airstrip moves with it. Among the many advantages of this mobile airstrip is the complete continuity of action on the home base as well as complete familiarity of the pilots with this base, thus avoiding distracting elements which might take their minds off the job at hand. The parallel between the airstrip and the carrier is fairly exact for the carrier provides the fuel and servicing for the aircraft as well as the combat direction and billeting for the crews.

Aircraft in warfare are often considered to be long-range artillery. In tactical situations this has validity, but with the added advantage that the firepower can be delivered from virtually any quarter, not just from along a relatively known static front-line of the battle area. This is particularly effective in naval engagements where dive-bombing and torpedo attacks can originate from every point of the compass or any vertical angle or altitude. From the carriers, they can strike swiftly and repeatedly, carrying out an old but certain prescription for military success of 'getting there firstest with the mostest'.

Originally, aircraft were accepted by the navies to be used for scouting/observation duties and to spot for the heavy guns of the fleet. Gradually, the aircraft evolved as the attack force itself. Single or small groups of aircraft operating from battleships or cruisers could harass opposing forces but rarely could they press home an attack of sufficient size and intensity to do significant damage to an enemy ship or fleet. To do so requires a large number of aircraft delivering repeated blows to keep the enemy force on the alert and unable to make the necessary repairs to remain in action. The destruction is cumulative, with the second, third and fourth attacks doing more damage than the first – if the attacks are in rapid succession and by sufficient numbers of aircraft. It is for this purpose that the carrier is designed – to keep the refuelling, repair and ordnance facilities close at hand. It is also important that carriers operate in groups to provide mutual support so that should one carrier deck be damaged, the remaining ships in the group are able to

service the aircraft of the damaged carrier.

While all the navies of the world had their own views and functional designations for their aircraft, the types generally desired were: Spotting Reconnaissance, Bombers, Fighters and Torpedo Bombers. In most cases the mission capability overlapped, such as in the case of fighter-bomber, scout-bombers and scout-observation. These multi-purpose aircraft resulted from the desire, if not the necessity, to keep the number of types as small as possible and to reduce the aircraft maintenance and supply problems to a minimum.

Carrier-based aircraft developed almost beyond recognition during the Second World War. The Mitsubishi A5M, the first monoplane carrier-based fighter, did not enter service until September 1937 but by 1945 high-performance monoplanes were the norm. In some roles, however, the biplane still soldiered on. The Fairey Swordfish, for example, remained in service throughout the war and took part in many important battles.

The United States was brought into the war by the biggest carrier operation so far, when 350 aircraft from six ships attacked Pearl Harbor, but within months this paled almost into insignificance as carrier fleets and their aircraft turned the tide of the war against the Japanese.

	Built		Under Construction	
Britain		Furious		Illustrious
		Argus		Victorious
		Eagle		Formidable
		Hermes		Indomitable
		Courageous		Implacable
		Glorious		Indefatigable
		Ark Royal		
United States		Lexington		Wasp
		Saratoga		Hornet
		Ranger		
		Yorktown		
		Enterprise		
Japan		Hosho		Shokaku
		Akagi		Zuikaku
		Kaga		
		Ryujo		
		Soryu		
		Hiryu		
France		Béarn		Joffre
Germany				Graf Zeppelin

Carrier strength of the Powers: 1939

The Landing Signals Officer aboard the escort carrier Ravager *signals instructions to a Grumman F6F Hellcat. Once on his landing run, the pilot was subject to the commands of the LSO, who also decided the rate at which aircraft could land*

The first form of arrester was the rope and sandbag system used by Ely during his landing aboard the USS *Pennsylvania* on 18 January 1911 and described previously. During the early period of carrier development a number of other systems were tried, among them the very unsatisfactory and potentially dangerous practice of 'ditching' alongside an escort destroyer. If the pilot was fortunate enough to make a good landing or ditching, inflatable flotation bags were provided to keep the plane afloat until the pilot could be rescued. This system also had the disadvantage of sacrificing the plane and engine.

A second system was tried at the Marine Experimental Aircraft Depot on the Isle of Grain, Kent, UK, in late 1915. It consisted of an inclined wire ropeway fitted over the stern of the ship. While one BE fitted with a special gear did succeed in landing on this equipment, the idea was dropped in favour of a return to the earlier sandbag system.

Another system tried consisted of fore-and-aft wires supported on blocks about six inches above the deck. The aircraft was fitted with a number of hooks mounted on the axle which engaged one or more of the wires. To complete this system, the pilot lowered a tail hook to engage a set of transverse wires which were attached to the now standardised sand bags. These transverse wires were spaced at 30-ft intervals. The axle-mounted hooks ensured a straight run down the deck.

All these tests, it should be remembered, were before the fitting of internal wheel brakes. The high probability of a lateral gust of wind causing the aircraft to slew around was ever present. This resulted in a great number of damaged aircraft landing gears, propellers and wing tips as well as severe twisting strain on the airframe itself. The same system or a slightly modified version was used on the USS *Langley*, the first aircraft carrier commissioned in the US Navy. This ship began its service as the collier *Jupiter* and was later modified to the configuration of an aircraft carrier and recommissioned as USS *Langley*.

Another variation of the longitudinal 'grid' cable system was installed on HMS *Argus* in 1919. At first no transverse arrester cables were used: instead an ingenious system allowed the longitudinal wires to serve as brakes as well as guides. The aircraft had the hooks suspended from the axle as before. The cables were laid on the deck fore-and-aft and flush with the deck. The clearance necessary to bring the cables into contact with the hooks was provided by lowering the aircraft elevator, which was located near the centre of the flight deck, about nine inches. When the plane, on its landing rollout, dropped onto the lowered elevator, the hooks engaged the wires. At the forward part of the elevator an 'artificial hill' ramp brought the plane back to deck level and at the same time created sufficient tension on the cables for friction to bring the plane to a halt.

At the same time the aircraft required unusually high, stilt-like landing gear to ensure that the propeller would clear the wires. This required extra weight to provide the strength to withstand the twisting strains when the aircraft swerved from side to side. As might be expected, a number of aircraft sustained varying degrees of damage which had to be repaired before they could be flown from the deck again. The number of accidents caused by this system

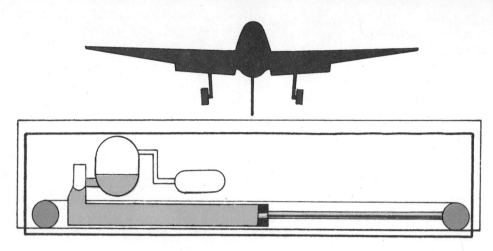

Approach
With the deck pendants raised, the arresting engines at battery, barrier cables raised and the landing area clear the aircraft carrier is ready to receive aircraft. The approaching plane has its wheels down, flaps down and arresting hook down preparatory to landing

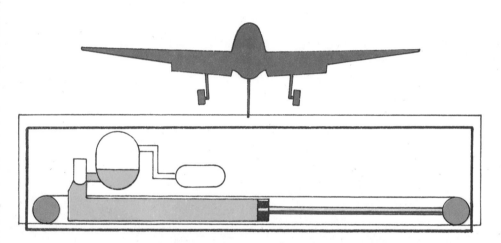

Engagement
The aircraft hook engages the cross-deck pendant pulling it forward, while the purchase cable is being pulled out from the deck edge sheaves

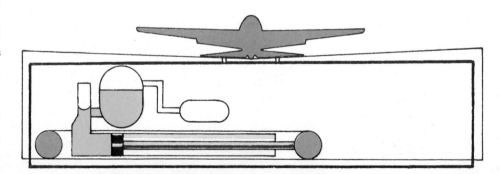

Arrestation
As the plane travels down the deck, purchase cable is pulled out causing the engine ram to be forced into the engine cylinder displacing hydraulic fluid under pressure through the control valve into the accumulator. This fluid metering process through the control valve restrains the pulling out of the purchase cable, and consequently the pendant cable

ARRESTED LANDING SYSTEMS

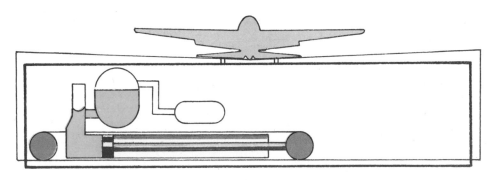

Arrestation Complete
The restraining action stops the motion of the plane, whereupon the control valve automatically closes, preventing it from being pulled back along the deck by the deck pendant, an action known as 'walkback'. 'Hookmen' run onto the flight deck and unhook the deck pendant from the plane. Barriers are lowered, plane moves forward and the pilot starts to fold his wings

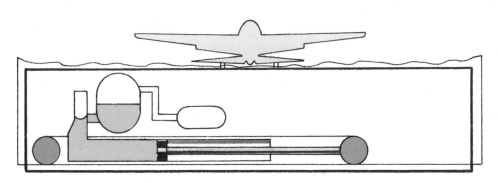

Taxiing from Arrester Gear and Retrieving
With the barrier down the plane moves over them and is 'spotted' ahead of the barriers or taken down the elevator to the hangar deck. Simultaneously the deck pendant is retrieved to its ready position by allowing the fluid from the accumulator to flow back into the cylinder and force the ram to battery position

Landing Signals Officer's Flag Signals

Everything OK

Landing hook not down

You're too slow— speed up

Too fast— slow down

You're low— climb a little

Cut engine and land

No good— go round again

Over this way a little

and equipment resulted in its abandonment seven years after its introduction. In 1924 the landing system reverted to that of the 1917 era, the rope and sand bag.

The sandbag system was improved by the addition of towers constructed on each side of the ship to support weights which looked like elevator weights. Via cables and sheaves from the deck, the weights were lifted in succession as the aircraft engaged the wires, much as sand bags had engaged in the older system. In the 1920s the 'Norden Gear' was installed in US Navy carriers. This machine consisted of a drum

An early arrester system used on the Royal Navy's carriers Argus *(below) and* Furious *(middle) consisted of longitudinal wires which were engaged by hooks mounted on the aircraft axle*

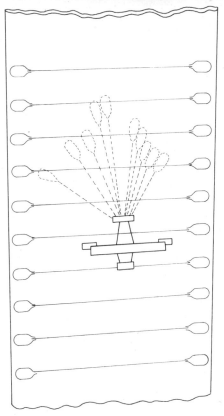

The simplest arrester gear comprised a series of transverse ropes attached to sandbags

approximately three feet in diameter which had spiral grooves machined in its surface to accommodate the cable used. To make the cable wind on the drum in level layers the drum was designed to slide along an axle shaft, rather than incorporating a moving guide for the cable. Each drum – one for each cable end – was equipped with a brake drum to slow it down and an electric motor to retrieve the cable after it was unhooked from the landed aircraft.

Because of the tendency for one drum to run out of cable before its mate, as a result of off-centre contact by the tail hook, it was decided to bring both ends of each deck line (or pendant) together and attach them to a single arresting engine. These hydraulic arresting machines consisted of a cylinder in which hydraulic fluid was compressed and forced through an orifice – whose size could be controlled – to an air-filled accumu-

lator. As the cable was paid out the fluid was compressed into the accumulator where the air was also compressed to provide the power for quick retrieval. The rate at which this hydraulic fluid was transferred was controlled by a valve which could be adjusted to allow for different aircraft.

To reduce the number of arrester gear units, the deck cables or pendants were attached in such a way that two pendants could be connected and both of them controlled by a single arrester.

In the process of landing aircraft aboard a carrier during the Second World War, one individual stood out above all others – even the ship's commander. This was the LSO or Landing Signals Officer. His judgment determined the condition and rate of acceptance of landing aircraft. Once on the final leg of an approach to the carrier, the pilot set his speed and power at pre-tested levels

and lined up at a predetermined altitude astern of the flight deck. From this point onward, he was subject to the commands of the LSO who communicated these instructions to the pilot by hand signals. Since hand signals are not readily visible, the LSO would use paddles similar to ping-pong paddles or other high visibility hardware which would ensure the visual communication of directions to the pilot.

Standing on a small platform at deck level near the aft end of the port side of the flight deck, the LSO would go through his signal routine for each aircraft. Part of his routine was standardised but most was based on experience of the incoming pilot, for the LSO quickly learned to know and anticipate any characteristics of the pilots and planes of his squadrons. He was in a very real sense a one-man act, and it was, as they say, 'a very difficult act to follow'.

CATAPULTS

Catapults used for aircraft launching are modern-day versions of those used by the Greeks and Romans as long ago as 340 BC to hurl missiles of stone against and into fortifications. In aviation history, assisted take-offs go back at least as far as the Wright Brothers and Dr Samuel P Langley, who was Secretary of the Smithsonian Institution in Washington, DC. It should be emphasised, however, that this does *not* include the first Wright plane of 1903, the first piloted heavier-than-air craft to fly under control in powered flight. The Wrights' catapult came later in 1904/5 and consisted of a tower on which was suspended a weight. Through a system of block and tackle, the weight was released and accelerated the plane up to flying speed.

The catapult of today dates back almost to the first association of aircraft with naval aviation. One of the first problems encountered in the marriage of the aeroplane with the ships of the fleet was the means of launching and retrieval of the aircraft without impairing the normal functioning of the ship. Realising this problem from the very beginning, Lt T G Ellyson, Naval Aviator 1, USN, and the head of the US Navy's Aviation Department, Capt W I Chambers, devoted time to producing at least two possible solutions to the problem.

The first, attributed to Glenn H Curtiss and Ellyson, was constructed and tried in 1911 at Hammondsport, NY, the home of Curtiss and the Curtiss Aeroplane & Motor Company. This device consisted of a cable 'slide' with the central cable fixed to a submerged post and the other end sloping upward from the shoreline to a platform. On each side of the main cable were two additional wires of comparatively smaller diameter which served as guides to keep the wings level until the aircraft attained control speed for the ailerons. Visualising a similar rig aboard ship, Ellyson made at least one successful flight from this slide. In doing so, he discovered that few problems were encountered with the control of the ailerons and the whole experimental take-off was over in a matter of seconds.

The second system, developed almost concurrently by Capt Chambers assisted by Naval Constructor H C Richardson and

Lt Ellyson, was a true catapult though primitive in construction and operation. Again, it was Lt Ellyson who made the first launch from this type of catapult, which was powered by compressed air. The date was 12 November 1912; the location was the Washington Navy Yard. The device consisted of a track mounted on a barge along which a wheeled dolly was propelled by compressed air. The aircraft, a Curtiss Model E (the Navy's A-3) with Ellyson piloting, was launched successfully. For all its simplicity, this catapult contained all the ingredients of the system which, with refinement, was still in use in 1922.

This first catapult was designed for installation on the turret of a battleship. In the end this proved impractical, but for years battleships and cruisers carried and launched aircraft from catapults which were deck mounted and independent of the turrets. The first major change from the compressed air type came in 1922 when a new catapult, designed to use gunpowder as the propellant, was designed by Lt Elmer Stone of the US Coast Guard and Mr C F Jeansen of the Bureau of Ordnance.

The development of catapults for use aboard carriers took place mostly during the Thirties when France, Germany and particularly England and the United States were carrying on secret developments. Japan, another of the nations involved in the development of aircraft carriers, did not carry out parallel programmes in catapult design. As far as is known, the Japanese did not have any satisfactory mechanical launching system for their carrier-borne aircraft until late in the war.

With the exception of the US, the other developments of carrier catapults relied on the obsolete and time-consuming use of a launching cradle which necessitated 'loading' each aircraft on the cradle prior to launching, and deck mounted tracks which obstructed movement of aircraft about the deck. The US, on the other hand, developed the expendable 'bridle' for flush deck operation. Using this very simple device it was possible to launch aircraft in rapid succession and with none of the complications inherent in stopping a heavy cradle at the end of each run. As a result, higher launching speeds and frequencies were possible

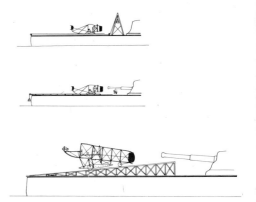

Early proposals for shipboard catapults included using weights to accelerate the aircraft under the force of gravity, but Eugene Ely relied on a simple ramp for his historic flight

and there were no tracks to restrict aircraft movement above the decks. The serious development of the flush-deck catapult began in 1934 at the Naval Aircraft Factory, Philadelphia, Pa. Carriers then under construction had these catapults installed but they were looked upon as a luxury rather than an everyday operational launching device. Remember, however, that aircraft weights and speeds were not great during that period. Under all but extreme sea or wind conditions the carrier deck was ample for take-offs and landings. Even during the early part of the Second World War its use was less than might be expected.

The real requirement for catapults developed when the CVE 'Jeep' carriers (also known as MAC – Merchant Aircraft Carrier – ships) were developed by converting cargo ships into carriers in 1942 to provide the necessary escorts for convoys in the Atlantic. It became apparent that if these little, slow converted merchant ships were to be of any value they would have to use catapults to launch anything other than lightweight aircraft. The restricted deck area, the top-heavy character of the ship and its high degree of movement at sea required the mechanical boost available from the catapult. When at sea in anything but the calmest weather, the roll and pitch of the CVE Jeep carrier made unassisted take-offs hazardous to both the plane and the ship. On the other hand, the catapult made a straight-line take-off a certainty and the aircraft was accelerated to a reasonable speed even when loaded to full military gross weight.

A Sea Hurricane about to be launched from a CAM ship. Each mission for one of these planes meant the loss of the plane as well as a ducking for the pilot

The same Jeep-type carrier made use of its full capability on numerous occasions including the delivery of Army Curtiss P-40 fighters to cover landing operations in North Africa in November 1942. At the invasion of Guadalcanal in August 1942, Marine fighter reinforcements were launched from the USS *Long Island*. In fact, a number of Army-type aircraft were equipped with quick-attach fittings for carrier launch should the need arise.

The advantages of using catapults are many, but the principal ones are:
1. The ability to carry a larger number of aircraft (up to 40% more) which can be larger and heavier and therefore more effective since the only limit is on the number that can be landed aboard. Greater numbers of aircraft can be spotted on deck for launching, since less deck area is used for take-off.
2. Night operations without the use of lights to see the deck can be carried out routinely. The catapult maintains the aircraft in a straight line and accelerates the plane to a safe flying speed. On clearing the deck, the pilot continues normal climb procedures on instruments.

3. Rough weather operations can be carried out almost as routinely as the night operations. Again, the catapult assures a straight take-off in spite of the deck position. Furthermore, launch can be timed to the roll or pitch of the ship to place the plane in the most favourable position and speed.
4. Finally, the aircraft can be launched in crosswind conditions – in fact it was common practice to launch right out of the hangar deck! In pre-catapult times, it was necessary to head the carrier into the prevailing wind to assure the flow of air down the centre line of the deck. While this seems reasonable, it was not always the most practical since the rest of the task force might, for tactical reasons, be headed in a different direction, as much as 180° to the prevailing wind. Under the old unassisted system this could force the carrier to steam away from the protective screen of the fleet force and then have to turn and catch up. The alternative might mean depriving the fleet of a tactical

advantage in order to protect the carrier. Neither of these was necessary with the availability of the catapult.

The catapults used during the Second World War were essentially the same as those developed earlier, but with two important differences. Compressed air was still the propelling medium but an accumulator was used with the air over oil rather than direct application from an air compressor to the aircraft launching shuttle (hook). In these oil-pneumatic catapults the oil became the energy-transmitting medium, thereby reducing the amount of air lost on each shot. Only the amount of air necessary for the shot was expended and recompression was accomplished by oil pumps rather than air compressors.

The other important feature was the absence of any cradle. The aircraft was supported and operated on its own landing gear, thereby reducing the mass and moving parts that would necessarily accompany the use of a cradle in the form of accelerating and decelerating shock-absorbing buffers. With this new system increased rate and speed of launching were made possible since there was no cradle to be retrieved.

Torpedo Bombers in Combat
AIMING A PUNCH WHERE IT HURTS

There is no denying the fact that the fighters and the dive-bombers are the glamour aircraft of carrier operations. However, the torpedo bomber certainly was one of the first types of carrier-borne aircraft, dating back to the First World War. The adaptation of the already developed torpedo to the new naval weapon, the aeroplane, was a natural evolutionary step. The torpedo was proving to be a potent alternative to the 16-in guns of the capital ships. It had been adapted to the submarine, the destroyer, the cruiser and the light, fast motor torpedo boat, giving each of these lesser fleet units the potential punch of the battleship. The problem, as always, was the delivery method.

Cruisers and destroyers usually did carry torpedoes as part of their ordnance complement but they were themselves sizeable targets for the big guns of an enemy fleet. The submarine, because of its stealth and difficulty of detection, had been the ideal and traditional delivery mechanism for the torpedo launching. But as the anti-submarine programme developed along with the submarine, the submarine as well as the motor torpedo boats (MTBs), became more vulnerable to attack from the air. Like the MTB, the aeroplane had the speed and the

manoeuvrability to take evasive action for its own protection while, at the same time continuing to press home an attack from any quarter, and it could be launched into an engagement from a floating or land base many miles from the scene of the battle. Each plane carried the same destructive punch as one of the large guns of the capital ships. Little wonder then that the torpedo was one of the first weapons to be adapted to the aeroplane.

The first attack
The concept of launching torpedoes from aircraft dates back to 1909 when T O M Sopwith built an aircraft known as the Cuckoo to a requirement suggested by Lt Murray Sueter, RN. The plane was not completed but served as an inspiration to Robert Blackburn who, having formed his own company, developed an improved version produced as the Blackburn Cuckoo. The earliest known success of aircraft torpedo attacks occurred in the First World War when two Short float seaplane aircraft from the seaplane carrier *Ben-my-Chree* each torpedoed a ship in the Sea of Marmara off Turkey.

Experience soon showed that launching seaplanes was at best a nuisance and at

worst a definite hazard since the carrier must necessarily slow to a near halt to launch and/or retrieve the aircraft. With the introduction of full-length flight decks on carriers, aircraft with wheeled undercarriages became the standard and made possible simplification of all operations. The torpedo carrier reconnaissance aircraft benefited in other ways too, since the weight and air resistance of floats had reduced performance to a degree which made the carriage of a torpedo only marginally possible. In one case, the Curtiss CT, in other respects quite an advanced aircraft, was a failure because the weight and drag imposed by the floats and struts did not permit the use of 1600-lb torpedoes. Otherwise, the CT was a very interesting aircraft. It was a twin-engine, low-wing monoplane developed at a time – 1920 – when biplanes were the standard.

A second major deterrent to the rapid development of the torpedo bomber was the torpedo itself. Directly adapted from the ship/submarine torpedo, the early airborne versions developed a number of problems when airlifted to their targets. Aerodynamic considerations and launching difficulties required very precise low level flying at the time of drop, imposing conditions on the

crew which made this branch of naval aviation little short of heroic. At the low altitude necessitated by the drop requirements, the torpedo plane was subject during its run not only to the hazard of direct hits: even a near miss could throw up a geyser which could be just as effective in deflecting the plane from its course.

Added to this ever-present barrage from a target or its supporting ships was the presence of defending fighters. These considered the heavily laden torpedo planes sitting ducks, particularly when they lined up for their run, for if the drop was to have any chance for success the bomber must hold its course – a very predictable course at low altitude, during which time fighters picked them off with discouraging regularity. Because of this, naval strategists did not consider the torpedo bomber a very practical weapon. The delicate structure and guidance mechanism of the Whitehead torpedo, which was designed for underwater or slightly above the water launching, made the low level aircraft delivery necessary. Consequently, anti-aircraft gunners of the fleets assumed that the torpedo craft would be like fish in a rain barrel. Records show these views to be unduly pessimistic, as the torpedo aircraft, particularly the Fairey Swordfish, gave a good account of themselves.

In spite of these normally hazardous conditions under which torpedo crews operated, this class of naval aircraft was considered to be very unspectacular until 11 November 1940 – when British Fleet Air Arm Fairey Swordfish (affectionately known as 'Stringbags') launched from the carrier HMS *Illustrious*, created havoc and sank or damaged a substantial number of ships of the Italian Battle Fleet in a daring strike on the Italian naval base at Taranto. This bold attack cost the British two Swordfish lost and two damaged – quite remarkable when one considers the volume

A Japanese Kate attempts to torpedo the USS South Dakota *during the Battle of Santa Cruz.* Inset: *A US Navy Avenger releases its torpedo in practice*

of anti-aircraft fire directed at the attackers.

During the Battle of Cape Matapan, Fairey Albacores and Swordfish, though insufficient in numbers, managed to divert a far superior Italian force from cutting off an outnumbered and outgunned British cruiser group. The torpedo planes succeeded in jamming the steering gear and flooding the Italian battleship *Vittorio Veneto* with about 4000 tons of water. This action slowed the ship sufficiently to allow the British Fleet to catch the battleship and its escorting cruisers and destroyers and blow them out of the water.

Relentless pounding

This was a long awaited test, for until this time torpedo bombers had not been tried in an open sea engagement. It was the beginning of a series of airborne torpedo attacks. During these battles the Italian fleet was repeatedly harassed by the Swordfish and the planes reduced the comfortable 100-mile lead of the Italian battleship to 30 or 40 miles in a matter of eight hours with repeated, relentless pounding. The cumulative damage principle took its toll. In the attempt to save the battleship, the Italians lost four cruisers and a number of destroyers which were sent to aid the badly mauled *Vittorio Veneto*. In spite of very heavy anti-aircraft fire and the almost pedestrian pace of the Swordfish, the British lost only one aircraft.

Again and again the torpedo bomber was to show its mettle by crippling some of the biggest and best-defended ships, as well as extracting a heavy toll of lesser fighting ships and supporting supply ships. In spite of the handicap of their torpedoes, which made them slow and lacking in manoeuvrability the torpedo planes of the

Royal Navy's Fleet Air Arm and the RAF managed to keep the waters around the European continent within their control.

The most dramatic service rendered by the Swordfish was the encounter with the *Bismarck*, the most powerful battleship then afloat. This super-ship, along with its escort, the battle-cruiser *Prinz Eugen*, broke out of the Baltic Sea into the North Atlantic on 23 May 1941 to attempt to destroy or at least harass the Atlantic 'bridge' of ships that was Great Britain's lifeline to North America. Virtually the whole of the British Home Fleet was concentrated on the efforts to destroy this threat to Britain's survival. Events that followed proved once again the importance of having an air arm in any fleet. The carrier HMS *Victorious*, only recently commissioned and carrying a large cargo of crated Hawker Hurricanes destined for Gibraltar, was pressed into service, though her complement of operational aircraft consisted of less than a dozen Swordfish and only half a dozen Fairey Fulmar fighters.

In a running fight with HMS *Hood* and *Prince of Wales,* the *Bismarck* emerged the victor with relatively minor damage but in need of dry docking before carrying out her intended mission. One of her fuel tanks had been damaged, reducing her cruising range measurably. During the night, *Victorious* proceeded to within striking range of her aircraft to deliver a night torpedo attack. The Swordfish, with the valuable assistance of the newly developed radar, succeeded in scoring a hit which did no significant damage, but the high speed manoeuvring necessary to avoid the torpedoes in the heavy weather increased the damage which had resulted from the running fight with the British battleships. The boiler-room of the *Bismarck* was flooded causing a further reduction in her speed. In the prevailing heavy weather, the *Bismarck* shook off her pursuers only to be rediscovered by an

RAF Catalina patrolling the area in mid morning on 26 May at a position only 11 hours away from Brest, the destination port, and only a few hours beyond the protective range of German land-based aircraft.

Once again, the Swordfish went into action, this time from HMS *Ark Royal* which had been despatched from Gibraltar. The second wave of 15 Swordfish, flying converging courses in low clouds and heavy weather, succeeded in severely damaging the *Bismarck's* propellers and steering gear and jamming the rudders. During the night, she circled helplessly while the British fleet gathered for the dawn attack. With the first light of dawn, *Rodney* and *King George V* pounded the *Bismarck* to ruins. The torpedo attack that followed from the cruiser *Dorsetshire* sent the pride of the German navy to the bottom of the ocean.

It is well to examine at this stage the conditions which prevailed during these engagements. One fact that stands out is the relatively small numbers of aircraft involved. As experience was gained, the aircraft were employed in progressively greater numbers and, instead of in-line attacks, the planes attacked simultaneously along converging courses. Poor weather and/or darkness also limited the fighter defensive cover, and out of it all came the Swordfish, the ungainly dinosaur of the aircraft world, certain game for defensive

fighters – though its manoeuvrability and slow speed succeeded on occasion in evading even the sleek monoplane fighters.

An inexpensive machine of the tube-and-fabric era, the Swordfish was easy to maintain. It could and usually did operate in the most deplorable weather conditions in spite of heaving decks that kept all other aircraft grounded.

Technically, the Swordfish was of a conventional design of composite construction, mainly steel tube and fabric with limited use of sheet metal sheathing adjacent to the engine, back to the diagonal line aft of the front cockpit and the cockpit enclosure from the upper longerons and back to the rear of the after cockpit. Its single nine-cylinder air-cooled Bristol Pegasus 30 radial engine was rated at 750 hp.

The Fairey Albacore, successor to the Swordfish, was from the same mould and the same manufacturer. The configuration was the same, that of a single-engine biplane with fixed landing gear. It was a 'cleaned up', modernised version of the Swordfish, designed to replace it, but in fact, the Swordfish outlived its successor. Reaching carrier operation status in late 1940, the Albacore took part in a number of actions, the most notable of which was the battle of Cape Matapan in March 1941.

Operated from shore bases as often as from carriers, Albacores provided protective cover for convoys and flew anti-submarine

patrols. They were prominent in minelaying and in flare dropping as well. Their service in North Africa during the Western Desert campaign was one of the highlights of their service career; there they dropped flares to illuminate Rommel's positions and concentrations of armour for RAF night bombers. During this operation, it is estimated that they released approximately 12,000 flares in addition to taking part in the bombing themselves.

While this action was taking place, a monoplane replacement was being developed. The Fairey Barracuda, developed under an Air Ministry R & D Specification S24/37, issued in January 1938, never enjoyed the confidence of its crews.

Following the first flight of the prototype on 7 December 1940, a long development period ensued resulting in a great number of structural, aerodynamic and powerplant 'fixes' that delayed its entry into operational service until September 1943. Coupled with the structural problems was that of retrain-

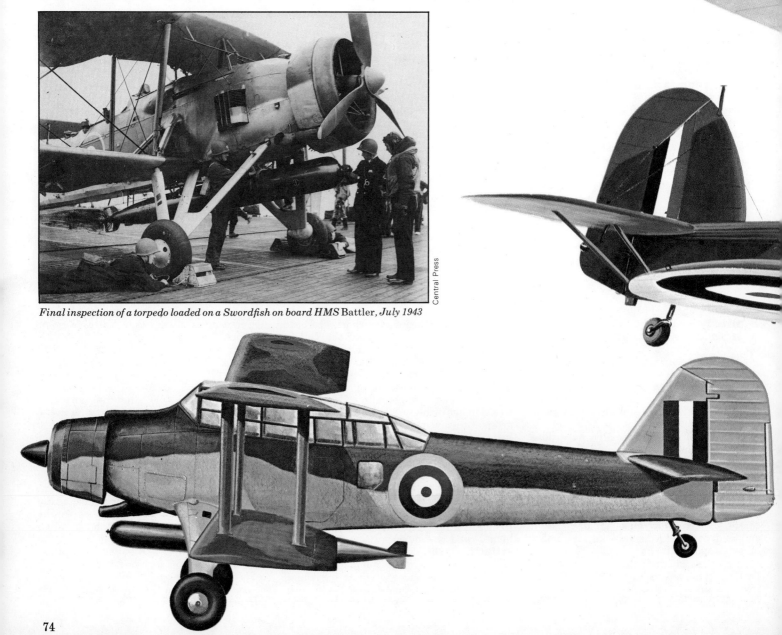

Final inspection of a torpedo loaded on a Swordfish on board HMS Battler, *July 1943*

ing crews from the slow, forgiving and highly manoeuvrable Swordfish and Albacore. Spins resulting from heavy application of the rudder while in a turn and the ensuing loss of altitude were most distressing and tiring to the pilots whose full attention was required to perform the necessary evasive attack manoeuvres.

In addition to its basic role of a torpedo bomber, the Barracuda was to be fitted out with a plethora of equipment with which to carry out a wide variety of additional duties. During its operational life it was to carry radomes, rockets, bombs, mines, lifeboats and containers for the dropping and supply of agents behind the front lines in France.

The aircraft retained the manoeuvrability necessary for torpedo attack but, in addition, was stressed to carry out the dive-bombing role.

The greatest successes attributed to the Barracuda were the attacks on the German battleship, *Tirpitz*, which was blockaded in a Norwegian fjord. In the neutralising of this battleship and her escorting cruisers, the Barracuda accounted for 176 sorties, of which 174 got through to the target, although it was well protected by both natural and man-made defences. Only two aircraft were shot down by anti-aircraft fire. Previous to this, the Barracuda had been giving a good account of itself in anti-shipping operations along the coast of Europe, using its dual capability as a dive-bomber to account for an impressive total of shipping damaged or destroyed.

Torpedoes in the Pacific

The Pacific theatre also had its share of torpedo activity with less lopsided results than in the European/Mediterranean theatre. As a rule, conditions in the Pacific were not as favourable to the torpedo plane. The weather was better, for a start, and the presence of large numbers of fighters with each of the opposing sides made torpedo launching a decidedly hazardous occupation – not that any combat category is safe, even in the most favourable conditions.

Beginning with the Japanese surprise attack on Pearl Harbor on 7 December 1941, 40 Nakajima B5N 'Kate' torpedo bombers gave a good account of themselves in successfully dropping torpedoes in the shallow harbour, with 104 additional Kates operational in their alternate role of horizontal bombers from altitude. In conjunction with the Aichi D3A 'Vals', the Kate wrought destruction on a scale rarely seen before or since Pearl Harbor. The first wave of attackers consisted of 40 Kates armed with torpedoes, with 50 additional Kates armed as horizontal bombers. The second wave of attackers included 54 Kates. At the conclusion of the attack, over 2400 Americans had been killed, almost 1200 wounded, four battleships were sunk, another beached and three others badly damaged. All of this was accomplished at a relatively small cost. Of the 354 Japanese aircraft involved in the attack, 5 Kates, 9 Zeros and 15 Val dive-bombers had been lost. As earth-shaking and successful as this attack was, it was a preview of the carrier task force which became the standard of naval operations during the Pacific War.

The B5N Kate and the less numerous Mitsubishi B5M were similar in configuration and structure – both were low-wing monoplanes built to the same specifications. The B5M was a bit more conservative in design and retained the fixed landing gear which was the principal identification detail between these two very similar aircraft.

Both had folding wings to facilitate stowage on board carriers and both carried their ordnance, whether torpedo or bombs, externally. Both were developed to meet a specification issued in 1935: the Nakajima entry, being more advanced in engineering concept, was chosen for large-scale production and assignment to carrier duties.

Fairey Swordfish I
The antiquated 'Stringbag' had the superb handling essential for carrier flying, and delivered cripplingly accurate torpedo attacks in actions from Taranto to the sinking of the *Bismarck*
Span: 45 ft 6 in *Length:* 36 ft 4 in
Engine: Bristol Pegasus 30, 750 hp
Armament: 1 Vickers mg; 1 Lewis mg *Max Speed:* 139 mph at 4750 ft *Ceiling:* 10,700 ft
Range: 546 miles *Bombload:* 1×18-in torpedo or 1500 lb bombs or mines or 8×60-lb bombs

Fairey Albacore
Overshadowed by the Swordfish for which the Albacore was planned as a replacement, this rugged biplane fought at Matapan and in the Western Desert on flare-dropping missions and proved a useful anti-submarine aircraft
Span: 50 ft *Length:* 39 ft 9½ in *Engine:* Bristol Taurus II, 1065 hp *Armament:* 1 Vickers mg; 2 Vickers 'K' mg *Max Speed:* 161 mph at 4000 ft *Ceiling:* 20,700 ft *Range:* 930 miles
Bombload: 1×18-in torpedo or 2000 lb bombs

With the outbreak of hostilities in the Pacific in 1941, a major part of the US fleet of capital ships was sunk or put out of action. Fortunately, the carriers *Lexington, Saratoga* and *Enterprise*, still at sea, escaped the fate of the battleships and cruisers at Pearl Harbor. Forming part of the aircraft complement of the three carriers were the venerable Douglas TBD Devastators, by this time five years old and suffering from old age in the form of intergranular corrosion of their structure and sheet metal skin.

Fairey Barracuda Mk II
The three-seat Barracuda served as the FAA's workhorse, carrying everything from bombs, torpedoes, mines and rockets to lifeboats. Forty-two Barracudas crippled the mighty *Tirpitz* in Kaafiord, Norway on 3 April 1944
Span: 49 ft 2 in *Length:* 39 ft 9 in
Engine: Rolls-Royce Merlin 32, 1640 hp
Armament: 2 Vickers K mg *Max Speed:* 228 mph at 1750 ft *Ceiling:* 16,600 ft *Range:* 1150 miles unloaded *Bombload:* 1×1620-lb torpedo or 4×450-lb bombs or 6×250-lb bombs

As a result the TBDs served only six months at the beginning of the war.

During this time they took part in the first action against the Japanese. Flying from the *Enterprise,* Torpedo Squadron VT 6, armed with bombs in a dawn attack, caused heavy damage to ships anchored at Kwajalein and, after re-arming with torpedoes, succeeded in accounting for two transports, two cargo ships, one cruiser and two submarines – which can be considered a good day's work. Later the same day, VT 6 bombed Taroa, destroying a number of grounded aircraft and an ammunition dump. At the same time VT 5 was busy bombing a large shore installation on Jaluit.

With these modest successes, the planes of the two squadrons suffered only minor hits by the shore anti-aircraft batteries.

Shortly afterwards, on 24 February 1942, the TBDs of VT 6 attacked Wake Island, followed by a raid on Marcus Island on 4 March. TBDs from the *Yorktown* and *Lexington* were equally busy with raids on Lae and Salamaua where they reverted to torpedo dropping to destroy 10 ships. On 7 May the planes of VT 2 and VT 5 succeeded in sinking the Japanese light carrier *Shoho* in co-operation with other aircraft in the fleet in coordinated attacks during the Battle of the Coral Sea.

Showdown at Midway
The most famous battle in which the TBDs participated was the Battle of Midway which began on 4 June 1942, with a combined total of 41 TBDs available from all the US carriers in the massed fleet. Aside from a few veterans of the actions previously listed, the bulk of the squadron crews were new and inexperienced, hastily assembled at the outbreak of the war, and most of them had never taken off with live torpedoes prior to this battle.

At Midway, the torpedo bombers faced a major part of the Japanese Navy including capital ships and four aircraft carriers bent on the destruction of Midway as an outpost of the US Navy. With this array of strength, which included the very capable, and by now well-proven, Zero navy fighters among its bag of weapons, the Japanese fleet was a most impressive adversary. The TBDs faced a 'stacked deck'. With good weather, but low clouds at about 2000 ft, with many

Nakajima B5N2 'Kate'
B5Ns were in the forefront of the attack on Pearl Harbor, and during the following year carrier-based Kates were to deliver fatal blows to the carriers *Lexington, Yorktown* and *Hornet*
Span: 50 ft 10 in *Length:* 33 ft 9 in
Engine: Nakajima Sakae II, 970 hp at 9845 ft
Max Speed: 235 mph at 11,810 ft
Ceiling: 27,100 ft *Range:* 1237 miles
Armament: 1×7·7-mm mg *Bombload:* 1764 lb bombs or torpedo

A US battleship blazes at Pearl Harbor. But the Japanese had failed to hit the vital carriers, which were fortunately still at sea when the attack occurred

Japanese ships to maintain an umbrella of anti-aircraft fire and the fighter squadrons of four Japanese carriers, the situation was at its worst for the TBDs. Added to this, the planes and their Mk 13 torpedoes were both outmoded and inadequate for the job, as events were to show.

The TBDs, with an approach speed of about 125 mph, were exposed to the murderous fire of the Japanese guns for about 15 minutes during their approach. The early models of the Mk 13 torpedoes could not be dropped at speeds above 100 mph or higher than 50 ft above the surface. Coupled with this was the necessity to aim for a quartering bow shot for these torpedoes with a maximum speed, under favourable conditions, of 30 knots could never catch a carrier or cruiser if launched from a rear quarter.

In the face of these odds, three squadrons of TBDs, the Torpedo Squadrons VT 8 from the *Hornet,* VT 6 from the *Enterprise* and VT 3 from the *Yorktown* pressed home the attack, only to lose the bulk of their planes and crew (the aircraft loss was 90%, the crew casualty rate was 85%). VT 8 lost all 15 planes with only one survivor, Ensign George Gray. VT 6 lost all but three aircraft and two aircraft of VT 3 survived, only to splash down just short of landing on board the *Yorktown*. Many concluded, incorrectly, that this was the end of the line for torpedo bombers.

The TBD was a conventional aircraft for its day, first entering service with the fleet in November 1937. It was of stressed skin construction and monoplane configuration. The low cantilever wing tapered in plan and profile from the root to the tips. About half-way out, at the flap/aileron juncture, each wing could be folded hydraulically, making it the first type of aircraft to have this feature. The oval cross-section fuselage accommodated the crew of three – pilot, navigator/bombardier and radio-operator/gunner. A special window beneath the pilot permitted the bombardier, lying prone, to use a bombsight for launching an externally mounted torpedo or bombs.

Douglas TBD-1 Devastator
The backbone of the US Navy's carrier torpedo forces at the outbreak of the Pacific War, the Devastator was already obsolete. With its light armament and slow approach speed, it was easy prey for Zero pilots
Span: 50 ft *Length:* 32 ft 6 in *Engine:* Pratt & Whitney R-1830-64, 900 hp *Max Speed:* 225 mph *Range:* 985 miles *Armament:* 1 × ·30-in mg; 1 × ·50-in mg *Bombload:* 1000-lb bomb or 1 × 21-in torpedo

Armament was minimal but typical of the times in which the TBD was designed. It consisted of one ·30 cal synchronised gun firing forward and one ·50 cal flexible-mounted gun in the rear cockpit. The Pratt & Whitney R-1830-64 engine developed 900 hp to give a weight to power ratio of over 11 lb per hp at 10,194 lb combat gross.

Replacement in the wings
At the Battle of Midway the heavy casualties suffered by the TBDs emphasised the need for an immediate replacement. Such a machine was in the wings, for Squadron VT 8 which had sustained such heavy losses at Midway was scheduled to be one of the first squadrons to be re-equipped with the Grumman TBF Avenger. In fact, six Midway-based Avengers of VT 8 attacked the Japanese fleet at Midway early on 4 June only to lose five aircraft in the ensuing battle. In this case it was not so much the quality of the aircraft involved as the numbers and the lack of coordinated fighter and dive-bomber attacks to keep the Japanese gunners' minds and guns off the torpedo planes as they began their attacks.

Two months later, on 7 August 1942, when the first amphibious assault began on Guadalcanal, the TBFs had replaced all the TBDs. From this date onward the TBFs were the standard torpedo bomber of the US Fleet and were used in very substantial numbers by the Royal Navy and other Allied navies. In the Pacific theatre alone, the TBFs took part in the Battles of the Eastern Solomons on 24-25 August 1942; Santa Cruz Islands (26-27 October 1942); Gilbert Islands (10 November to 10 December 1943); the Marshall Islands (29 January to 23 February 1944) and the Battle of the Philippine Sea, 19-24 June 1944.

A rugged aeroplane, the TBF was quite obviously a near relative to the F6F Hellcat fighter – so much so that at least one Japanese pilot, Saburo Sakai, one of the most famous fighter aces of all time, mistook a flight of Avengers for Hellcats. He proceeded to attack from below and to the rear only to find himself trapped in the concentrated crossfire from the ventral stinger guns in the TBF flight. This was the first torpedo plane to carry its load, whether the new 22-in, 2000-lb torpedo or the equivalent weight in 500-lb bombs, internally, thereby

Nakajima B6N2 Tenzan (Heavenly Mountain) 'Jill'
The Japanese Navy had high hopes for this big carrier attack bomber, but in action its high landing speed restricted it to the larger carriers, while it proved an easy target for US Hellcats
Span: 48 ft 10 in *Length:* 35 ft 8 in *Engine:* Mitsubishi MK4T Kasei 25, 1680 hp at 6880 ft *Max speed:* 299 mph at 16,075 ft *Ceiling:* 29,660 ft *Range:* 1085 miles *Armament:* 2 × 7·7-mm mg *Bombload:* 1764-lb bombs or torpedo

cutting down on air resistance and increasing the maximum speed to around 250 mph, a good 80–100 mph faster than the old TBD.

Part of this increase was, of course, attributable to the nearly 1000 extra hp provided by the Wright R-2600 engine. This additional power also improved take-off performance, making it possible to get off the carrier decks in as little as 650 ft. In the case of the small CVE Jeep carriers, the additional boost required to launch the heavily laden TBFs led to accelerated development of the flush deck catapults for all-weather operations. The use of small merchant ships converted to CVEs was one of the most important steps in maintaining anti-submarine patrols with the Atlantic convoys, as well as providing close support for amphibious landings and anti-submarine patrols and resupplying the larger attack carriers after battle losses in the Pacific. The TBFs were an important and integral part of both of these operations.

Contrary to earlier concepts of torpedo plane design, the TBF was fat and business-like in appearance and in combat it grossed at nearly eight tons, an impressive load for a single-engine aircraft, and one which accounted for its relatively poor rate of climb. Testimony to the ruggedness of the TBF, usually referred to as the 'Turkey' by its crews, is the fact that even now, Avengers are still in demand and still in use as 'water bombers' in delivering fire-extinguishing chemicals for forest fire control.

The TBF and the F6F Hellcat were initially produced side-by-side, but increased demand for the F6F made it necessary to secure a second source of production for the TBF. A contract was negotiated with the Eastern Aircraft Division of General Motors at their Trenton, NJ plant and signed on 23 March 1942. In December 1943, Grumman, the parent plant, ended production of the TBFs after producing in excess of 2290 planes. Eastern Aircraft Division then became the primary constructor under the designation of TBMs, producing a total of 7546 planes.

A mid-wing monoplane of rather portly dimensions, the Avenger had accommoda-

tions for a three-man crew above the wing in a greenhouse canopy, the aft end of which was rounded off by a glazed ball turret. The wing, in plan form, had a straight centre section out to the folding point, at which juncture there was an almost equal taper of the leading and trailing edges of the outboard panels. The centre section housed the main fuel tanks and the retractable landing gear fittings and struts. Under the wing was a fairly spacious bomb-bay which could totally enclose the Mk 13 torpedo or alternatively four 500-lb bombs or an auxiliary fuel tank for long-range reconnaissance or ferrying. The wheels themselves were fully enclosed in the outer panels of the wings when the gear was retracted outward during flight. In spite of this outward retraction feature, the tread was quite generous, unlike the Messerschmitt Bf 109 and the Spitfire, both of which had a similar disposition of the undercarriage.

The big 18-cylinder Wright R-2600-8 was a powerful engine, developing 1700 hp initially, but was prone to overheat, requiring careful management by the pilot. Armament consisted initially of one ·50 cal machine-gun mounted on the starboard side of the cowling, synchronised to fire through the propeller (later models were fitted with two wing guns), and a single ·50 cal gun mounted in a Grumman-designed turret covering the upper rear field of fire. This single gun was mounted on the starboard side. Finally, in the bombardier's ventral position was a single ·30 cal machine-gun. Primary ordnance was the torpedo which increased in weight and improved in reliability as the war progressed. In addition, the TBF could carry bomb loads of up to 2000 lb, ranging from 100-lb bombs in salvo to single 2000-lb bombs, often supplemented by wing-mounted rocket launchers when engaged in supporting amphibious assaults.

Designed as a replacement for the Kate, the Nakajima B6N2 Tenzan (Heavenly Lightning) 'Jill' was the last Japanese aircraft designed as a carrier-based torpedo bomber to see action during the Second

Grumman TBF-1 Avenger
The Avenger had the defensive qualities and
strike capability of a twin-engined aircraft,
combined with the size and handling of a carrier
aircraft. Carrying bombs, depth charges or
torpedoes, the type was outstanding in US and
Royal Navy service

Span: 54 ft 2 in *Length:* 40 ft *Engine:* Wright
Cyclone GR-2600-8, 1850 hp
Armament: 2×·5-in mg in wings; 1×·3-in mg in
ventral position; 1×·5-in mg in dorsal turret
Speed: 259 mph at 11,200 ft *Ceiling:* 23,000 ft
Range: 1000 miles loaded *Bombload:* 1×22-in
torpedo or 2000 lb bombs

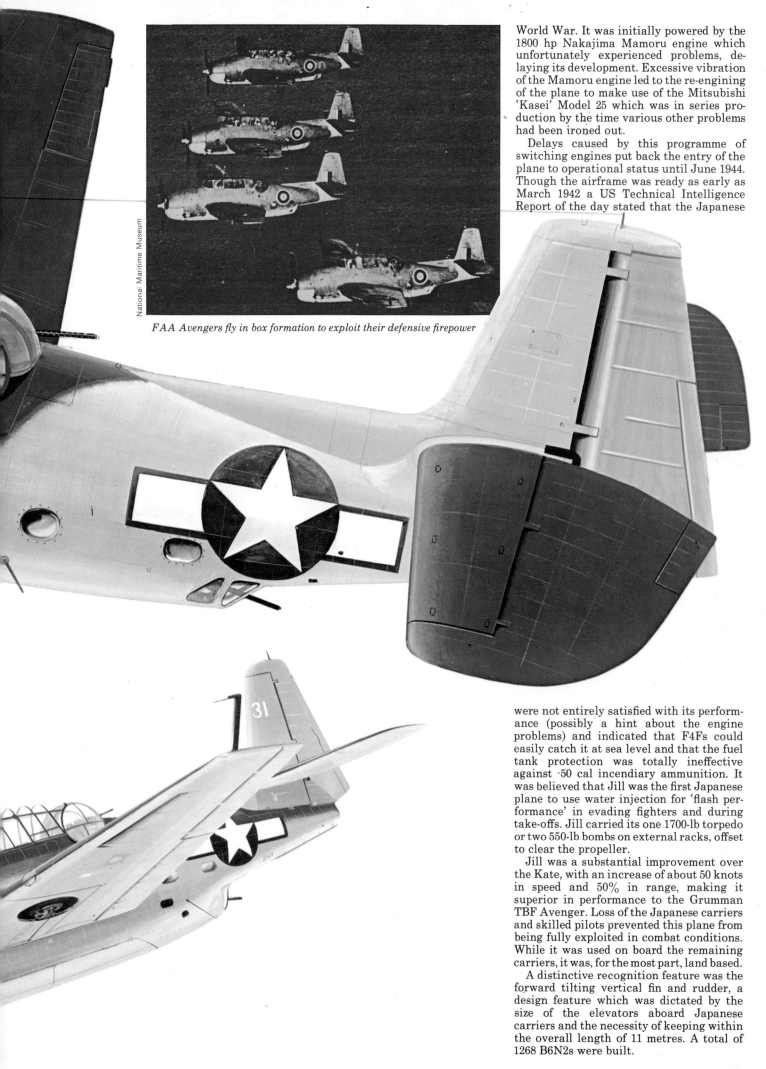

World War. It was initially powered by the 1800 hp Nakajima Mamoru engine which unfortunately experienced problems, delaying its development. Excessive vibration of the Mamoru engine led to the re-engining of the plane to make use of the Mitsubishi 'Kasei' Model 25 which was in series production by the time various other problems had been ironed out.

Delays caused by this programme of switching engines put back the entry of the plane to operational status until June 1944. Though the airframe was ready as early as March 1942 a US Technical Intelligence Report of the day stated that the Japanese

FAA Avengers fly in box formation to exploit their defensive firepower

were not entirely satisfied with its performance (possibly a hint about the engine problems) and indicated that F4Fs could easily catch it at sea level and that the fuel tank protection was totally ineffective against ·50 cal incendiary ammunition. It was believed that Jill was the first Japanese plane to use water injection for 'flash performance' in evading fighters and during take-offs. Jill carried its one 1700-lb torpedo or two 550-lb bombs on external racks, offset to clear the propeller.

Jill was a substantial improvement over the Kate, with an increase of about 50 knots in speed and 50% in range, making it superior in performance to the Grumman TBF Avenger. Loss of the Japanese carriers and skilled pilots prevented this plane from being fully exploited in combat conditions. While it was used on board the remaining carriers, it was, for the most part, land based.

A distinctive recognition feature was the forward tilting vertical fin and rudder, a design feature which was dictated by the size of the elevators aboard Japanese carriers and the necessity of keeping within the overall length of 11 metres. A total of 1268 B6N2s were built.

A Japanese dive-bomber swoops on USS Hornet while a torpedo plane circles, Battle of Santa Cruz

Dive Bombers
'WHEN WE SAY DIVE WE MEAN STRAIGHT DOWN'

Scout-bomber/strike-reconnaissance attack aircraft are better known as dive-bombers, dive-bombing being their most spectacular and devastating form of attack. Though tried in limited form by the Royal Flying Corps during 1918, the first true dive-bombing was carried out by the US Marines in 1919 in Haiti and later in Nicaragua in 1928, using Curtiss Helldivers, when the lives of their comrades on the ground would have been endangered by any less precise bombing method.

As early as 1927 the US Navy began to practise dive-bombing with all types of aircraft except the VPB patrol bombers and VTB torpedo bombers, using such machines as the Curtiss BFC and BF2C (redesignated Hawk III and Hawk IV). These were developments of the Hawk I and II export Hawks and the US Navy's F11 C-2 fighters. During his many visits to the US, Ernst Udet was intrigued by this form of bombing, which was then being demonstrated at air shows by Maj Al Williams, USMC Ret, and others. Using his Gulfhawk I, a Curtiss F6C owned by the Gulf Oil Company, Williams was a regular performer and crowd-pleaser as he roared straight down to deposit a bag of flour or a dummy bomb on a target in front of the grandstand with almost unerring accuracy.

Udet was sufficiently impressed to persuade his old First World War chum, Hermann Göring, to purchase two of the export Hawks for demonstration and testing back in Germany. These two aircraft, with manufacturer numbers 80 and 81, were delivered during the first two weeks of October 1933 and cost the then high price of $11,500 each. When Udet took delivery he promptly christened them Iris and Irik and set out to convince the budding Luftwaffe that this was the way of the future. Unfortunately one of the Hawks crashed in 1934 and the other was relegated to the Berlin Museum after having been flown extensively in demonstrations and outlived its usefulness. At the end of the Second World War this remaining Curtiss Hawk ended up in the Air Museum at Krakow, Poland.

The tactic of dive-bombing was continuously practised by the US Navy, to a lesser extent by the Fleet Air Arm and, presumably, by the Imperial Japanese Navy. The nature and size of ships make them very elusive targets, especially when they take evasive action, and there is little possible benefit from near misses by bombs dropped in salvo. Unless it is a very near miss, causing hull damage by concussion, conventional salvo bombing could waste a lot of bombs with little or no effect on the target. With a dodging and turning ship, the difficulty of getting a direct hit is increased many times.

'Battleship Row', Pearl Harbor, 7 December 1941
Bomb-aimer's view of stricken US Pacific Fleet

Single-engined aircraft normally used by the Navy do not carry many bombs, so it is necessary to use bombs of sufficient size to do meaningful damage and to place those bombs with great accuracy. Payloads rarely exceed 1½ tons, making it normal practice to use smaller bombs in quantity only against land or harbour targets. This does not mean that level bombing is not used in battle, for the sheer magnitude of bombs raining down on a fleet of ships or a landing zone from whatever source lends substantial assistance to the attacking force as a destructive and distractive element. There is also a strong possibility of a hit or near miss silencing a ship's anti-aircraft guns.

Dive-bombing, on the other hand, is a reasonably accurate delivery method in which the plane is lined up with the target so precisely that it is almost like sighting down the barrel of a gun. Evasive action is still possible, but the pilot can correct for this with small movements of the controls of his aircraft until the instant of release, which can be at a very low altitude, depending on the skill, daring and physical tolerance of the pilot.

Dive-bombers try to approach a target at high speed taking advantage of any cloud cover and, when possible, diving out of the sun in order to increase the problems for the defending anti-aircraft gunners. While speed is an asset in getting to the target, and away from it after the bomb is released, it is a disadvantage to build up too much speed in the dive. To do so increases the difficulty in aiming, as well as the stress on a plane

and crew during the pull-out. Aerodynamically clean, the dive-bomber would build up a tremendous speed if not retarded by some means. It is therefore necessary to fit these aircraft with speed-retarding dive brakes. These enable the pilot to adjust his dive speed to be fast enough to press home the attack and still slow enough to pick up the target and make a good recovery.

Confusing the Gunners
The ideal is a true vertical dive which enables the pilot to confuse the ship's gunners by giving him a choice of any angle for recovery. Simply by rolling the plane while in the vertical position, the pilot can avoid giving away his intended direction of recovery and thus confuse the gunners who would normally try to 'lead' him like a clay pigeon during his recovery trajectory, when the plane is most vulnerable. The pull-out rate and altitude is determined more by what the pilot can stand, physically, than by what the plane can take.

Dive-bomber pilots are quick to point out that 'when we say dive, we mean straight down'. However, it did not always work out that way in practice, for the pull-out often caused the pilot to black out due to blood being driven from the pilot's head by centrifugal force (referred to as 'Gs'). Medical scientists and technicians combined forces to develop anti-G suits to retard the flow of blood from the pilot's head by exerting pressure on arterial pressure points and the stomach area, reducing, or at least delaying, the normal tendency to black out.

Contrary to general belief, a pilot does not just line up a target, particularly a moving target, in his sights and hold this position. He continues to fly the plane, adjusting for wind, target movement and, most probably, bursts of flak. During the dive he must avoid skidding or the bomb will be deflected away from the aiming point. Finally, the pull-out point must be determined and this varies with the pilot's personal tolerance for the centrifugal force and the type of bomb, since he wants to be levelled out and well on his way before the bomb bursts.

Among the advantages of dive-bombing is the fact that anti-aircraft fire never has succeeded in stopping a dive-bombing attack, and it is far more accurate than other systems. Ideally, an attack should be a coordinated effort between the dive-bombers to disable the target ship and torpedo bombers to come in for the kill. As one wag put it, 'If you want to let in air, you use bombs, and if you want to let in water you use torpedoes'.

The spectacular aspect is well known but the second, and equally important, function of this type of aircraft is scouting for an enemy force. The strike-reconnaissance/scout-bomber must have the range to carry out this mission as well – and sometimes both missions must be combined. Such was the case when Lt-Cdr C Wade McClusky set out to find the large Japanese fleet which was headed for Midway Island.

The fleet had been reported by a US Army B-17 to be headed toward the island, but numbers and types of ships were missing from the brief radio transmission. McClusky led an air group of 33 Douglas SBDs of VB 6 and VS 6 off the *Enterprise* in search of the enemy force. Unknown to McClusky, the Japanese Fleet had turned and was steaming north-east instead of toward the island. Not finding them in the expected position, he continued to search until he made contact and began the attack that was to become the Battle of Midway. A few minutes later a second group, VS 3 and VS 5 from the *Yorktown*, led by Lt-Cdr Max Leslie, joined the battle. In the ensuing action, the Japanese lost four carriers, the *Kaga, Akagi, Hiryu* and *Soryu*. This decisive victory was accomplished at a cost of 32 casualties and the loss of all but six of the 41 torpedo bombers from VT 8 and VT 6.

At the outbreak of the Second World War the aircraft considered to be in this combat grouping were the British Blackburn Skua, the Japanese Aichi D3A Val and the US Douglas SBD Dauntless. As the war progressed, lessons learned in the various engagements were incorporated in the aircraft under development. Among the planes of this second grouping were the Nakajima B6N1/2 Jill and the Aichi B7A1 Grace, the Curtiss SB2C and the Fairey Barracuda

(discussed under the heading of torpedo bomber/attack aircraft). The Barracuda, as noted, was designed or adapted to do virtually everything and ended up doing none of its tasks exceptionally well.

One of the least known aircraft of the war was the Blackburn Skua. This lack of recognition would be strange except that at the time the Skua was making its mark in history, censorship was the order of day. The Skua was not produced in any great quantities so it was not seen sitting around every airstrip as were Moths and Cubs. In fact records show that only 165 were manufactured. But among its accomplishments it is credited with the destruction of the first German plane by a British aircraft during the war. The event took place on 25 September 1939, when a Skua shot down one of three Dornier Do 18 flying boats which were shadowing British fleet units off the coast of Norway.

State of the art

The Skua, like the Aichi Val and the Douglas SBD, represented the state of the art of the late 1930s, each reaching fleet operation status in 1937–39 and all scheduled for replacement just prior to the outbreak of war. HMS *Ark Royal* received six Skuas in November 1938, just in time for the opening action of the war. Operationally, the Skua played a very active role in the early days of the war, not because of great faith in dive-bombing on the part of the Royal Navy who favoured the torpedo as a weapon, but because in many instances it was the only aircraft available.

Blackburn Skua
The Royal Navy's first operational monoplane was conceived as a dual purpose fighter and dive-bomber, and saw combat in Norway, over Dunkirk and Dakar
Span: 46 ft 2 in *Length:* 35 ft 7 in
Engine: Bristol Perseus XII, 890 hp
Armament: 4 Browning mg; 1 Lewis mg *Max Speed:* 225 mph at 6500 ft *Ceiling:* 19,100 ft
Range: 760 miles *Bombload:* 1 × 500-lb bomb

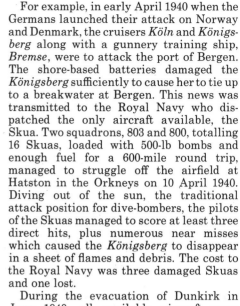

Blackburn Roc
The tactical concept of the Roc – bringing its four-gun turret to bear in broadside attacks on enemy aircraft – proved a failure and the type saw little combat, ending its days as a target tug
Span: 46 ft *Length:* 35 ft 7 in *Engine:* Bristol Perseus XII, 890 hp *Armament:* 4 × ·303 Browning mg *Max Speed:* 223 mph at 10,000 ft *Ceiling:* 18,000 ft *Range:* 810 miles

For example, in early April 1940 when the Germans launched their attack on Norway and Denmark, the cruisers *Köln* and *Königsberg* along with a gunnery training ship, *Bremse*, were to attack the port of Bergen. The shore-based batteries damaged the *Königsberg* sufficiently to cause her to tie up to a breakwater at Bergen. This news was transmitted to the Royal Navy who dispatched the only aircraft available, the Skua. Two squadrons, 803 and 800, totalling 16 Skuas, loaded with 500-lb bombs and enough fuel for a 600-mile round trip, managed to struggle off the airfield at Hatston in the Orkneys on 10 April 1940. Diving out of the sun, the traditional attack position for dive-bombers, the pilots of the Skuas managed to score at least three direct hits, plus numerous near misses which caused the *Königsberg* to disappear in a sheet of flames and debris. The cost to the Royal Navy was three damaged Skuas and one lost.

During the evacuation of Dunkirk in June 1940, all available aircraft were pressed into service to provide air cover. Skuas from 801 and 806 Squadrons took their place along with other aircraft types to provide much needed cover for the beleaguered British Expeditionary Force. After Dunkirk, the Skuas saw action in the Mediterranean, where 800 and 803 Squadrons, on board the *Ark Royal*, attacked units of the French Fleet, dive-bombing and putting out of action the new 35,000-ton battleship *Richelieu*.

There followed several engagements aiding convoys en route to the besieged island of Malta. Finally, in 1941, the Skuas were replaced by Fairey Fulmars for operational flying, but continued in service as trainers and for target towing. The rapid pace of aircraft development with the beginning of the war proved too fast for the sturdy Skua which had been designed in 1934 and first flown in 1937.

The Skua was an all-metal, single-engine monoplane. The fuselage, in compliance with specifications 0.27/34, was designed to be waterproof. It was divided into three watertight compartments to provide flotation should a ditching at sea be necessary. This was a valuable foresight as a number did ditch.

Production aircraft were fitted with the Bristol Perseus XII sleeve-valve engine – a unique engine, substituted for the Bristol Mercury which was required to outfit the Bristol Blenheim.

The Skua was the first all-metal mono-plane to reach operational status with the Fleet Air Arm and was the first British aircraft designed specifically for dive-bombing. One surprising detail in view of its slow speed (225 mph max) was its alternative role of fighter and the location of the fuel tanks in the fuselage between the front and rear cockpits. A similar tank location in the De Havilland DH-4 of the First World War earned for it the unenviable name of 'Flying Coffin', but this was before self-sealing fuel tanks were developed.

The rugged but awkward angled landing

gear and tail hook, plus the folding wing panels, completed the Skua's fitting-out for carrier service. Range was 760 miles; endurance was 4.5 hours at cruising speed of 145–165 mph.

Its armament was modest. Typical of that found in aircraft at the beginning of the war, it consisted of four forward-firing ·303 cal Browning machine-guns mounted in the wings and a single ·303 cal Lewis gun in a flexible mount in the rear cockpit. Ordnance consisted of one 500-lb bomb carried externally on a fork mount to ensure clearance of the propeller and up to eight 30-lb bombs on external wing racks. The latter were used primarily for practice since the only bombs of any value in this weight class were anti-personnel fragmentation bombs.

The Aichi D3A 'Val', built in 1937, was by far the most important of the Japanese dive-bombers and was considered obsolete by the time it was used so effectively at Pearl Harbor. Although the Yokosuka D4YI Suisei (Comet), code named by the Allies 'Judy', was in the development stage, it was not to see service until February 1944 off Truk Island, so the Val really had the war to itself in the dive-bomber class. It was the first all-metal dive-bomber built by the Japanese and was based on engineering knowledge obtained from the Heinkel He 118 which had been purchased by the Japanese for study purposes.

Slow and vulnerable
The Val was not too popular because of its relatively slow top speed of 232 mph and was also quite vulnerable in spite of the agility characteristic of Japanese aircraft of that period. Like its contemporaries it carried a single 550-lb bomb externally. For shorter ranges this load was supplemented by two smaller bombs fitted to wing racks, each of about 130 lb.

The devastation of Pearl Harbor was largely due to the Val. Following that historic attack the Val's next appearance was in the Indian Ocean in April 1942 where, for the second time, the Japanese convinced an anxious world that sea power was at the mercy of air power, particularly if the ships did not have adequate defensive air power of their own. It was an expensive lesson in ships and men, for the British carrier *Hermes* and the cruisers *Cornwall* and *Dorsetshire* all were sunk.

Following the major battles of Midway and Coral Sea, where the Japanese lost the major part of their trained and experienced

The American battleship USS Arizona *reduced to a blazing hulk by Japanese dive and torpedo bombers*

'Vals' in formation. They were the first Japanese type to bomb US targets

aircrews, the accuracy of their bombing fell to 10% hits in contrast to the 80% and 82% hit ratio that prevailed when they attacked the British ships in the Indian Ocean. The Japanese never managed to replace the experienced pilots lost in these battles.

Failure of the Yokosuka D4Y Judy to meet the operational requirements resulted in a continuation of production of the Val in an improved model, the Aichi D3A2, fitted with a more powerful engine, the Kinsei 54, and additional fuel capacity to increase the operating range.

From China to Leyte Gulf

In addition to the Pearl Harbor attack and the fateful battles of the Coral Sea and Midway, the Val was present in the earlier operations in China, at Wake Island, Darwin, Eastern Solomons, Santa Cruz, Philippine Sea (known as the 'Marianas Turkey Shoot') and finally the Battle of Leyte Gulf. By this time, Japan no longer had a carrier force and all navy aircraft, regardless of their intended use, were forced to operate from land bases. From this point onward, attacks by the Japanese consisted mostly of Kamikaze attacks. For this, the remaining Vals were converted to single seat configuration.

The Val was a single engine, low-wing monoplane whose fixed landing gear had streamlined covering over the legs and pants over the wheels. The fixed landing gear was one of the most obvious identification characteristics and contributed to lack of speed but was considered an asset when the plane was in its bombing dive. To facilitate stowage aboard carriers, the wing tips could be folded at a point six feet inboard from the tips. Like other aircraft of this period, its armament was not highly regarded. It carried two 7·7-mm guns firing

Aichi D3A2 'Val'

This rugged carrier-borne dive-bomber was in the forefront of the attacks on Pearl Harbor and on the Royal Navy in the Indian Ocean, and sank more Allied fighting ships than any other Axis aircraft type
Span: 47 ft 2 in *Length:* 33 ft 5 in
Engine: Mitsubishi Kinsei 54, 1100 hp at 20,000 ft *Armament:* 3×7·7-mm mg *Max speed:* 267 mph at 9845 ft *Ceiling:* 34,450 ft *Range:* 840 miles *Bombload:* 1×550-lb plus 2×132-lb bombs

forward and a single 7·7-mm gun mounted in the rear cockpit for defensive purposes and for strafing the decks of enemy ships as the bomb run was completed.

A total of 1294 Vals were produced between 1937 and 1944, 478 of which were the earlier model 11s (D3A1), powered by the 1075 hp Mitsubishi Kinsei 43 radial air-cooled engine. The second variant, the Model 22, powered by the Mitsubishi Kinsei 54, a twin-row 14 cylinder engine, boosted the power to 1200 hp and increased the speed to 266 mph. A total of 816 of the Model 22s (D3A2s) were built between 1942 and 1944.

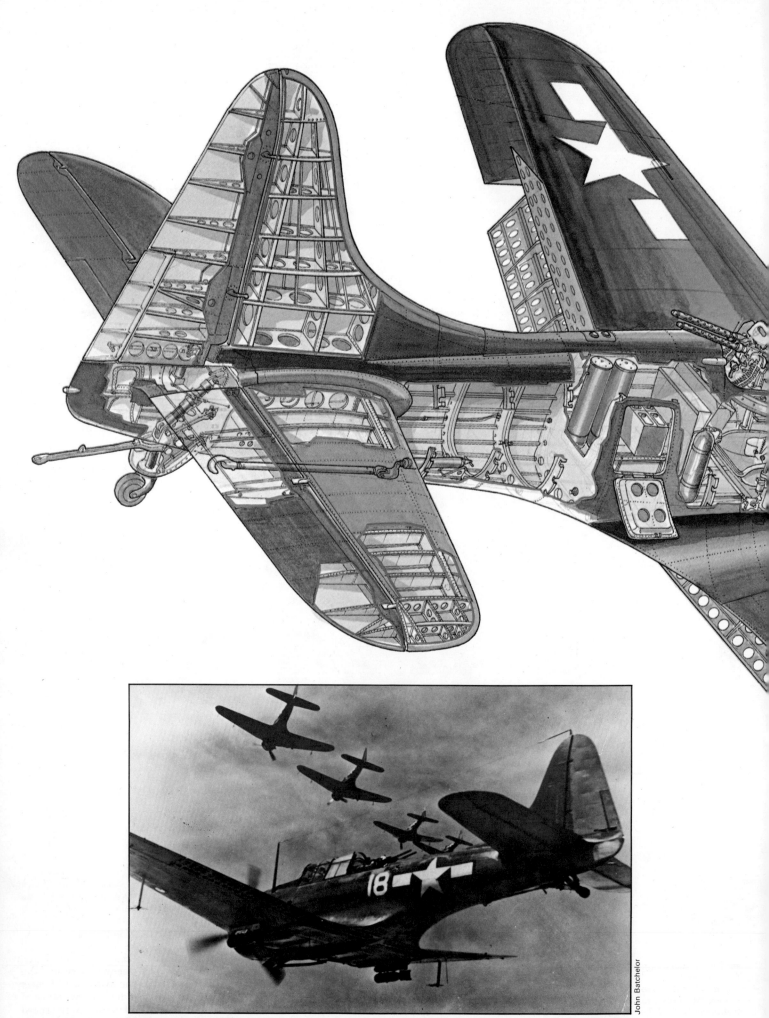

A flight of US Navy Dauntless dive-bombers heads for the Japanese base at Palau in the western Pacific

John Batchelor

Douglas SBD Dauntless
The SBD dive-bomber, approaching
obsolescence by 1941, was one of the most
important instruments in the American victories
and still outperformed its successor, the Helldiver
at Coral Sea, Midway, and the Philippine Sea
Span: 41 ft 6 in *Length:* 33 ft *Engine:* Wright
Cyclone, 950 hp *Max speed:* 255 mph
at 14,000 ft *Ceiling:* 25,200 ft *Range:* 773 miles
Armament: 2 × ·5-in mg *Bombload:* 1 × 500-lb bomb

Designed in 1938 and accepted by the US
Navy in February 1939, practically on the
eve of war, the Douglas SBD Dauntless
nevertheless represented pre-war technology. Fortunately, its design was quite
adaptable, within limits, to changes dictated by combat experience. Above all it
was a compact, rugged machine that could
take a lot of punishment at the hands of both
friend and foe. Friends were likely to expect
too much from it in load carrying and
handling and an enemy target or aircraft
could be expected to throw everything at it.

The SBD had only barely passed its
teething period when war broke out. The
first planes were accepted in February 1939
and the first contract for 57 SBD-1s was
negotiated during the first week of April
1939. Following the outbreak of hostilities,
these orders were substantially increased
with successive model changes indicating
responses to lessons and tactics learned in
the European war. These included increases in fuel, self-sealing fuel tanks and

armour plate for the crew, as well as a more
powerful engine, a Wright-Cyclone R 1820
delivering 1000 hp, to maintain the performance. Pearl Harbor added new urgency
to production lines, and an additional 500
SBDs were ordered. By this time the armament had changed from two ·30 cal cowling-
mounted guns to two ·50 cal machine-guns.
A second ·30 cal gun was added to the rear
cockpit. The SBDs produced under this
expanding programme, plus the remaining
SBD-2s, played a major role in the crucial
battles of the Coral Sea and Midway.

The SBDs gave a good account of themselves in every enagagement of the Pacific
theatre and, like the Aichi Vals, had a
reprieve. This resulted from delays in
getting the Curtiss SB2C, their intended
successor, fully acceptable and modified for
carrier operations. All told, they accounted
for most of the damage sustained by the
Japanese carriers and other enemy ships
they encountered.

Like its counterpart in the Japanese
Navy, the Val, the SBD almost had the war
all to itself for its successor, the Curtiss
SB2C did not satisfy operational requirements until late in 1943. In fact one eminent
naval historian, Samuel Eliot Morison, in
recording the Battle of the Philippine Sea,
stated that 'the new Helldiver was outshone
by the two remaining squadrons of Dauntless dive bombers . . . here the Dauntless
fought her last battle'.

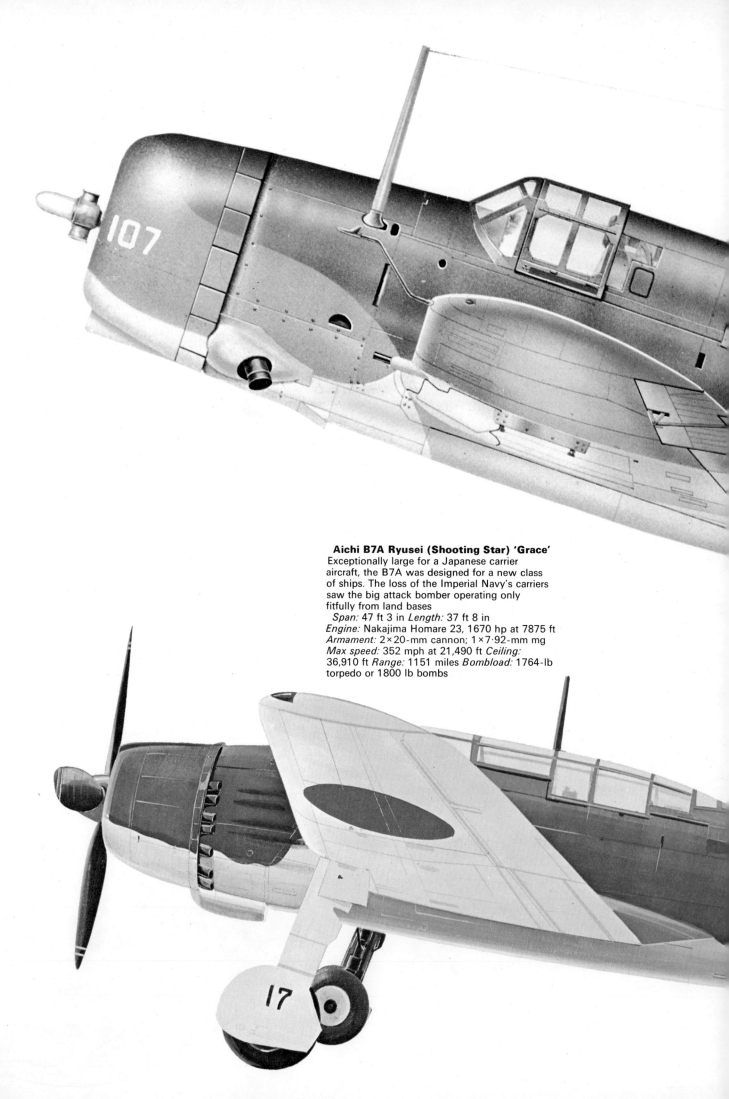

Aichi B7A Ryusei (Shooting Star) 'Grace'
Exceptionally large for a Japanese carrier
aircraft, the B7A was designed for a new class
of ships. The loss of the Imperial Navy's carriers
saw the big attack bomber operating only
fitfully from land bases
  Span: 47 ft 3 in *Length:* 37 ft 8 in
Engine: Nakajima Homare 23, 1670 hp at 7875 ft
Armament: 2×20-mm cannon; 1×7·92-mm mg
Max speed: 352 mph at 21,490 ft *Ceiling:*
36,910 ft *Range:* 1151 miles *Bombload:* 1764-lb
torpedo or 1800 lb bombs

Armament of the SBD-5 (the most numerous variant of the type) consisted of two ·50 cal guns mounted in the top deck of the cowl and a brace of ·30 cal flexible-mounted guns in the rear cockpit for the radio-operator.

Ordnance could consist of a variety of loads including (published specifications to the contrary) a 1600-lb bomb on the centre rack plus two 100-lb bombs on wing mounts, all externally mounted. In a scouting configuration, drop-tanks could be attached to the wing mounts for greater endurance.

In the final version of the SBD-6, the engine was the 1350 hp Pratt & Whitney

Curtiss SB2C Helldiver

Designed to fit the standard US carrier deck-elevator, the Helldiver suffered constant stability problems but it won honours in the USN's last dive-bomber action at Leyte Gulf, and in the attacks on the Japanese super-battleships *Yamato* and *Musashi*

Span: 49 ft 9 in *Length:* 36 ft 8 in
Engine: Wright R-2600-8, 1700 hp *Max speed:* 294 mph *Ceiling:* 23,000 ft *Range:* 695 miles

R-1820-66 and the published weights were 6554 lb empty and 10,882 lb at gross take-off weight. Unlike most of its contemporaries, the SBDs did not have folding wings to improve their shipboard stowage ability. Instead they had the same basic wing construction as their parent, the Northrop XBT-2 (XSBD-1), the Northrop Gamma and the ubiquitous DC-3 Dakota. The similarities of design are more than incidental.

Designed to replace the Douglas SBD, the Curtiss SB2C Helldiver was long overdue in combat. A succession of problems and modification programmes delayed the first squadron delivery of SB2C-1s until December 1942, a full year after Pearl Harbor. The original contract for the XSB2C-1 had been negotiated and signed in May 1939. Between these two dates a seemingly endless series of problems conspired to delay production. Difficulty with stability and control tests, cooling problems and loss of test aircraft kept engineers and test pilots busy for many months trying to resolve the problems as they occurred. In addition to design problems there was the question of engineering the plane for production by the thousand. Parts that normally would have been handmade out of a number of small components now were redesigned for mass production, often resulting in single unit forgings to economise on both man-hours and weight.

Weight reduction was an ever-present

albatross around the necks of the SB2C engineers. The SB2C was designed to carry bombs 50% heavier than those carried by the SBD it was to replace, and this added weight was to be carried in an internal bomb-bay. This was difficult to accomplish for two reasons. Firstly, increasing loads were being hung on the SBD in response to combat necessity and bombs 50% heavier were also larger, making it difficult to carry them internally. Secondly, external racks, while increasing the frontal drag, also permitted a wider variety of sizes and configurations.

By the time the problem areas were determined and the appropriate corrections made by modifications, the war was well under way. Most of the really big and decisive battles were over by 11 November 1943 when Squadron VB 17 from the *Bunker Hill* equipped with SB2Cs attacked the harbour at Rabaul. From this date until the end of hostilities the Helldiver was the standard dive-bomber, USN, replacing the SBD in all remaining major actions of the war.

Only a small number of SB2Cs were ordered by Allied forces. The Royal Australian Air Force ordered 150 A-25As, a land-based Army version, but took delivery of only ten, since by this late date there was no longer a requirement for land-based dive-bombers. Twenty-six SBW-1Bs were delivered to the Royal Navy from Canadian Car & Foundry Production. Like the Helldiver, which carried on a traditional Curtiss name, the A-25As were also to carry a traditional name of 'Shrike'.

The 'Beast', as it was called by its crew, was not particularly well liked, although it established a good record before the end of the war. It could carry up to 2000 lb of bombs in the bomb-bay and was tested to carry a Mk 13 torpedo though this was never used during the service life of the aircraft. In a similar vein the SB2C-2 was tested with floats with the idea of using it for close support of expeditionary landings. This configuration was never to see combat use. Depending on the dash number, the SB2Cs were armed with either four ·50 cal machine-guns or two 20-mm cannons plus two ·30 cal machine-guns in a flexible mount for the rear seat gunner.

Cancellation recommended
Directional stability was to plague the design during all its operational life. The short fuselage required to fit two aircraft on to each of the 40 ft × 48 ft elevators contributed to this. To improve the directional stability, the engine was moved forward one foot and compensating area added to the fin and rudder. On shake-down carrier qualification tests aboard the *Yorktown*, the SB2Cs had many problems, including structural failure, collapsed tail wheels and missed hook contact. Based on this experience, the ship's commander, Capt J J Clark recommended cancellation of the entire contract. This was in June 1942, only six months after Pearl Harbor when all the emphasis was on planes to win the war.

This was hardly the climate to start over again with a new design. As a result all parties pressed on, throwing good money after bad to make it work in spite of all its deficiencies. Under any other circumstances Captain Clark's recommendation would have spelled the end of this plane. The production lines turned out 600 SB2Cs before all the bugs were under control. The 601st plane was the first to be delivered

without a stop-over at one of the modification centres.

With the Pacific war nearly over and most of the Japanese carriers destroyed or damaged beyond repair there was really little left for the Helldivers to do. The one exception was the Battle of the Philippine Sea, where the SB2Cs gave a good account of themselves. They were to be the last dive-bombers of the Second World War.

After undergoing additional modifications to make them suitable for different tasks, the SB2Cs and their derivatives the A25s, were phased out of service and most of them scrapped.

Of limited importance during the Second World War, but built to requirements and from lessons learned in combat, the Aichi B7A1 *Ryusei* (Shooting Star) 'Grace' did

not establish any record of action from carriers although it was designed as a follow-on to the Nakajima B6N2 Jill and the D4Y Judy. Only 105 of these aircraft plus nine prototypes were completed before the end of hostilities and after the destruction of the Japanese carrier fleet.

The Grace was the first Japanese aircraft to be designed for internal stowage of a 1760-lb torpedo. In addition, it could carry a second torpedo externally. It was distinctive in design, having an inverted gull-shaped wing for the same reason as the Vought F4U Corsair, namely the need to shorten and therefore reduce weight of the retractable landing gear. It also featured coordinated droop ailerons (10°) which provided additional drag and lift when the flaps were lowered.

An 1825-hp Nakajima 'Homare' 12 engine made the Grace substantially faster than its predecessors with 356 mph being achieved during tests. Unfortunately, the engine was not fully developed, needed time-consuming maintenance and lacked reliability.

Among the dive-bomber category the Junkers Ju 87 is not generally known as a carrier-based type though as a dive-bomber it is probably better known than any other plane. The fact that it was considered and even stressed and fitted with catapult and arrester hook escapes any but the most intense researcher.

At the beginning of the war Germany had under construction an aircraft carrier, the *Graf Zeppelin*, which was abandoned early in the war. The principal dive-bomber, the Ju 87C or Stuka as it was best known, was to have been the dive-bomber assigned to this ship. The Ju 87C was a special modification of the Ju 87B-1 and was fitted with jettisonable landing gear in anticipation of the probability of a ditched landing. This

Towards the end of the war, many types of Japanese

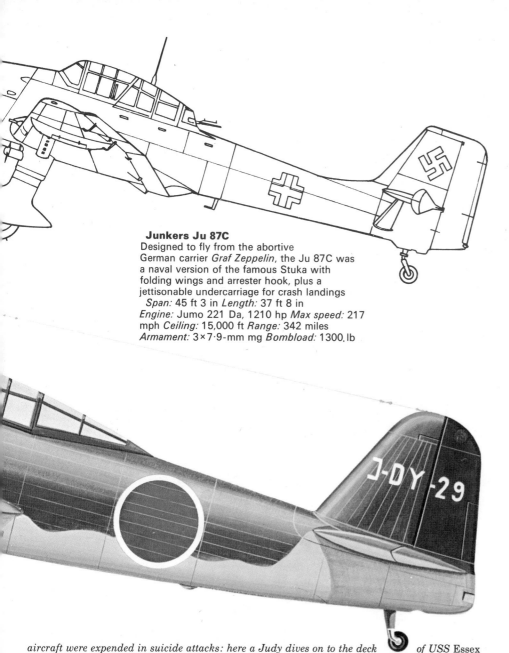

Junkers Ju 87C
Designed to fly from the abortive German carrier *Graf Zeppelin*, the Ju 87C was a naval version of the famous Stuka with folding wings and arrester hook, plus a jettisonable undercarriage for crash landings
Span: 45 ft 3 in *Length:* 37 ft 8 in
Engine: Jumo 221 Da, 1210 hp *Max speed:* 217 mph *Ceiling:* 15,000 ft *Range:* 342 miles
Armament: 3 × 7·9-mm mg *Bombload:* 1300, lb

aircraft were expended in suicide attacks: here a Judy dives on to the deck   *of USS* Essex

modification feature, to the best of our knowledge, was not used by Germany's ally Japan in the design of the Aichi D3A Val.

Only a few were produced and these were converted back to the Ju 87B-1 configuration when the carrier plans were abandoned.

The last of the carrier-based attack bombers or dive-bombers built by the Japanese was the Yokosuka D4Y1 *Suisei* (Comet), Allied code name 'Judy', which first entered service in its scout-reconnaissance role during the Battle of Midway. It was produced in a variety of models and in surprisingly large numbers – 2038 – which exceeded the production of Curtiss SB2Cs, even though Japan was under direct attack during the latter days of the war and disruption was certain to prevail during this time.

The Judy was interesting in a number of respects, one of which was the use of the liquid-cooled Aichi AE1A Atsuta 12 engine which produced 1200 hp. Most carrier-based aircraft, with the notable exception of the D4Y1 and D4Y2 Judy and the British Fairey Barracuda and Fulmar used air-cooled engines. Even the later versions of the Judy, D4Y3 and D4Y4, used air-cooled radial engines, the Mitsubishi Kinsei Model 62.

In each of these exceptions to the existing tradition, the resulting aircraft was very attractive. The Aichi Atsuta 12 was a version of the German Daimler-Benz engine built under licence. Poor reliability prompted the Aichi engineers to suggest changing the engine to the 1560-hp Mitsubishi Kinsei 62, an air-cooled radial. This modification was designated D4Y3. Of the 2038 D4Ys produced, at least 822 were powered by radial air-cooled engines.

Reconnaissance only
Like all naval carrier aircraft, the Judy was of a multi-purpose design, for dive-bombing/attack, night-fighter and finally as special attack (Kamikaze) aircraft. Until March 1943 the Judy experienced wing flutter when tested as a dive-bomber. As a result they were restricted to their reconnaissance configuration when they made their combat debut, flying from the aircraft carrier *Soryu* during the Battle of Midway. The D4Y2, powered by the 1400-hp Aichi Atsuta 32, had the airframe strengthened, making it serviceable in its intended principal role of dive-bomber. Unfortunately, time was running out for the Japanese fleet, much of which had slipped beneath the Pacific waters. During the period when the type was being strengthened, those produced were in action as reconnaissance aircraft flying from all the carriers remaining in action.

The night-fighter conversion was an interesting but relatively ineffective modification designed to attack B-29s which were then making regular runs over Japan. In this conversion a 20-mm cannon was fitted in the fuselage to fire upward at a 30° angle. Interesting as it was this was not an effective weapon since the plane itself had very poor performance. It had a 50 to 80 mph speed advantage over its predecessor, the D3A Val, and the contemporary SB2C. However, the latter carried at least twice the load of the D4Y and had almost twice the range.

Due to the pressure of the American forces moving steadily toward the Japanese homeland, desperate measures were adopted. The Kamikaze groups used specially designed aircraft, as well as modified production aircraft. Like the remaining Vals, the Judy was also used for this duty.

US Navy

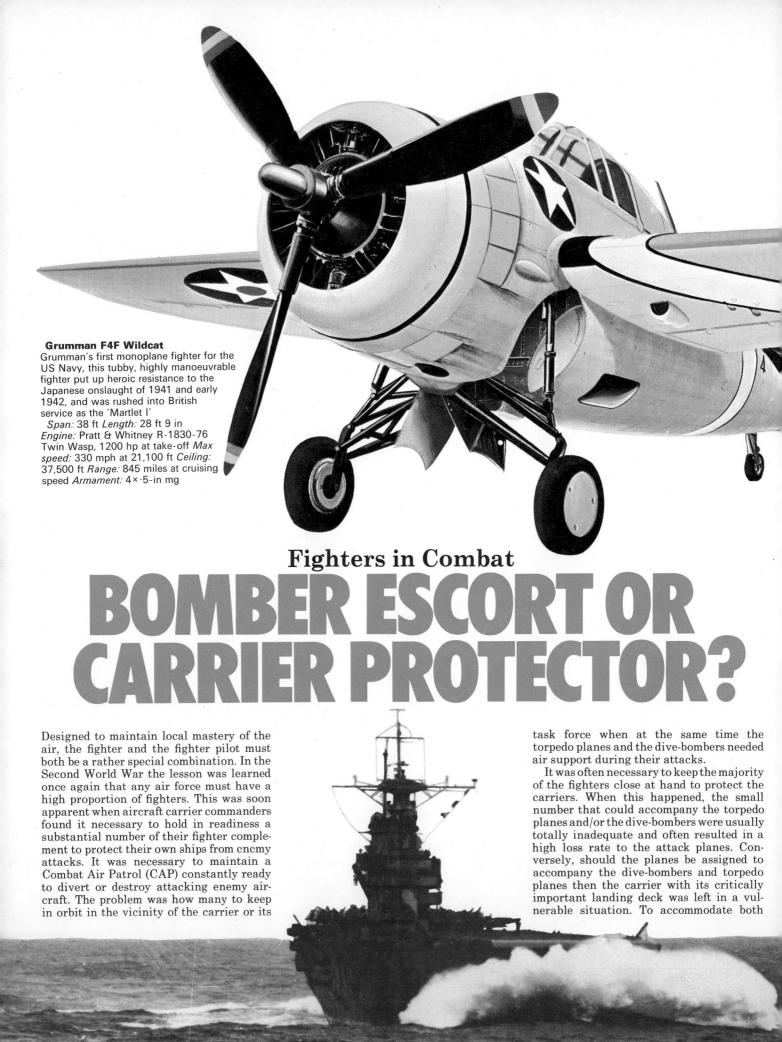

Grumman F4F Wildcat
Grumman's first monoplane fighter for the US Navy, this tubby, highly manoeuvrable fighter put up heroic resistance to the Japanese onslaught of 1941 and early 1942, and was rushed into British service as the 'Martlet I'
Span: 38 ft *Length:* 28 ft 9 in
Engine: Pratt & Whitney R-1830-76 Twin Wasp, 1200 hp at take-off *Max speed:* 330 mph at 21,100 ft *Ceiling:* 37,500 ft *Range:* 845 miles at cruising speed *Armament:* 4 × ·5-in mg

Fighters in Combat
BOMBER ESCORT OR CARRIER PROTECTOR?

Designed to maintain local mastery of the air, the fighter and the fighter pilot must both be a rather special combination. In the Second World War the lesson was learned once again that any air force must have a high proportion of fighters. This was soon apparent when aircraft carrier commanders found it necessary to hold in readiness a substantial number of their fighter complement to protect their own ships from enemy attacks. It was necessary to maintain a Combat Air Patrol (CAP) constantly ready to divert or destroy attacking enemy aircraft. The problem was how many to keep in orbit in the vicinity of the carrier or its task force when at the same time the torpedo planes and the dive-bombers needed air support during their attacks.

It was often necessary to keep the majority of the fighters close at hand to protect the carriers. When this happened, the small number that could accompany the torpedo planes and/or the dive-bombers were usually totally inadequate and often resulted in a high loss rate to the attack planes. Conversely, should the planes be assigned to accompany the dive-bombers and torpedo planes then the carrier with its critically important landing deck was left in a vulnerable situation. To accommodate both these requirements, the percentage of fighters in relation to other types of aircraft rose from roughly 18% to 60% of the aircraft complement of the carrier.

Another factor which made these aircraft ratios necessary was the increasing use of fighters in an attack role, loaded with ordnance almost beyond belief. In these cases, the fighters operated in the role of fighter-bombers delivering bombs, rockets and/or napalm on the first attack wave, and reverting to their fighter role after

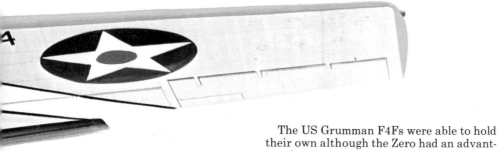

dropping their ordnance stores. It was partially because of the multitude of attack functions taken over by the fighters that scout-bombers became less and less necessary as the war progressed.

In fighter aircraft superior speed, while an important consideration, is not adequate in itself, nor is rate of climb the whole answer. Manoeuvrability by itself is also meaningless, but to combine the three in a machine superior to those of an opponent is the goal of the aircraft designer.

In the case of naval aircraft, additional requirements are imposed by their operation at sea and often far from friendly land bases. Among these requirements is adequate endurance and the strength to withstand launching and retrieval. Prior to the Second World War, two-seater fighters were purchased, and well into the early part of the war such planes as the Fairey Fulmar were operated – not because of any outstanding superiority but because of a lack of anything better. They were adequate when attacking slow bombers or reconnaissance aircraft but were at a grave disadvantage when opposed by single-seat fighters. The additional crew member and the accommodations for him penalised the plane's action. The most successful and most numerous naval fighters of the Second World War were single-seat planes.

Japan, among the major naval powers, had the best shipboard fighters when the war began. The French were woefully inadequate, as were the British, and the US was only slightly better off. The European nations had almost totally neglected sea-based airpower for a variety of reasons. The US was still suffering from short rations and shortsightedness, a hangover from the depression years.

The Mitsubishi A6M2 was the outstand-

ing fighter aircraft in the opening days of the Pacific war and came as a considerable surprise to most military authorities. The intensive security maintained by the Japanese largely accounted for this surprise. The A6M2, better known as the Zero or Zeke because of the designation of the aircraft as the Navy type '0' carrier fighter, was much maligned in the US as being a copy of one or more well known US aircraft. The Zero nevertheless gave a good account of itself and its pilots.

The US Grumman F4Fs were able to hold their own although the Zero had an advantage in most categories. By being able to absorb a lot of battle damage and still carry on, the F4F's four ·50 cal machine-guns were capable of tearing up the light structure and unprotected fuel tanks of the Zeros. High on the list of design criteria for the Japanese naval fighters was high manoeuvrability and high speed. To obtain these, it was necessary to compromise by using a light structure and by elimination of frills such as self-sealing fuel tanks and armour plate protection for the pilot and vital parts of the aircraft. They were, in fact, the correct choice for the war 'game-plan' of the Japanese commanders for a fast-moving war of short duration. Their misfortune was in not destroying the *Lexington* and *Enterprise* at Pearl Harbor.

New generation

The well-trained and heroic pilots of the US Navy, flying the rugged Wildcats and other carrier aircraft, held on and turned the tables when the new generation of planes was ready for combat operations. US planes like the Grumman F6F Hellcat were designed with the specific purpose of attaining air superiority over the Zero. The Japanese, on the other hand, did not have access to industrial resources to match those of the US, which was able to maintain production lines of F4Fs and SBDs while at the same time design and build the second generation aircraft.

The Japanese, in the meantime, were hard pressed to accomplish the same results although in retrospect one can only admire their determination, the variety of aircraft types and numbers produced during the war. The Zero, along with the Zeke and other

variations, was the principal Japanese carrier fighter from the beginning to the end of the war.

In the European theatre the British Navy paid a high price for peacetime lethargy or perhaps for the honest ignorance of fiscal and military officialdom. When the war clouds were growing in intensity, the Fleet Air Arm, which attained an independent status in May 1939, was still using the Gloster Sea Gladiator, a conversion of the RAF's last biplane fighter.

The success of the Hurricane and Spitfire prompted the Royal Navy to request a monoplane fighter. This resulted in the Fairey Fulmar, a two-seater which was to become the Navy's first all-metal monoplane fighter. The Blackburn Skua, previously mentioned, was to have been an all-purpose machine supposedly capable of operating as a fighter as well as a dive-bomber, but as a fighter it was badly outclassed.

With this situation Britain, hardpressed on many fronts, built Fairey Fireflys and adopted the Grumman Martlet I, basically the F4F with the single row Wright R-1820 instead of the more normal twin row Pratt & Whitney R-1830. These Martlets were originally ordered by the French and were diverted to the Fleet Air Arm after the French capitulation in June 1940. They were well tested and coming off production lines at a rate to satisfy US and British requirements.

Holding the line

The plane that held the line and kept the Imperial Japanese Navy busy during the early stages of the war was the Grumman F4F, a comparatively small single-engine, mid-wing monoplane. A pugnacious looking machine in the air, it was almost ugly on the deck, propped up on its narrow tread retractable landing gear. In the early models, the gear was manually retracted by thirty turns of a crank at the pilot's right hand. This feature was never particularly liked by pilots for more often than not it resulted in a porpoising flight path just after lift-off. In any event it was better than that of the Polikarpov I-15, the little Russian biplane fighter used by the Republicans in Spain. In the I-15, each landing gear leg had to be cranked up independently by hand, resulting in a roll, or partial roll, first one way and then another.

The F4Fs, christened 'Wildcats', were just coming into carrier service when war broke out. The fall of France in June 1940 resulted in increased orders for the Wildcat which, up to this point, was going through the normal peacetime development progression of service trials leading to full acceptance by the Navy. The original design competition was announced in 1935 to replace the Grumman F3F-1 biplane then in

USS Hornet, *the carrier that launched Doolittle's raid on Tokyo and was later sunk off Guadalcanal*

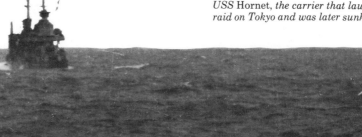

service. The competition was won by the Brewster F2A Buffalo but the US Navy gave Grumman a contract for a new prototype, designated XF4F-3. This turned out to be a very fortunate occurrence because, in service, the Buffalo showed a distressing weakness of the landing gear.

However, the Buffalo could easily out-manoeuvre the Wildcat in simulated combat but, on returning to the carrier, the odds were in favour of an unserviceable plane – not because of combat damage but because of landing damage. The F4F on the other hand was rugged and reliable in all situations but was lacking in climb and manoeuvrability when compared with its antagonist, the Japanese Zero. It more than made up for these deficiencies in its firepower of four (and later six) wing-mounted ·50 cal machine-guns, self-sealing fuel tanks and armour for pilot protection. The merit of these features was clearly demonstrated by the nearly seven to one combat-kill ratio over its opponents, many of them Japanese Zeros.

One design feature which caused problems and resulted in one fatal crash was inflation, in the air, of the specified flotation air bags. Elimination of these and the mechanism for hydraulically folding the wings provided space in the wings and weight reduction which made it possible to add another pair of guns and ammunition to bring the armament up to six ·50 cal machine-guns. This battery of guns proved to be the answer to any other deficiencies the Wildcat might have had, for when the pilot got on a target there was little doubt about the outcome.

Having quickly learned of the manoeuvrability and climb characteristics of the Zero, the US Navy pilots concentrated on head-on or diving attacks. In the head-on attack the Wildcat had the advantage of the high velocity ·50 cal guns, while the Japanese 7·7-mm machine-guns barely scratched the Wildcat and their slow-firing, low-velocity 20-mm cannon were quite inaccurate. The diving attack used the strength of the Wildcat, while its ability to manoeuvre even at high speed was another plus factor since the Zero was found to have problems with aileron control at the higher speeds encountered in dives. The F4F was never redlined for terminal dive speeds which is testimony to its durability.

The Wildcat was considered to be a transitional fighter by the US Navy, intended to hold on until a second generation could be produced. Whatever the intent, it is recorded fact that the F4F was present and gave a good account of itself and its pilots in most of the major engagements in the Pacific and in the Atlantic as well.

The F4F was present at Pearl Harbor, where 11 Wildcats were caught on the ground and nine destroyed. As the war progressed the Japanese pushed on with their attacks on Wake Island. This was one of the most heroic defensive battles, and one which was to spur the American war production efforts, bringing the Wildcat to the attention of the American public. With seven of the newly arrived Wildcats destroyed during the first Japanese attack, the remaining aircraft, never more than three in the air at the same time, succeeded in destroying a twin-engine Japanese bomber and at least one Zero in air combat. In addition, Capt Henry T Elrod, USMC,

Fairey Fulmar I
The Royal Navy's first 8-gun fighter, the Fulmar kept the two-seater layout for a navigator/observer and was outmatched by its land-based contemporaries and their naval derivatives
Span: 46 ft 5 in *Length:* 40 ft 3 in
Engine: Rolls-Royce Merlin VIII, 1080 hp
Max speed: 280 mph *Ceiling:* 26,000 ft
Range: 800 miles *Armament:* 8 × ·303-in mg

Blackburn Firebrand TF 5
Conceived as early as 1939, the Firebrand torpedo-fighter was dogged by development difficulties, and became operational in 1945, too late to see action
Span: 51 ft 3½ in *Length:* 38 ft 9 in
Engine: Bristol Centaurus IX, 2520 hp
Armament: 4 × 20-mm cannon *Max speed:* 340 mph at 13,000 ft *Ceiling:* 28,500 ft *Range:* 740 miles *Bombload:* 1 × 1850-lb torpedo or 2 × 1000-lb bombs

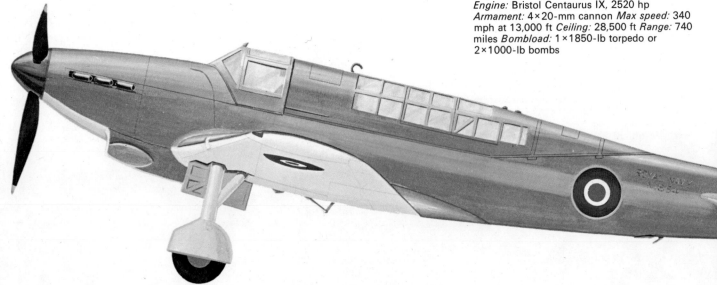

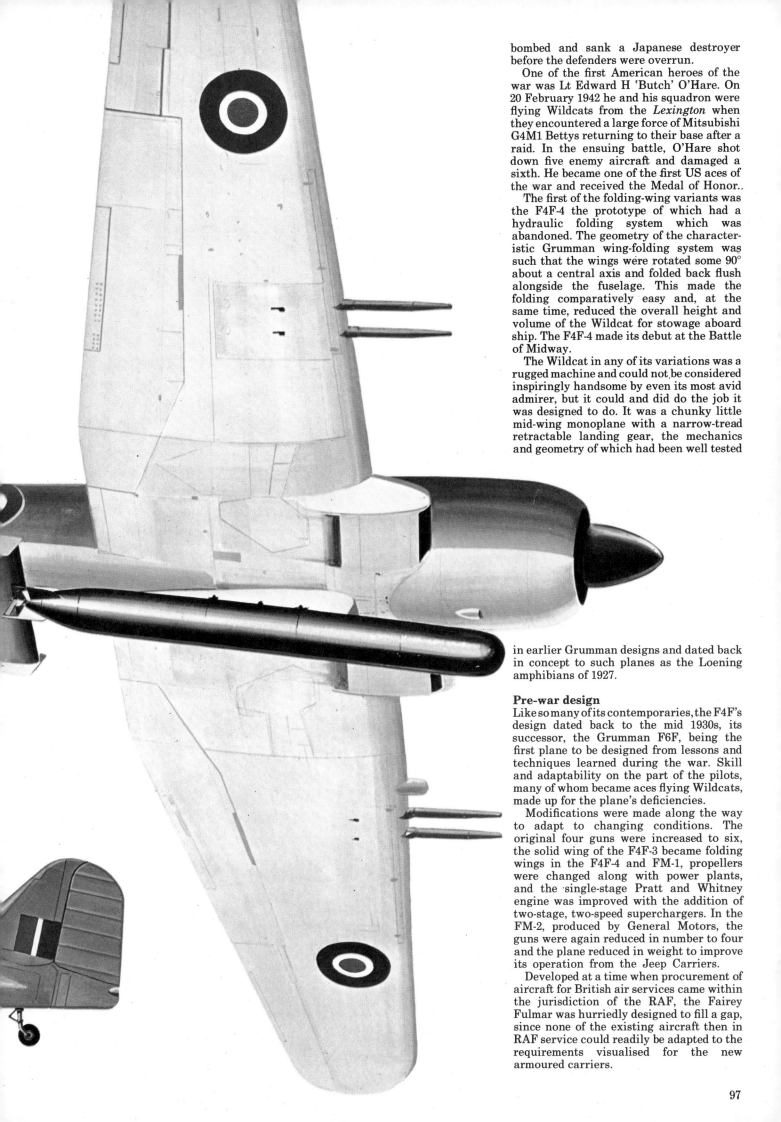

bombed and sank a Japanese destroyer before the defenders were overrun.

One of the first American heroes of the war was Lt Edward H 'Butch' O'Hare. On 20 February 1942 he and his squadron were flying Wildcats from the *Lexington* when they encountered a large force of Mitsubishi G4M1 Bettys returning to their base after a raid. In the ensuing battle, O'Hare shot down five enemy aircraft and damaged a sixth. He became one of the first US aces of the war and received the Medal of Honor..

The first of the folding-wing variants was the F4F-4 the prototype of which had a hydraulic folding system which was abandoned. The geometry of the characteristic Grumman wing-folding system was such that the wings were rotated some 90° about a central axis and folded back flush alongside the fuselage. This made the folding comparatively easy and, at the same time, reduced the overall height and volume of the Wildcat for stowage aboard ship. The F4F-4 made its debut at the Battle of Midway.

The Wildcat in any of its variations was a rugged machine and could not be considered inspiringly handsome by even its most avid admirer, but it could and did do the job it was designed to do. It was a chunky little mid-wing monoplane with a narrow-tread retractable landing gear, the mechanics and geometry of which had been well tested in earlier Grumman designs and dated back in concept to such planes as the Loening amphibians of 1927.

Pre-war design

Like so many of its contemporaries, the F4F's design dated back to the mid 1930s, its successor, the Grumman F6F, being the first plane to be designed from lessons and techniques learned during the war. Skill and adaptability on the part of the pilots, many of whom became aces flying Wildcats, made up for the plane's deficiencies.

Modifications were made along the way to adapt to changing conditions. The original four guns were increased to six, the solid wing of the F4F-3 became folding wings in the F4F-4 and FM-1, propellers were changed along with power plants, and the single-stage Pratt and Whitney engine was improved with the addition of two-stage, two-speed superchargers. In the FM-2, produced by General Motors, the guns were again reduced in number to four and the plane reduced in weight to improve its operation from the Jeep Carriers.

Developed at a time when procurement of aircraft for British air services came within the jurisdiction of the RAF, the Fairey Fulmar was hurriedly designed to fill a gap, since none of the existing aircraft then in RAF service could readily be adapted to the requirements visualised for the new armoured carriers.

Some allowances should be made for the shortcomings of the Fulmar when compared with other fighters, for it was designed to a different set of conditions as reflected in the specifications. The RAF had reserved for itself and its aircraft the task of defending ships while they were in range of land-based enemy aircraft. With these segments accounted for, if not tested in practice, the Royal Navy's fighter requirements were reduced to that of accompanying torpedo and strike/dive-bomber aircraft and driving off any reconnaissance aircraft. To meet

these requirements, the Fulmar was designed to incorporate two seats, the rear one for an observer/navigator/telegrapher. Note that the term 'gunner' is conspicious by its absence, as the rear seat occupant was already burdened with three jobs. In any case a good number of observers would have willingly taken on the gunnery duty as well if the designers had only had the foresight to include one or more guns for the rear seat. Thus it was that the observer was 'along for the ride' when the combat situation was at its worst. The pilot could not count on enemy fighters to avoid a direct stern attack.

With its several shortcomings, including lack of armour protection for the pilot, the Fulmar did give a good account of itself during the opening days of the war in the European theatre, accounting for 112 enemy aircraft shot down and 80 more damaged, which was about one third of the total Royal Navy victories.

Liquid-cooled engine
The Admiralty's preference for an air-cooled engine was not incorporated in the design, making the Fulmar one of the few aircraft designed for carrier operation that used liquid-cooled engines. As designs for the Fairey Barracuda were firmed up, it was proposed and accepted to use the same engine, the Rolls-Royce Merlin 30 in both the Barracuda and the Fulmar II. This was intended to reduce the maintenance parts problem, although no great performance gains resulted from the change.

In armament the Fulmar was equal to the Hawker Hurricane, having eight wing-mounted ·303 cal machine-guns which were impressive in number, but not in range. With the development of radar, the spacious rear cockpit made the Fulmar a logical plane for the Fleet Air Arm to use as a night fighter where its lack of speed would be less detrimental. In addition, the range of the Fulmar would allow it to remain airborne for five hours or more when fitted with auxiliary fuel tanks.

In combat service, the 15 Fulmars of 806 Squadron did provide air superiority for the Fleet operating in the eastern Mediterranean until they were overcome by Luftwaffe aircraft in early January 1941. In most of

Mitsubishi A5M4 'Claude'
This single-seat carrier fighter had fought over China and given Japanese Navy fighter pilots combat experience. Although obsolescent by 1941, the last 'Claudes' (the Allied code-name) were expended as Kamikaze suicide aircraft *Span:* 36 ft 1 in *Length:* 24 ft 10 in *Engine:* Nakajima Kotobuti 41, 785 hp at 9485 ft *Armament:* 2×7·7-mm mg *Max speed:* 252 mph at 6890 ft *Ceiling:* 32,150 ft *Range:* 746 miles

Mitsubishi A6M5 Reisen (Zero Fighter) 'Zeke'
Universally known as the 'Zero', the potency of the A6M fleet fighter gave the Allies a shock during the Japanese onslaught of 1941 and 1942, but the A6M5, the final production version, was outclassed by the new generation of US carrier fighters from 1943 *Span:* 36 ft 1 in *Length:* 29 ft 11 in *Engine:* Nakajima Sakae NK1F, 1100 hp at 9350 ft *Armament:* 2×7·7-mm mg; 2×20-mm cannon *Max speed:* 351 mph at 19,685 ft *Ceiling:* 38,520 ft *Range:* 1194 miles

the actions in which the Fulmars participated they accounted for more enemy planes down than they lost themselves. Considering relative performance, these results are quite remarkable and a tribute to the crews. Only one specimen is known to survive: NI 854, in the Fleet Air Arm Museum, RNAS Yeovilton, Somerset.

Rude awakening

Until the surprise attack on Pearl Harbor, the Mitsubishi A6M2 'Zero' was comparatively unknown even to the organisation most likely to encounter it, the US Navy. Although it had been reported by Gen Claire Chennault in 1940 after his 'Flying Tigers' had encountered a number of them over China, little effort was made to determine the capability of this new fighter. Even if an attempt had been made to learn more, it is quite unlikely that any results would have been forthcoming, for the Japanese were the most security conscious of nations at that time.

As a result of the lack of knowledge of the Zero, the Allies of the Pacific theatre, particularly the US, suffered a rude awakening by the attack at Pearl Harbor and the seeming invincibility of the onrushing Japanese war machine as it pushed steadily down the Asian Coast and through the islands of the western Pacific. Following these surprises, intelligence teams and engineering and military analysts groped for an explanation of this successful design. It was reputed to be a copy of the best features of the Vought V-143, the Hughes Racer and, possibly, one or two other aircraft for good measure.

The fact was that this, like any other plane of that date, was 'a copy of all that preceded it' according to the designer, Jiro Horikoshi, who had been assigned to lead the Mitsubishi design team. It was in fact an example of the state of the art when the Zero was designed. It could not be attributed to any one or more designs as a copy. Like the bee, the design team sampled many designs, taking the best and blending them to achieve the results required.

With the outbreak of hostilities between Japan and China in July 1937, the performance requirements increased as a result of combat experience. Specifications had

Associated Press

The slightly damaged USS Maryland *against a backdrop of smoke after the Pearl Harbor attack*

99

increased to such a degree that a Nakajima design team elected to concentrate on other projects, pulling out of the competition and leaving the project and problems with the Mitsubishi team. They succeeded to a remarkable degree and produced a plane that will be remembered along with the First World War Spad and Fokker D VII.

It was a classic and exceptionally fine compromise, as all aircraft designs must be. The design started with a compromise choice of engine, the 875 hp Mitsubishi Suisei 13 engine, although the designer favoured the larger, more powerful but heavier Mitsubishi Kinsei 40 engine. It wasn't until much later – too late – in the war that the Kinsei was to be adopted. Contrary to general belief, the lack of protective armour for the pilot was not an oversight, or a result of disregard for the crew, but a hard compromise choice dictated by the performance characteristics considered to be essential. The gamble almost paid dividends, for the Japanese had things pretty much their way at first and for several months until the Zero's weaknesses were found and exploited by the US pilots.

The Zero's first flight
The first prototype, the A6M1, made its first flight on 1 April 1939. Storm clouds were gathering in Europe and the US Exclusion Act of 1924 was still a very sore point with the Japanese, not so much because of its results but because it implied that Japan was less than a major international power.

The aircraft was officially designated Navy type 0 carrier fighter on 31 July 1940, and shot down its first enemy aircraft on 13 September 1940 when 13 planes flying over China surprised and downed 27 Polikarpov I-15s and I-16s without suffering any losses themselves. At this time General Claire Chennault, who was then reorganising the Chinese Air Force, advised his colleagues in the US of this new fighter, but his warning was either ignored or forgotten.

The high point of the A6M2's service was the Pearl Harbor attack of 7 December 1941 and the invasion of Wake Island soon after. There followed a succession of victories as the Japanese pushed further south, eventually attacking Port Darwin, Australia, on 15 February 1942, destroying eight Australian aircraft in air combat and an additional 15 on the ground – again without losses to themselves. Following this, the Japanese fleet under Admiral Nagumo headed for the Indian Ocean where they sank the British fleet units consisting of HMS *Dorsetshire,* HMS *Cornwall* and the carrier HMS *Hermes.*

The Japanese were now riding high on wings of victory, but at the same time the

Mitsubishi A6M2 Zero
Jiro Horishoki's brilliant fighter design first saw action in September 1940 when A6M2s destroyed 99 Chinese aircraft for the loss of 2 Zeros. The A6M2 was the model in service during the 1941–42 period of runaway Japanese victories
Span: 39 ft 4 in *Length:* 29 ft 9 in
Engine: Nakajima NK1F Sakae 12,950 hp at 13,780 ft *Max speed:* 331 mph at 16,000 ft
Ceiling: 32,810 ft *Range:* 1160 miles
Armament: 2×20-mm cannon; 2×7·7-mm mg

USS Yorktown *listing heavily after a savage battering during the Battle of Midway. But her Dauntlesses had smashed two Japanese carriers*

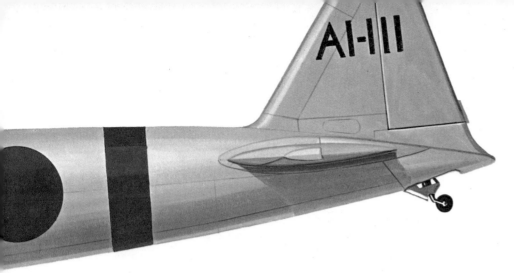

Japanese force consisting of less than 200 Zeros leapfrogged its way through the Philippines and down the coast of Asia, concentrating on the defeat of a hodgepodge of obsolescent aircraft such as Brewster F2A Buffaloes, Curtiss CW-21Bs, Hawk 75s, P-40s and Hawker Hurricanes.

The Zero was built in a number of variants and model improvements including the A6M2, Zero (Zeke), A6M2-N (float fighter 'Rufe'), A6M2-K (two-seat trainer), A6M3 'Hamp' (Models 22 & 23) and A6M5 Zeke 52 which itself had a number of variations.

By mid 1943, the Zero and the Hamp had been surpassed by most Allied fighters yet they were always potent adversaries when flown by an experienced pilot. The Grumman F6F in particular and the Vought F4U were to provide air superiority over the Zeros.

Inevitable end

In one last desperate role, the A6M2s were used as Kamikaze weapons. Equipped with one 500-lb bomb, the Zeke was used in the much described spectacular attacks on US ships. While the A6M2 Kamikaze accounted for a high percentage of the attacks and actual hits, the effort was not worth the price, for the US attacks had reached a crescendo of such proportions and determination that, at best, the Kamikaze could only hope to delay the inevitable.

The Vought F4U Corsair was unique in several respects, one of the war's most versatile aircraft, an excellent fighter and a dive-bomber/attack plane. It was capable of lugging and delivering external ordnance loads up to a total of 4000 lb. It was this dual capability that reduced the requirement for additional dive-bombers and other specialised aircraft such as the Curtiss SB2Cs.

The Corsair was the first fighter to be powered by a 2000 hp engine, and in later configurations such as the Goodyear-built F2G was powered by the 3500 hp Pratt & Whitney R-4360 engine. To use this high power at high altitudes it was necessary to install a large, slow-turning propeller. To provide ground clearance for this propeller and still keep the landing gear short and rugged for arrested landings was a problem which was solved by the unusual bent wing configuration. The resulting wing position made unnecessary the extensive filleting usually required to smooth out the air flow at the juncture of the wing and fuselage. The short landing gear also served as a dive brake, with the added advantage of retracting backward into the wing.

This configuration improved pilot visibility on the approach and final leg of landing and when landing, the stall occurred in the trough of the gull close to the fuselage.

US was marshalling its military strength and heading for the Battle of the Coral Sea on 7/8 May 1942, the first battle ever to be fought entirely by aircraft with the surface ships out of sight of each other. It was at this point of the war that the tide began to turn. The Grumman F4Fs held the line and each carrier force had one carrier seriously damaged, and the Japanese lost the light carrier *Shoho*.

Shortly afterwards, on 3/4 June 1942, the Battle of Midway was underway. Again, the Zero extracted a heavy price, but this time the victims were mostly the TBDs which, through an error in timing, were left unprotected during their run. In turn, the Japanese paid an extremely heavy price with the loss of most of their carrier force and their complement of aircraft and crew was sadly depleted as well. These carrier losses included the *Kaga, Akagi* and *Soryu*, and the *Hiryu* which was set afire, but not before her aircraft crippled the *Yorktown*.

In connection with this battle, a diversionary attack was made on the Aleutians during which one Zero was forced to land due to fuel loss. Though wrecked on landing in a bog and killing the pilot, this Zero was to play an important role. Salvaged and restored to flying condition, it was thoroughly tested at Anacostia and North Island Naval Air Stations, and its strong and weak points documented. With this final bit of technical intelligence, the US aircraft industry was able to finalise the design of aircraft then in production, notably the Grumman F6F Hellcat and the Vought F4U Corsair. The Hellcat was, in fact, the first fighter designed specifically to gain mastery over the Zero. Despite the fact that the Zero had been improved, it was no match for a plane built right from the start to conquer it.

With the Japanese carrier fleet no longer a threat, the remaining Zeros were forced to operate from land bases, where they distinguished themselves and their crews by having their endurance and that of their pilots developed to a degree that amazed everyone. During the first year of the war a

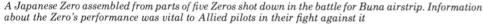

A Japanese Zero assembled from parts of five Zeros shot down in the battle for Buna airstrip. Information about the Zero's performance was vital to Allied pilots in their fight against it

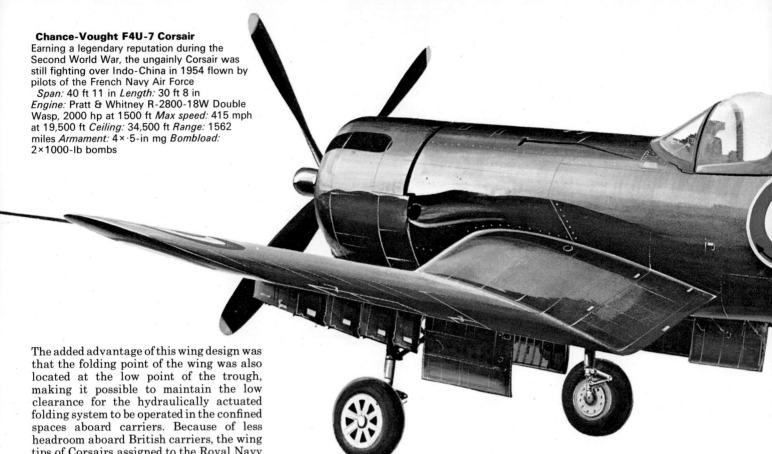

Chance-Vought F4U-7 Corsair
Earning a legendary reputation during the
Second World War, the ungainly Corsair was
still fighting over Indo-China in 1954 flown by
pilots of the French Navy Air Force
Span: 40 ft 11 in *Length:* 30 ft 8 in
Engine: Pratt & Whitney R-2800-18W Double
Wasp, 2000 hp at 1500 ft *Max speed:* 415 mph
at 19,500 ft *Ceiling:* 34,500 ft *Range:* 1562
miles *Armament:* 4×·5-in mg *Bombload:*
2×1000-lb bombs

Fleet Air Arm Corsair II fighters in echelon formation. The type provided cover for the Tirpitz *raids*

The added advantage of this wing design was
that the folding point of the wing was also
located at the low point of the trough,
making it possible to maintain the low
clearance for the hydraulically actuated
folding system to be operated in the confined
spaces aboard carriers. Because of less
headroom aboard British carriers, the wing
tips of Corsairs assigned to the Royal Navy
were shortened by removal of eight inches
from each wing tip resulting in a squared
off wing tip and a slightly higher stalling
speed – but little else was changed.

The structure of the F4U was simplified by
using large single panels whenever possible
and fabricating these by arc welding whenever practical. One unusual feature was the
rather generous use of fabric in a plane of
this late date.

Veterans of the Second World War will
readily recall the distinctive sounds of
aircraft which caused instinctive reactions
among ground crews and particularly anti-
aircraft gunners and troops in the front
lines. The engine exhaust, propeller or
cooling system produced distinctive sounds
which inspired fear or exhilaration. In the
case of the Corsair, the whistling sound
generated by the wing root air intakes was
so pronounced that enemy troops referred
to it as 'Whistling Death', for it extracted
a high price in air combat and an even
greater one among the ground troops in its
role as an attack plane, bombing, launching
rockets and strafing.

Because of its rather unconventional
appearance it was also known by US and
Allied personnel as the 'Bent-wing Bird'.
With the exception of the Stuka and the
Grace, there was no other Second World
War aircraft with this unusual wing con-
figuration.

The Corsair had a prolonged adolescence.
While it was designed for carrier operation,
a variety of idiosyncrasies, including a
bounce when landing aboard carriers, kept
it from its intended role until 1944, although
the first 22 F4Us had been proclaimed
combat-ready as early as December 1942.
In spite of its early rejection from carrier
qualification it was operated by Marine
and Navy squadrons VMF 124 and VF 17
from land bases, establishing a victory/loss
ratio of better than 11 to 1.

The first action in which Corsairs took
part was to escort Consolidated PB4Y-2,
single-finned Navy Liberators, all the way

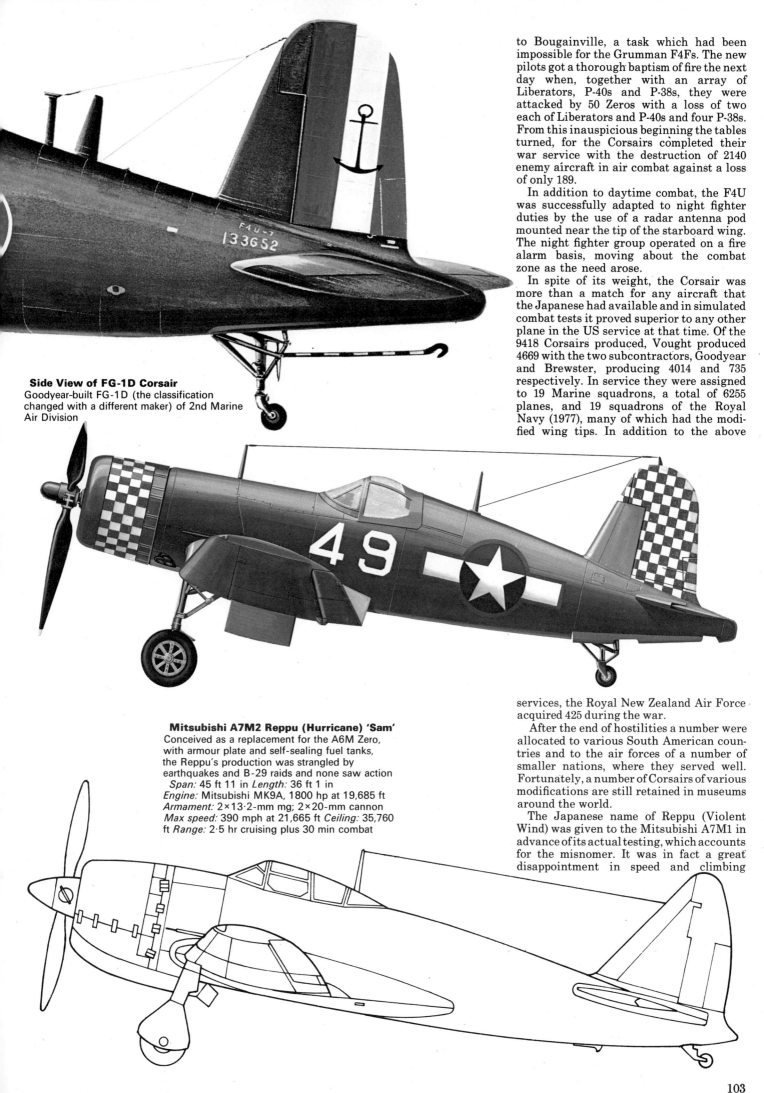

to Bougainville, a task which had been impossible for the Grumman F4Fs. The new pilots got a thorough baptism of fire the next day when, together with an array of Liberators, P-40s and P-38s, they were attacked by 50 Zeros with a loss of two each of Liberators and P-40s and four P-38s. From this inauspicious beginning the tables turned, for the Corsairs completed their war service with the destruction of 2140 enemy aircraft in air combat against a loss of only 189.

In addition to daytime combat, the F4U was successfully adapted to night fighter duties by the use of a radar antenna pod mounted near the tip of the starboard wing. The night fighter group operated on a fire alarm basis, moving about the combat zone as the need arose.

In spite of its weight, the Corsair was more than a match for any aircraft that the Japanese had available and in simulated combat tests it proved superior to any other plane in the US service at that time. Of the 9418 Corsairs produced, Vought produced 4669 with the two subcontractors, Goodyear and Brewster, producing 4014 and 735 respectively. In service they were assigned to 19 Marine squadrons, a total of 6255 planes, and 19 squadrons of the Royal Navy (1977), many of which had the modified wing tips. In addition to the above

Side View of FG-1D Corsair
Goodyear-built FG-1D (the classification changed with a different maker) of 2nd Marine Air Division

Mitsubishi A7M2 Reppu (Hurricane) 'Sam'
Conceived as a replacement for the A6M Zero, with armour plate and self-sealing fuel tanks, the Reppu's production was strangled by earthquakes and B-29 raids and none saw action
Span: 45 ft 11 in *Length:* 36 ft 1 in
Engine: Mitsubishi MK9A, 1800 hp at 19,685 ft
Armament: 2×13·2-mm mg; 2×20-mm cannon
Max speed: 390 mph at 21,665 ft *Ceiling:* 35,760 ft *Range:* 2·5 hr cruising plus 30 min combat

services, the Royal New Zealand Air Force acquired 425 during the war.

After the end of hostilities a number were allocated to various South American countries and to the air forces of a number of smaller nations, where they served well. Fortunately, a number of Corsairs of various modifications are still retained in museums around the world.

The Japanese name of Reppu (Violent Wind) was given to the Mitsubishi A7M1 in advance of its actual testing, which accounts for the misnomer. It was in fact a great disappointment in speed and climbing

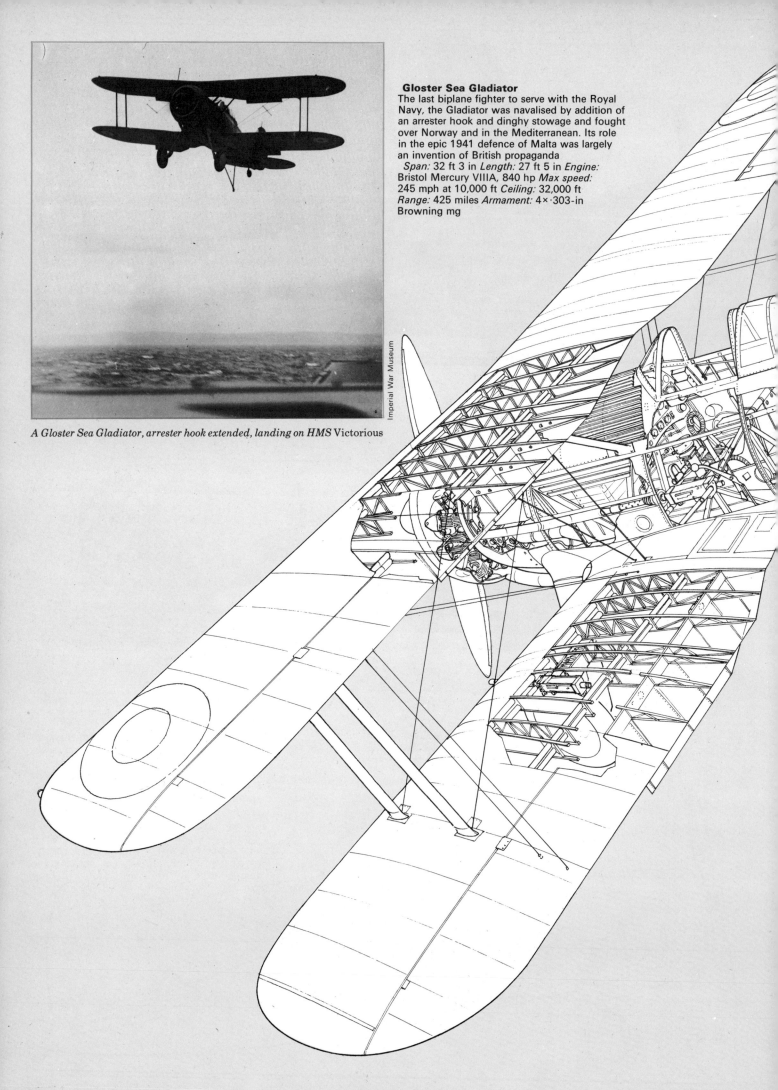

Gloster Sea Gladiator

The last biplane fighter to serve with the Royal Navy, the Gladiator was navalised by addition of an arrester hook and dinghy stowage and fought over Norway and in the Mediterranean. Its role in the epic 1941 defence of Malta was largely an invention of British propaganda

Span: 32 ft 3 in *Length:* 27 ft 5 in *Engine:* Bristol Mercury VIIIA, 840 hp *Max speed:* 245 mph at 10,000 ft *Ceiling:* 32,000 ft *Range:* 425 miles *Armament:* 4×·303-in Browning mg

A Gloster Sea Gladiator, arrester hook extended, landing on HMS Victorious

Imperial War Museum

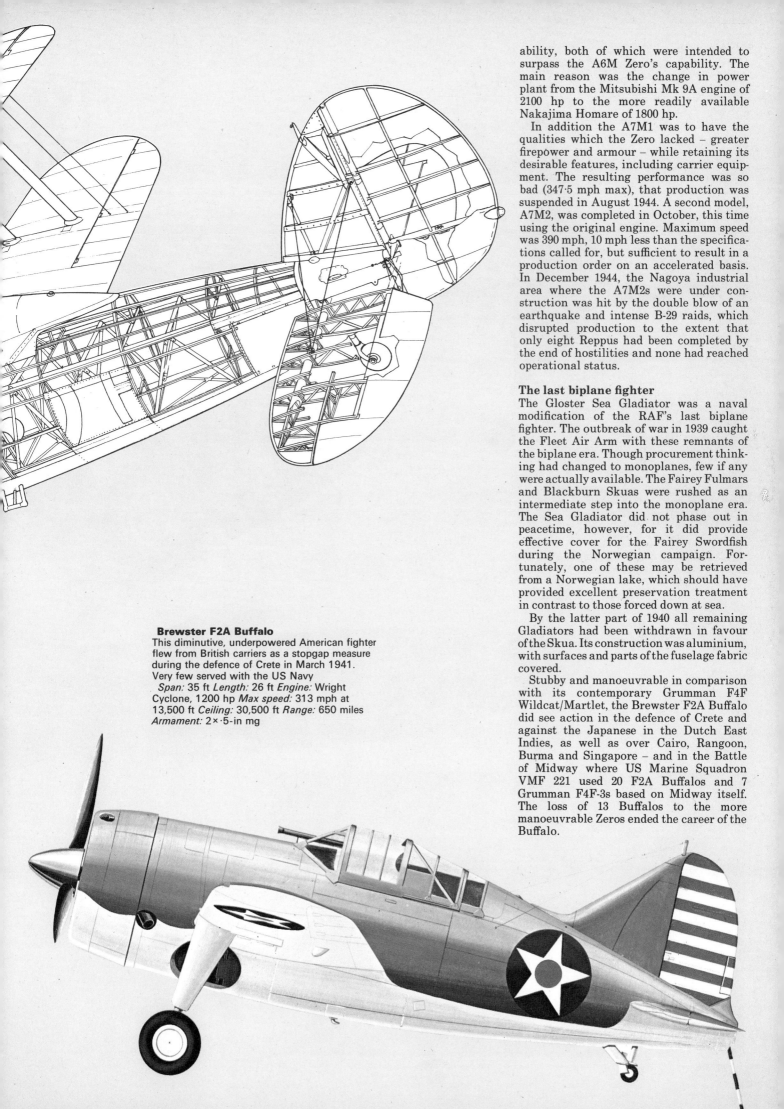

ability, both of which were intended to surpass the A6M Zero's capability. The main reason was the change in power plant from the Mitsubishi Mk 9A engine of 2100 hp to the more readily available Nakajima Homare of 1800 hp.

In addition the A7M1 was to have the qualities which the Zero lacked – greater firepower and armour – while retaining its desirable features, including carrier equipment. The resulting performance was so bad (347·5 mph max), that production was suspended in August 1944. A second model, A7M2, was completed in October, this time using the original engine. Maximum speed was 390 mph, 10 mph less than the specifications called for, but sufficient to result in a production order on an accelerated basis. In December 1944, the Nagoya industrial area where the A7M2s were under construction was hit by the double blow of an earthquake and intense B-29 raids, which disrupted production to the extent that only eight Reppus had been completed by the end of hostilities and none had reached operational status.

The last biplane fighter

The Gloster Sea Gladiator was a naval modification of the RAF's last biplane fighter. The outbreak of war in 1939 caught the Fleet Air Arm with these remnants of the biplane era. Though procurement thinking had changed to monoplanes, few if any were actually available. The Fairey Fulmars and Blackburn Skuas were rushed as an intermediate step into the monoplane era. The Sea Gladiator did not phase out in peacetime, however, for it did provide effective cover for the Fairey Swordfish during the Norwegian campaign. Fortunately, one of these may be retrieved from a Norwegian lake, which should have provided excellent preservation treatment in contrast to those forced down at sea.

By the latter part of 1940 all remaining Gladiators had been withdrawn in favour of the Skua. Its construction was aluminium, with surfaces and parts of the fuselage fabric covered.

Stubby and manoeuvrable in comparison with its contemporary Grumman F4F Wildcat/Martlet, the Brewster F2A Buffalo did see action in the defence of Crete and against the Japanese in the Dutch East Indies, as well as over Cairo, Rangoon, Burma and Singapore – and in the Battle of Midway where US Marine Squadron VMF 221 used 20 F2A Buffalos and 7 Grumman F4F-3s based on Midway itself. The loss of 13 Buffalos to the more manoeuvrable Zeros ended the career of the Buffalo.

Brewster F2A Buffalo
This diminutive, underpowered American fighter flew from British carriers as a stopgap measure during the defence of Crete in March 1941. Very few served with the US Navy
Span: 35 ft *Length:* 26 ft *Engine:* Wright Cyclone, 1200 hp *Max speed:* 313 mph at 13,500 ft *Ceiling:* 30,500 ft *Range:* 650 miles *Armament:* 2 × ·5-in mg

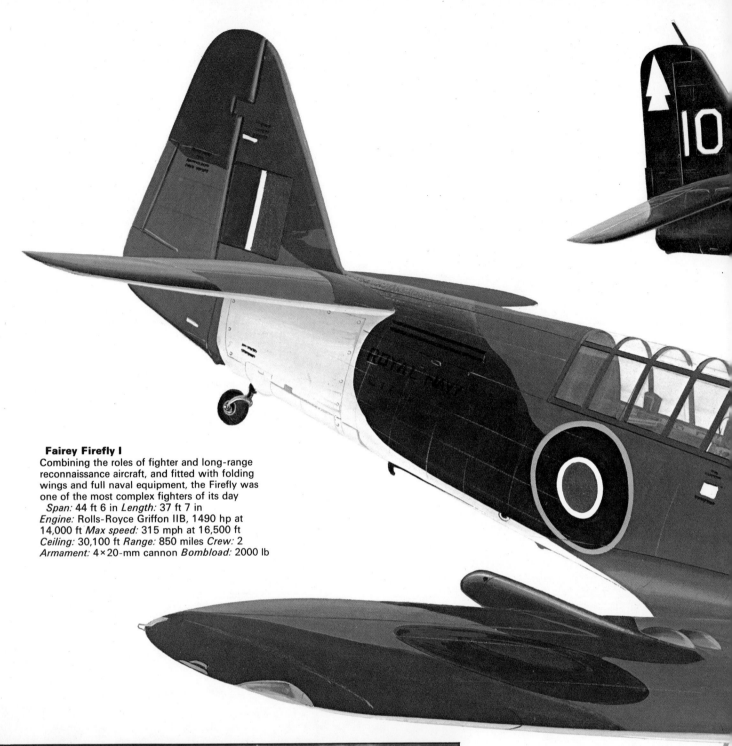

Fairey Firefly I
Combining the roles of fighter and long-range
reconnaissance aircraft, and fitted with folding
wings and full naval equipment, the Firefly was
one of the most complex fighters of its day
Span: 44 ft 6 in *Length:* 37 ft 7 in
Engine: Rolls-Royce Griffon IIB, 1490 hp at
14,000 ft *Max speed:* 315 mph at 16,500 ft
Ceiling: 30,100 ft *Range:* 850 miles *Crew:* 2
Armament: 4×20-mm cannon *Bombload:* 2000 lb

A formation of US Navy Grumman Hellcats, the type that replaced the Wildcat at war against the Zero

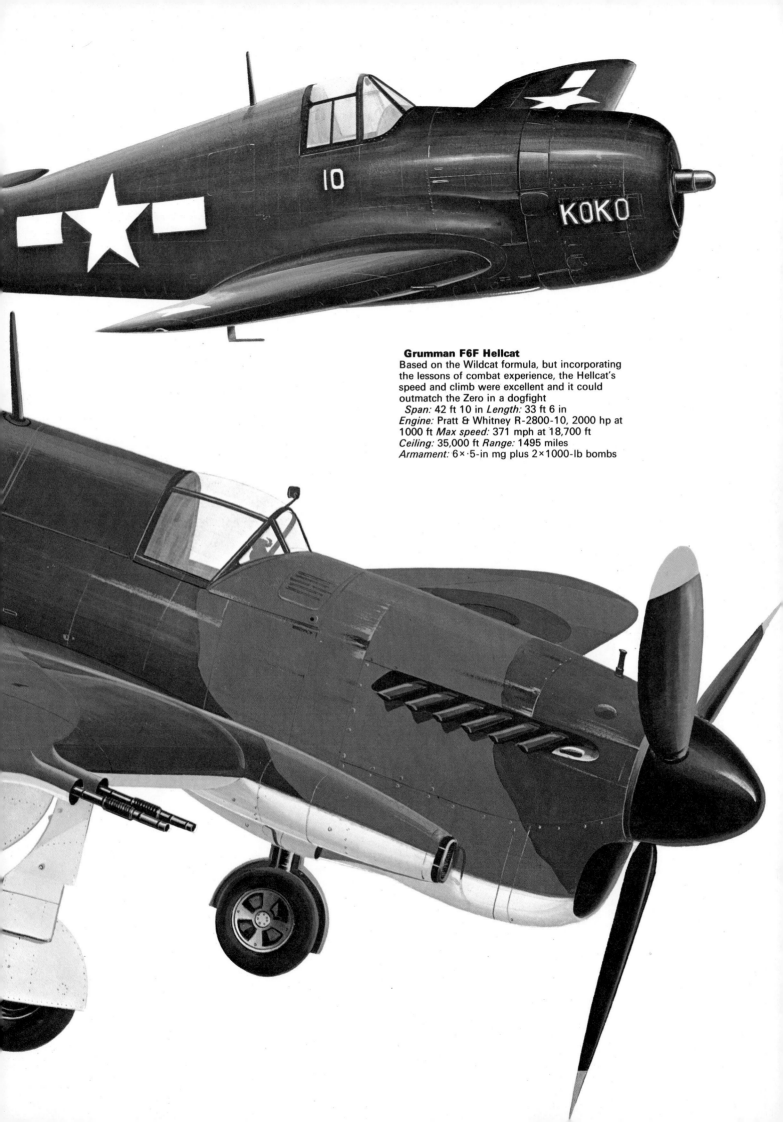

Grumman F6F Hellcat
Based on the Wildcat formula, but incorporating
the lessons of combat experience, the Hellcat's
speed and climb were excellent and it could
outmatch the Zero in a dogfight
Span: 42 ft 10 in *Length:* 33 ft 6 in
Engine: Pratt & Whitney R-2800-10, 2000 hp at
1000 ft *Max speed:* 371 mph at 18,700 ft
Ceiling: 35,000 ft *Range:* 1495 miles
Armament: 6×·5-in mg plus 2×1000-lb bombs

The Buffalo had the unique distinction of winning the US Navy design competition against the Grumman F4F and still falling by the wayside. Production was not one of the Brewster Company's strong points, either with the Buffalo and Buccaneer/Bermuda of their own design or when they were called upon as a second source for the Vought F4U/F3A.

The US Navy found the Buffalo particularly susceptible to deck landing damage due to a weakness in the landing gear. As a result, the Grumman Wildcat superseded the Buffalo to become the standard carrier fighter of both the US Navy and the Fleet Air Arm until the Vought F4U and Grumman F6F replaced them.

In comparative tests with the Hurricane I, the Buffalo was slightly more manoeuvrable but slower to accelerate in a dive. Though designed for carrier operation, when sold to the British it was found to be one foot too large in wing span and could not be accommodated on carrier elevators. Instead it was used in the Near East over Cairo, where the fine silt was less harmful to the air-cooled radial engine than it had been to other planes' close tolerance liquid-cooled engines.

Other features which prevented it from assignment to serious combat were lack of firepower (the Buffalo had two ·50 cal and two ·30 cal machine-guns) and of armour plate, which was neither thick enough nor large enough. These were its major failings, its other deficiencies being sufficient to relegate it to training missions or desperation defence requirements.

A two-seat fighter/reconnaissance aircraft, the Fairey Firefly was built to a requirement dating back to the mid-1920s and as a replacement for the stop-gap Fairey Fulmar, which served well if not spectacularly during the early part of the war.

The war was well under way in Europe and the US was recovering from the shock of Pearl Harbor, the complete tally of the disaster not yet fully appreciated, when the Firefly prototype was first flown on 22 December 1941. While resembling the Fulmar in general plan and profile – making it hard to differentiate between them at a distance – the Firefly was, aerodynamically, an improvement, while the substitution of the 1730 hp R-R Griffon II B and later the 1990 hp Griffon XII did much to improve the performance with an immediate 40 mph increase in top speed.

Along with the increased performance, the armament was changed from the eight ·303 cal guns of the Fulmar to the four 20-mm cannon of the Firefly. The wing plan form adopted was quite similar to that of the graceful, elliptical wings of the Supermarine Spitfire. Were it not for the generous expanse of clear glass aft of the wing, the Firefly might easily have been mistaken for the Spitfire. The Firefly got a comparatively late start, but by the end of 1946 over 950 Mk 1s and night fighter modifications had been built, over 800 of them by the Fairey plants. The remainder were built by General Aircraft Company.

The Firefly distinguished itself in action in the Far East as an attack plane launching rockets against important targets such as the oil refineries in Sumatra in January 1945, effectively knocking out the major source of petroleum products for Japanese ships and aircraft. Earlier attempts by British Engineers to destroy refinery storage tanks during the retreat from the Malay Peninsula resulted in amusing and embarrassing results when the high octane fuel refused to burn. The intensity of fumes snuffed out attempts to ignite it with any of the normal – and some far from normal – forms of incendiary materials.

Night fighter Firefly

One of the principal variants of the Firefly Mk 1 was that of night fighter. As in the case of the Fulmar, the spacious rear cockpit was quite adequate for the radar equipment; however, the early forms of radome successfully cluttered up the otherwise clean aerodynamics, resulting in lower speeds, and the weight of the early radar equipment altered the centre of gravity, making it necessary to move the engine 18 inches forward to compensate. This combination of pilot and radar operator is practically standard for current combat aircraft including fighters. The radar/counter measures crew member in currently operational fighters is regarded as essential to the performance and safety of the aircraft. In the days of the Firefly, however, the second crew member was a definite obstacle to high performance in an aircraft when compared with the single-seat, single-engined contemporaries. Its top speed was 316 mph, only slightly greater than that of the Brewster Buffalo, whose every

performance was surpassed rather quickly and early in the war.

During the preliminaries to the sinking of the German battleship *Tirpitz*, the Firefly was used to attack auxiliary ships and silence anti-aircraft gun emplacements in preparation for the battleship's destruction by RAF Lancasters.

The Grumman F6F Hellcat, successor to the F4F Wildcat/Martlet, was built in the Grumman tradition of robust, rugged structure with good flight control characteristics and, in this case, performance adequate to gain air superiority over the Japanese Zero.

During the first 16 months of the Pacific War, the Wildcat was on its own and did a remarkable job considering that normal terms of measurement would have shown it to be inferior to its enemy, the Zero. The brutish Hellcat was designed to remedy the situation with speed and climb ability superior to the Zero's. It was the first plane built after Pearl Harbor and incorporated the features demanded by Navy pilots allowing them to initiate ·or break off combat at their choosing.

Grumman F8F Bearcat
The Bearcat appeared too late to see combat, but had brought the Grumman fighter design precepts to perfection. Lighter than the Hellcat by 3000 lb, its superior performance was gained at the expense of firepower
Span: 35 ft 6 in *Length:* 28 ft *Engine:* Pratt & Whitney R-2800-22W Double Wasp, 2100 hp at take-off *Max speed:* 424 mph at 17,300 ft *Ceiling:* 33,700 ft *Range:* 955 miles *Armament:* 4×·5-in mg *Bombload:* 2000 lb or 4×5-in rockets

The results of tests on the Zero forced down in the Aleutians established the design parameters for the Hellcat which was then being designed. It was, in fact, designed to better the performance of the Zero as its primary mission. That reserves in structural strength were there also was important but almost of secondary importance at this time.

Like its sister-ship on the Grumman production lines, the TBF Avenger, the Hellcat was big and spacious inside and of simplified rugged structure to ensure ease of production and maintenance aboard carriers. Carrying this simplification further, the wings were folded manually with the locking pins operated hydraulically from the cockpit and made safe by manually controlled lock pins. For stowage aboard ship the wings were rotated about the front spar and then folded backward alongside the fuselage, leading-edge downward, like those of the Wildcat and the Avenger.

The landing gear rotated 90° as it retracted rearward, like that of the Curtiss P-40 and Vought F4U. Cover plates smoothed over the wheels and struts when fully retracted. When in the extended position, a cover plate at the upper end of the gear leg added to the drag produced by the gear. The six ·50 cal machine-guns were mounted in the panels just outboard of the line where the wings broke for folding.

The fuselage was a semimonocoque structure with rings and stringers, covered by stressed skin. Adequate armour plate was installed for pilot protection and a turn-over structure was incorporated as well.

Performance had been improved, with the speed 60 mph faster than the F4Fs. Range was increased and the ammunition carried was 400 rounds per gun – nearly doubling the capacity of the F4F. Most important, the Hellcat could be flown and flown well by the inexperienced pilots who were then coming into combat theatres fresh from the training centres.

The first flight of the XF6F-3 took place in July 1942 and the first full squadron of Hellcats was delivered by December of the same year. The F4F and the TBF production was farmed out to General Motors where the designation was changed to FM-1 and TBM, but little else changed as production continued unabated. Fourteen months from design to production was a record of which Grumman could be proud and one that instilled pride in the workers for the esprit de corps of Grumman employees was the envy of the other wartime manufacturers, especially their neighbour, Brewster.

The first combat flown in F6Fs was a VF 5 flight, in support of the strike aircraft from Task Force 15, consisting of *Essex*, light carrier *Independence* and the second *Yorktown* in their attack on the Marcus Islands on 31 August 1943. Numerous encounters further endeared the Hellcat to its pilots and improved their skills for the big battles just over the horizon. The Battle of the Philippine Sea, 19-20 June 1944 (known as the 'Marianas Turkey Shoot'), was one of the most decisive battles of the war. On 19 June aircraft of Task Force 58 destroyed 402 enemy aircraft, and by 10 August carrier aircraft had sunk 110,000 tons of enemy ships and destroyed 1223 enemy aircraft.

Staggering losses
The date, 20 June, was memorable for other reasons. In a dusk battle at extreme range, Task Force 58 lost 104 aircraft out of 216 launched. Of the Hellcats six were lost in the vicinity of the Japanese fleet of Admiral Ozawa, while 17 splashed down with dry tanks on the way home. The dive-bombers (SB2C – Helldiver) and torpedo bombers (TBF – Avenger) lost 60% or more of their planes over the target or en route back to Task Force 58. This battle and the Battle of Leyte Gulf, 23-26 October, resulted in 1046 enemy aircraft destroyed during the month of October and another 770 during November. The staggering losses in planes and aircraft carriers, as well as other surface ships, spelled the end of the once powerful Japanese carrier aviation.

In all these battles the Hellcat played an important role in protecting the strike force and defending the massed US carrier force against the determined and suicidal attacks of the Japanese carrier pilots.

The Hellcat also found favour with the Fleet Air Arm and was used extensively in Atlantic operation, notably from HMS *Emperor*, which carried out anti-shipping attacks along the Norwegian coast and provided fighter cover during eight attacks on the German battleship *Tirpitz* from April to August of 1944. Most of the Fleet Air Arm action took place in the Pacific where the F6F-5 (Hellcat II) was the standard. All told, the Royal Navy used over 1260 Hellcats. It was designed to do a job well and, by any standard, it succeeded.

The Hawker Sea Hurricane ('Hurricat' or 'Catafighter') was used as a stopgap measure when the German submarine and long-range Focke Wulf Fw 200 Condor became a menace in early 1941. The age of the Hurricane design made it unwise to expend design and fabrication effort to develop folding wings. Therefore, the plane was used as it was by catapulting it off CAM (Catapult Armed Merchantmen) ships. Each flight ended in a ducking for the pilot and loss of the aircraft, which probably accounts for the fact that only one Hurricane I is known to exist of all those that fought in or during the Battle of Britain. This one remaining Hurricane is on exhibition in the Science Museum in London.

The only situation where plane and pilot were recovered was during training, in port, or possibly when the convoy of which the CAM ship was a part was within range of land. Otherwise the normal method was for the pilot to take to his parachute and Mae West life preserver, hopefully to be picked up by ships of the convoy after the danger of attack was passed.

In addition to the CAM operation, a number of Hurricane IBs were adapted to operate from carriers by reinforcing the airframe to permit catapulting, and addition of an arrester hook. A number of variants were introduced with the addition of four 20-mm cannon mounted in the universal wing and, with a change in engine to the Merlin XX, these became Hurricane IICs.

Fleet Air Arm pilots originally flew the Hurricats off the CAMs but later were relieved by RAF pilots who well remember the shock of the catapult launching.

Of the carrier-based Sea Hurricanes, some were assigned to the CAM escort carrier HMS *Avenger* on the Russian Convoy PQ 18 to Murmansk, after the previous Convoy, PQ 17, which was without air cover, was pounded continuously en route by German aircraft based in Norway and Finland. On this convoy, the Sea Hurricanes accounted for five German aircraft destroyed and 17 more damaged with a loss of one pilot and four Hurricanes. They were to give a good account of themselves for some time, taking part in the defence of Malta and escorting convoys as late as August 1942 and during the North African Torch landings on 8–11 November 1942. By this time replacement aircraft, Seafires and Grumman F6F Hellcats were being placed aboard the carriers. The remaining Sea Hurricanes were stripped of their sea-going gear and returned to land duties.

The Supermarine Seafire was a well-tried and proven design modified to naval operating standards. The rather unusual configuration of the Seafire III, when the wings were folded for storage aboard carriers, led to the nickname of 'Praying Mantis'. The tips were folded downwards at the wing tip joint at the outboard aileron gap; then the main panels, outboard of the coolant radiators, were folded upward to form an almost equilateral triangle. The main panels were unbolted by unscrewing locking bolts inside the wheel wells. The wings were supported in their folded position by tele-scoping tubes which were normally stored in lateral slots in the upper wing surface. Folding was accomplished by a three or four man crew and reduced the original span to 13 ft 4 in, which was 23 ft less than the unfolded span of 36 ft 10 in.

Earlier Seafires made do with the non-folding standard Spitfire wing as most of them were conversions of existing standard models. Seafires were used extensively, taking over from the Sea Hurricanes in 1941 after it was shown that fast, single-engined, single-place fighters were needed aboard carriers and in naval operations.

On the offensive

The first operational use of the Seafire was from HMS *Furious*, *Formidable* and *Argus* flying in support of Operation Torch, the Allied landings in North Africa on 8–11 November 1942. Then, on 10 July 1943 the Seafires took to the offensive again, flying from HMS *Furious* and *Indomitable* in support of the Allied landings in Sicily. During this campaign, which lasted until 18 August, Allied airmen lost 274 planes and accounted for 1691 enemy aircraft.

Operation Avalanche, the invasion of the Italian mainland, began on 2 September. Fleet Air Arm squadrons operating from the escort carriers *Attacker*, *Battler*, *Hunter*, *Stalker* and *Unicorn* provided the total air cover for the beachhead during the early stages of this engagement. For the landing troops, the low wind velocity experienced was a pleasure since sea sickness was minimised but the Seafire pilots operating from

A Seafire Mk XV touches down aboard the Pretoria Castle. *Note the sting-type arrester hook*

A Hawker Hurricane 1A being catapulted from a Catapult Armed Merchantman (CAM ship). The Hurricane provided valuable cover for Atlantic and Arctic convoys. Each mission meant the loss of the plane, but the Hurricane was becoming obsolescent, and was unsuitable for conversion to a proper carrier plane. Mk 1B specifications: Span: 40 ft Length: 31 ft 5 in Engine: Rolls-Royce Merlin II, 1310 hp Max Speed: 298 mph at 16,400 ft Ceiling: 30,000 ft Armament: 8 × ·303 mg

the Jeep carriers soon realised that the maximum speed for the CVEs, about 17–18 mph, was not the best speed for the take-off and landing of the Seafire. During these hectic days amid low wind conditions a number of Seafires were damaged during deck operations, usually landings, when they came in too fast and tore the arrester hook from the aircraft.

The Seafires continued to serve well, flying top cover for the attacks on the *Tirpitz* and whenever their presence was needed, whether from shore or carrier base. The last action for the Seafires in the European theatre was in the Aegean Sea area during the latter part of 1944.

Meanwhile, in the Pacific theatre, the Seafires found themselves at a disadvantage, for ranges (or endurance) which had been quite acceptable in the European theatre were not adequate in the broad expanse of the Pacific. The normal two-hour endurance of the Seafire limited its usefulness as well as that of its carriers. The decision was made to retire the Seafires in favour of the F6F Hellcats and F4U Corsairs after nearly 1700 Seafires had been built or converted.

Although the Seafire was without a doubt the finest low-level fighter produced by the Allies, its range, firepower and ordnance capabilities did not match those of the later developed Hellcat and Corsair that had been designed from the outset for long endurance, heavy firepower and incredible ordnance capacity. These same features eventually made redundant such specially designed dive-bombers as the Curtiss SB2C.

Supermarine Seafire Mk III
A straightforward adaptation of the Spitfire, fitted with arrester hook and catapult spools, the Mk III had double-jointed folding wings (inset) to clear the low hangar ceilings typical of British aircraft carriers
Span: 36 ft 8 in *Length:* 30 ft *Engine:* Rolls-Royce Merlin 55, 1470 hp *Armament:* 4 × ·303-in mg; 4 × 20-mm cannon plus 1 × 500-lb or 2 × 250-lb bombs *Speed* 342 mph at 20,700 ft *Ceiling:* 37,500 ft *Range:* 508 miles

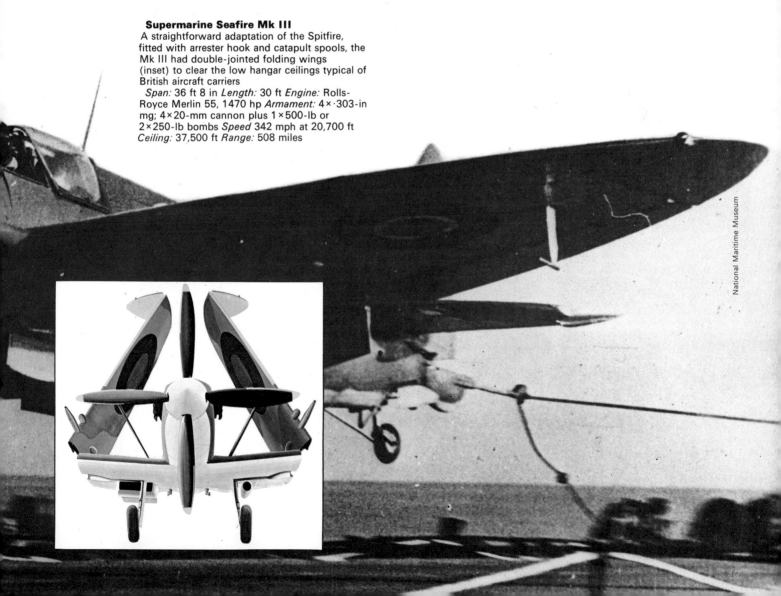

National Maritime Museum

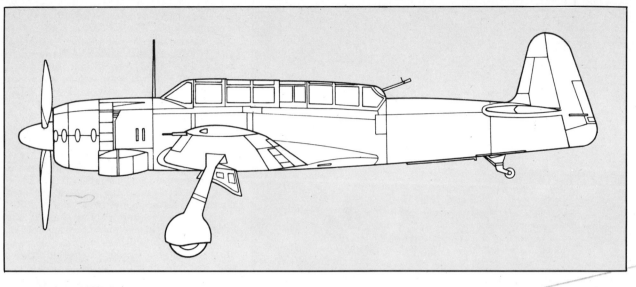

**Nakajima C6N1 Sauiun
(Painted Cloud) 'Myrt'**
Conceived exclusively as a carrier
reconnaissance aircraft, the C6N was a very
effective fleet shadower, its range and speed
(almost equal to those of the Hellcat) making it
almost immune to interception
  Span: 41 ft *Length:* 36 ft 1 in *Engine:* Nakajima
NK9H Homare, 1600 hp at 6560 ft
Armament: 1 × 7·92-mm mg *Max speed:* 379 mph
at 20,015 ft *Max range:* 3300 miles

Airspeed Fleet-Shadower Prototype
Built just before the Second World War but
never put into production, the type was
conceived as a means of extending a task force's
range. With an 8-hour endurance and speed of
only 45 knots, the type could pace an enemy
fleet, but its extreme vulnerability, and the fact
that aircraft already in service could do the job
made it somewhat redundant

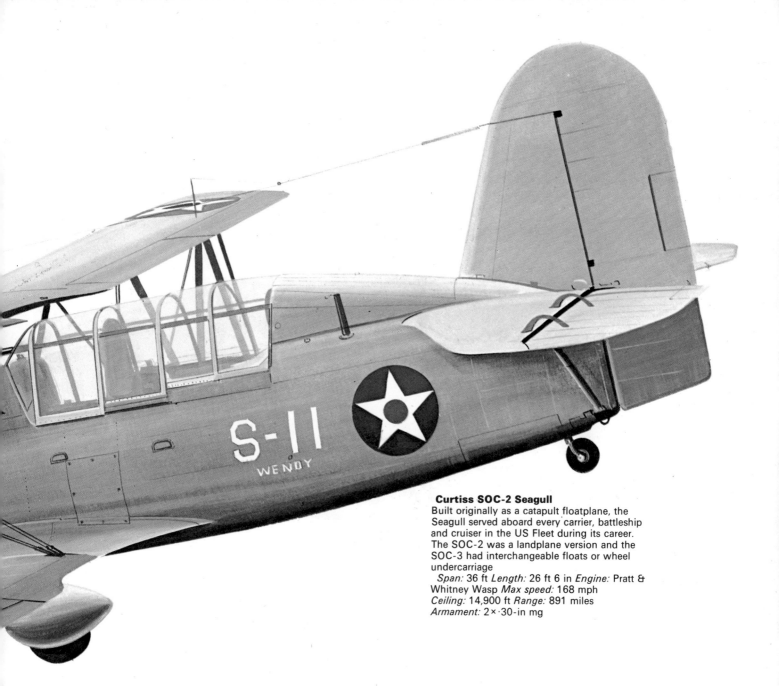

Curtiss SOC-2 Seagull
Built originally as a catapult floatplane, the Seagull served aboard every carrier, battleship and cruiser in the US Fleet during its career. The SOC-2 was a landplane version and the SOC-3 had interchangeable floats or wheel undercarriage
 Span: 36 ft *Length:* 26 ft 6 in *Engine:* Pratt & Whitney Wasp *Max speed:* 168 mph *Ceiling:* 14,900 ft *Range:* 891 miles
Armament: 2 × ·30-in mg

Useful Obsolescence
TRY HARDS AND TRAINERS

Among the aircraft intended for carrier use and fitted with arrester hooks was the Curtiss SO3C Seagull which was originally designed as a catapult-launched observation aircraft. Fitting a fixed landing gear of narrow tread to enable it to land aboard carriers or on land did little to improve its worth or acceptability. The instability of wheel gear dissuaded pilots of both the US Navy and British Fleet Air Arm (where it was known as the Seamew) from using this aircraft type. It is doubtful whether these were ever carried or operated from carriers. They were used to train radio operators and gunners and as radio-controlled targets. One unusual feature was the use of an air-cooled 12 cylinder inverted V engine, the Ranger SGV-770-6.

Also intended for carrier use were the aircraft designed to specifications as Fleet Shadowers. These aircraft, Airspeed 39 and General Aircraft Ltd 38, were designed to meet Air Ministry specifications S23/27 for

carrier operation to shadow enemy fleets during the night. Such activity was thought to require slow speeds and long endurance. As events developed, other aircraft normally carried by the carriers for scouting, bombing and fighting could accomplish the same mission, working in relays from carriers or from shore bases. These were preferred to the extremely vulnerable, slow and underpowered Fleet Shadower.

Relegated to training
Finally, there were several aircraft that mercifully did not get into serious combat action, for the events which unfolded during the early stages of the war would have made their use suicidal. Two of these were the Curtiss SBC-4 Helldiver biplanes, known as Clevelands in France and Britain, which were on their way to France during the first days of the war and were unloaded in Martinique when France capitulated in June 1940; and the Vought SB2U-1 Vindicator,

Curtiss SBC-4 Helldiver
The last combat biplanes to be manufactured in the USA, 186 SBCs were on strength with the US Navy and Marine Air Corps at the time of Pearl Harbor, although none saw action.
 Span: 34 ft *Length:* 27 ft 6 in *Engine:* Wright R-1820-34 radial, 950 hp *Max speed:* 237 mph at 15,200 ft *Ceiling:* 27,300 ft *Range:* 555 miles *Armament:* 2×·30-in mg *Bombload:* 1000 lb

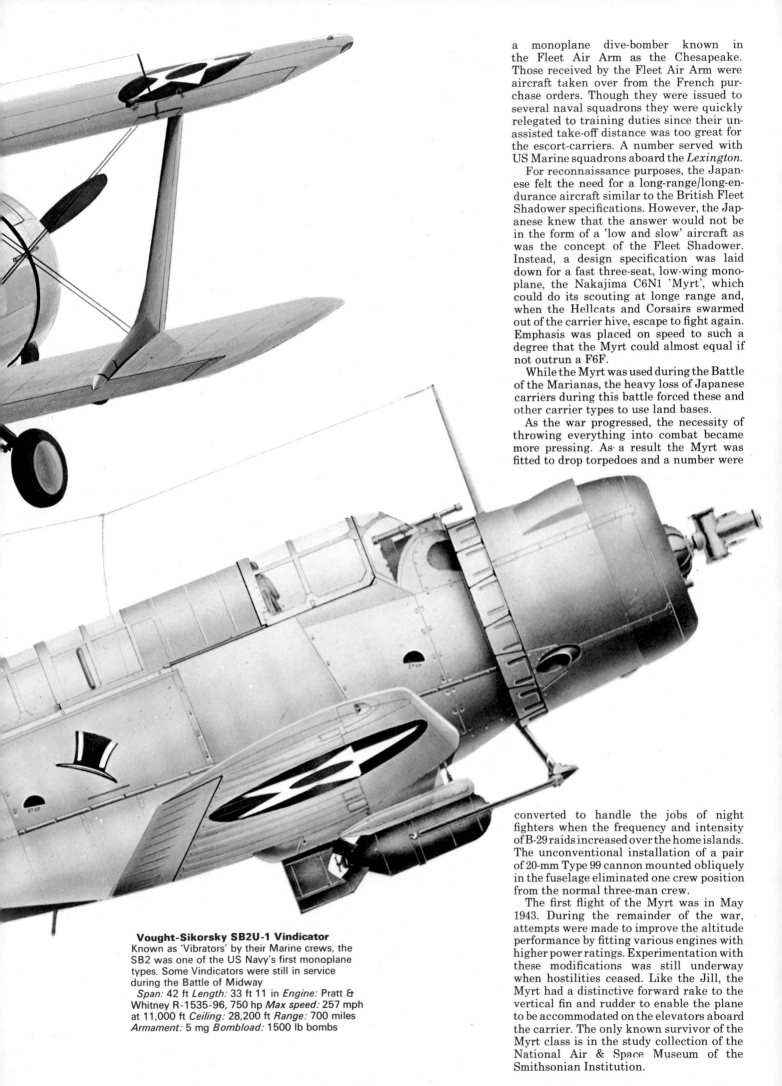

a monoplane dive-bomber known in the Fleet Air Arm as the Chesapeake. Those received by the Fleet Air Arm were aircraft taken over from the French purchase orders. Though they were issued to several naval squadrons they were quickly relegated to training duties since their unassisted take-off distance was too great for the escort-carriers. A number served with US Marine squadrons aboard the *Lexington*.

For reconnaissance purposes, the Japanese felt the need for a long-range/long-endurance aircraft similar to the British Fleet Shadower specifications. However, the Japanese knew that the answer would not be in the form of a 'low and slow' aircraft as was the concept of the Fleet Shadower. Instead, a design specification was laid down for a fast three-seat, low-wing monoplane, the Nakajima C6N1 'Myrt', which could do its scouting at longe range and, when the Hellcats and Corsairs swarmed out of the carrier hive, escape to fight again. Emphasis was placed on speed to such a degree that the Myrt could almost equal if not outrun a F6F.

While the Myrt was used during the Battle of the Marianas, the heavy loss of Japanese carriers during this battle forced these and other carrier types to use land bases.

As the war progressed, the necessity of throwing everything into combat became more pressing. As a result the Myrt was fitted to drop torpedoes and a number were converted to handle the jobs of night fighters when the frequency and intensity of B-29 raids increased over the home islands. The unconventional installation of a pair of 20-mm Type 99 cannon mounted obliquely in the fuselage eliminated one crew position from the normal three-man crew.

The first flight of the Myrt was in May 1943. During the remainder of the war, attempts were made to improve the altitude performance by fitting various engines with higher power ratings. Experimentation with these modifications was still underway when hostilities ceased. Like the Jill, the Myrt had a distinctive forward rake to the vertical fin and rudder to enable the plane to be accommodated on the elevators aboard the carrier. The only known survivor of the Myrt class is in the study collection of the National Air & Space Museum of the Smithsonian Institution.

Vought-Sikorsky SB2U-1 Vindicator
Known as 'Vibrators' by their Marine crews, the SB2 was one of the US Navy's first monoplane types. Some Vindicators were still in service during the Battle of Midway
Span: 42 ft *Length:* 33 ft 11 in *Engine:* Pratt & Whitney R-1535-96, 750 hp *Max speed:* 257 mph at 11,000 ft *Ceiling:* 28,200 ft *Range:* 700 miles *Armament:* 5 mg *Bombload:* 1500 lb bombs

TORPEDOES

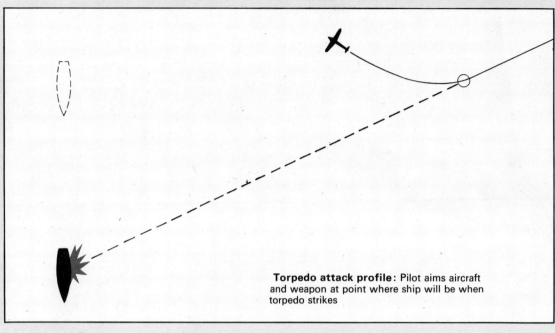

Torpedo attack profile: Pilot aims aircraft and weapon at point where ship will be when torpedo strikes

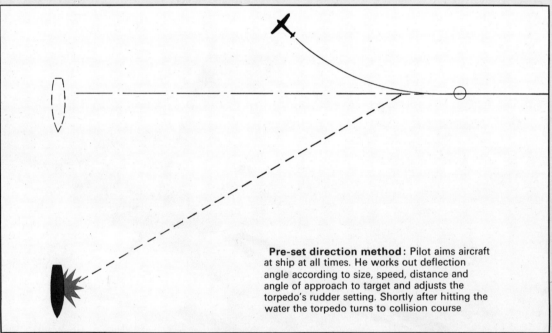

Pre-set direction method: Pilot aims aircraft at ship at all times. He works out deflection angle according to size, speed, distance and angle of approach to target and adjusts the torpedo's rudder setting. Shortly after hitting the water the torpedo turns to collision course

US Mk 13 Airborne Torpedo
A development of the original Whitehead torpedo, with vastly improved range and speed. Fully developed, the Mk 13 could deliver 600 lb of explosive at better than 40 knots over ranges of several miles. Thirteen feet long, with a 22·42-in diameter, the torpedo weighed about a ton. The steering mechanism and 700 hp steam engine were located in the rear of the torpedo, compressed air, fuel and water tanks in the middle, and the explosive in the nose

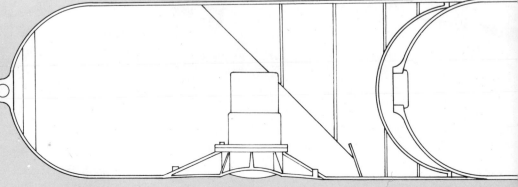

The USS California *settles low in the water amid clouds of smoke after being torpedoed at Pearl Harbor*

Probably the most effective airborne anti-shipping weapon is the torpedo. The earliest known success with a torpedo dropped from a plane was in the Gallipoli campaign in the autumn of 1915, when two Short torpedo bombers carrying 14-in (diameter) torpedoes succeeded in sinking two ships, one a 5000-ton supply ship. The only basic differences between airborne torpedoes and the original torpedo designed by Robert Whitehead for the Austrian Navy in 1862 were a more precise directional gyro and improved propulsion systems.

Against the Whitehead torpedo's speed of 6 knots and range of several hundred yards, its Second World War counterpart had a speed of 30 knots and a range of over 4000 yards. In view of the experience gained in naval battles in the Pacific, notably the Battle of Midway, the all-round performance of the US Mk 13 torpedo was improved to the point where speeds exceeded 40 knots and combat ranges were increased to several miles. The latest development also included target-seeking capability and proximity fuse exploders. Moreover, the torpedoes could be dropped at up to 300 knots and from altitudes approaching 1000 ft.

The earlier US airborne torpedoes, such as the 18-in diameter Mk 7, required that the pilot fly a very precise attitude and altitude of about 50 feet at the instant of drop. To do otherwise could destroy the torpedo by breaking its back, or cause it to skip on impact with the surface of the water. Experience with the earlier torpedoes led to the development of a torpedo tailored to the aircraft's conditions and limitations.

The US Navy developed the Mk 13 as an aircraft torpedo and then adapted it for use on the PT torpedo boats as well, since its rugged construction was well suited to the severe conditions encountered by these high-speed boats. It was, in effect, a miniature submarine designed to carry a sizeable quantity (600 lb) of high explosive and detonate it against an enemy ship. If placed well, the torpedo could burst the plates of a battleship, but only if exploded below the protective armour belt which surrounded the hull at the waterline. To ensure maximum destructive capability, the depth settings ranged from 2–3 ft for shallow draught barge-type shipping to 10 ft for destroyers, cruisers or submarines on the surface and about 22 ft for battleships and aircraft carriers. When proximity fuses were used, the depth would be somewhat greater, causing the torpedo to explode under the ship to do the most damage.

The Mk 13 in its developed form weighed a little over one ton, and was powered by a very compact engine which developed about 700 hp to drive the torpedo at speeds in excess of 30 knots. The US favoured rotary engines, while European manufacturers preferred reciprocating engines with pistons displaced radially around the shaft. Though not used extensively, the Germans developed an electric motor which was claimed to be over 95% efficient and, more important, did not leave a trail of air bubbles to mark its course.

Limited usefulness

The 18-in US Mk 7 torpedoes were tried but attained only limited success as was the case with the 21-in Mk 14 and Mk 15 torpedoes. The Mk 14 was developed for use in submarines and the Mk 15 for use on destroyers. Both these types were 21 ft long and weighed about 1½ tons each, which limited their usefulness to larger patrol bombers such as the Catalina flying boats.

The Mk 13 was much shorter, 13 ft long, slightly larger in diameter (22·42 in), and weighed about one ton. In addition, the Mk 13 required several attachments to make it operate successfully. To complete the torpedo for air drop, an air stabiliser, a plywood box-shaped fin, was fitted outside of the shroud ring which surrounded the counter-rotating propellers. The second accessory was a drag ring or blunt nose which was also made of wood and dubbed a 'pickle barrel'. This was fitted to the nose of the torpedo to take the initial shock of entry into the water and also to prevent skipping. Both of these fractured on impact with the water and dropped away. In the event that the torpedo was not housed inside the aircraft, as in the case of the TBDs, Barracudas and Swordfish, a streamlined cap was added forward of the pickle barrel drag rig. This cap pulled off at the time the torpedo was dropped.

In addition to the very precise driving mechanism, an extremely intricate guidance system was required to withstand the shock of launching and still keep it on course and at the required depth. The main charge was not easily exploded by impact. It was necessary therefore to add an exploder. Unfortunately, the mechanical impact exploder used on early models was a very temperamental device and caused a number of otherwise good hits to be wasted.

Early in the war these exploders were mechanically similar to bomb fuses and were not as reliable in operation as development and production costs would lead one to expect. Later versions set off a detonator of fulminate of mercury at the time of impact. The explosion of this detonator set off a booster charge which in turn ignited the main charge. In addition to the standard exploders, a magnetic proximity fuse was developed similar to those used for artillery and anti-aircraft shells. These were designated Mk 9 Exploders and made a near miss as effective as a direct hit.

The control mechanism was located in the rear third of the torpedo along with the powerful engine. The centre section housed an air flask with air pressures up to 2800 lb/sq in, and the fuel and water tanks for the steam engine. The nose section housed the explosive head.

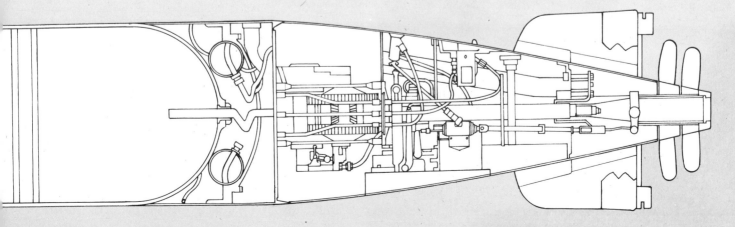

BOMBS

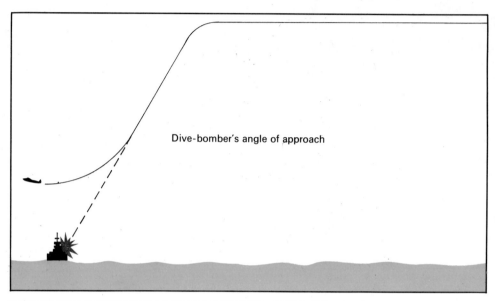

Dive-bomber's angle of approach

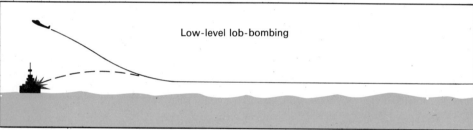

Low-level lob-bombing

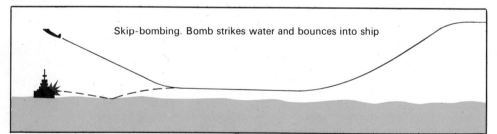

Skip-bombing. Bomb strikes water and bounces into ship

Smoke and flames billow from the deck of USS Bunker Hill, *under kamikaze attack off Okinawa*

In addition to torpedoes, carried-based aircraft could normally be expected to deliver three other major classes of ordnance: bombs, mines and rockets.

Of these three, bombs probably would constitute the largest group from several points of view. They could be subdivided by weight, type and fusing. Weights, for combat, ranged from the relatively light fragmentation bombs in the 20/25-lb weight range, up to the 2000-lb bombs.

Bombs are classed according to use, such as general-purpose (GP), armour-piercing (AP), semi-armour-piercing, fragmentation and depth. In addition to these, there is a whole range of chemical bombs which are classified according to the filler used or incendiary, the latter being rated as an intensive or scatter incendiary.

The shapes vary, as do the proportions, but they generally follow a streamlined form with directional stabilising fins attached to the rear of the bomb. Later, after the war, bombs were stream-lined to become low-drag bombs. Not that it made much difference to the bombing aspect but it did make a difference to the plane carrying the bomb. The low-drag bomb could add several miles per hour to the speed of a supersonic plane when carried instead of the old standard bomb. In some cases low-profile bombs were required if the aircraft was to get airborne.

Packed with explosive

The General Purpose (GP) bomb is packed with explosive which amounts to some 50% of the bomb weight. It is suitable for attack on unarmoured ships, ground targets, personnel and other targets generally susceptible to blast effect and earth shock. The bomb casing is about half an inch thick, which gives it enough rigidity to penetrate through buildings or through several decks of unarmoured ships. GP bombs range in weight from 100 lb up to 2000 lb. They are normally double-fused, nose and tail, to ensure detonation in case of malfunction of the nose fuse as a result of impact with the plating or building structure. On occasion, the tail fuses are delayed action to further ensure the detonation. When operating from land bases, an additional fuse, a hydrostatic fuse, might be added in an athwartship fuse pocket of the bomb.

However, this is not a general practice when operating from carriers. In the event of the aircraft returning with a 'hang up', there is always the possibility of its breaking loose on the arrested landing and rolling down the deck. Should this occur, the probability of the bomb going overboard and exploding beneath the Home ship is quite high.

Armour-piercing (AP) bombs were developed for use in penetrating the heaviest deck armour or reinforced concrete. To accomplish this, the nose is machined to a smooth, long ogival shape. Because its main purpose is penetration, the nose and casing is very thick, resulting in the explosive being the smallest part of the bomb – approximately 15% of the total weight. Anticipating contact with a highly resistant surface, the nose fuse is not used on this bomb, for the impact would almost certainly crush the fuse, preventing its functioning. The most common fusing is a tail fuse, with a possible athwartship fusing to give a back-up capability. Unless this bomb is right on target in the case of a ship, no great damage can be expected.

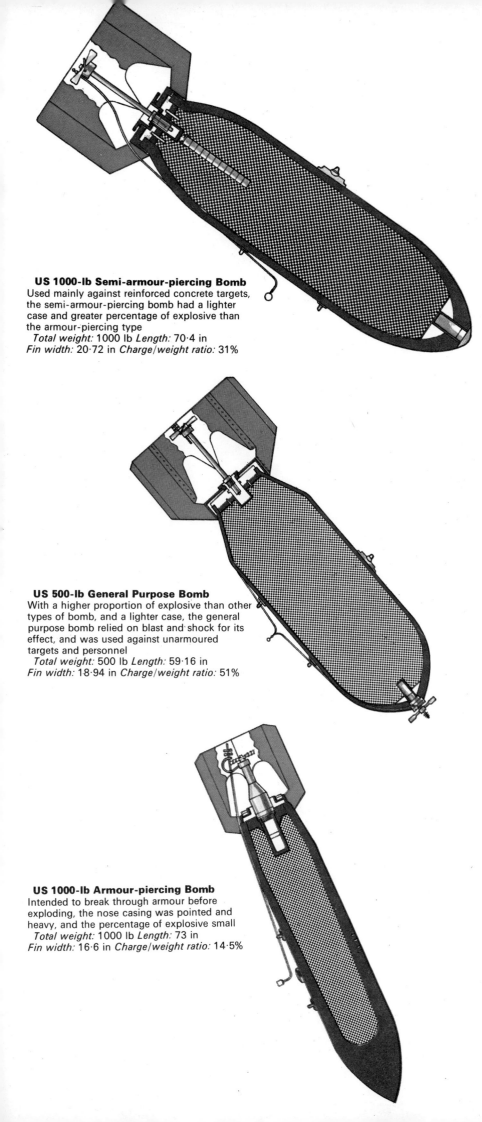

US 1000-lb Semi-armour-piercing Bomb
Used mainly against reinforced concrete targets, the semi-armour-piercing bomb had a lighter case and greater percentage of explosive than the armour-piercing type
Total weight: 1000 lb *Length:* 70·4 in
Fin width: 20·72 in *Charge/weight ratio:* 31%

US 500-lb General Purpose Bomb
With a higher proportion of explosive than other types of bomb, and a lighter case, the general purpose bomb relied on blast and shock for its effect, and was used against unarmoured targets and personnel
Total weight: 500 lb *Length:* 59·16 in
Fin width: 18·94 in *Charge/weight ratio:* 51%

US 1000-lb Armour-piercing Bomb
Intended to break through armour before exploding, the nose casing was pointed and heavy, and the percentage of explosive small
Total weight: 1000 lb *Length:* 73 in
Fin width: 16·6 in *Charge/weight ratio:* 14·5%

A variation, the semi-armour-piercing bomb, is intended primarily for reinforced concrete and is lighter than the AP bomb, making it possible to use a greater percentage of explosive.

Depth bombs were intended for submarines or other underwater targets. They have comparatively thin shells since they rely on the pressure wave against the hull of a submarine or other ship. They are armed for impact, air burst or hydrostatic detonation. They have an explosive load of up to 70% of the total weight.

One little-known use for these bombs was to encourage enemy troops to come out of lateral caves dug into the hills of Pacific Islands. The fuses used in this instance were nose contact or VT (proximity) fuses to give an air burst on or slightly above the ground, producing a blast effect rather than a penetrating effect. The hydrostatic fuses could be set to 25, 50, 75, 100 or 125 ft.

Fragmentation bombs might be mixed in with other more destructive ordnance mostly to reduce the activity or effectiveness of anti-aircraft gunners, with an additional possibility of use on parked aircraft to cause widespread damage if not destruction. Fragments piercing an aircraft might render the plane unserviceable with multiple shrapnel holes through cockpits, tyres and possibly fuel and oil tanks.

Mines were to account for a large amount of shipping sunk during the war, much of it by those placed by aircraft. The term 'mine' goes back to the first use of this system, which involved miners tunnelling under a defensive position to place a demolition charge. Early mines were contact mines with external horns which, when bumped by a ship, would trigger an explosive charge. In the Second World War modern versions of these, and more advanced types such as magnetic mines, were sown by aircraft in harbours, along coastlines and in frequently used channels to reduce the amount of shipping and resupply operations. Aircraft were perfect for this task, for they could sow the original mine fields and, as they were exploded or swept clear by the defenders, it was a simple matter for one or more planes to 'bolster' the mine field.

Some measure of the effectiveness of aerial mine-laying can be gained by the tonnage destroyed – 649,736 tons, with 1,377,780 tons damaged. British and German aircraft were particularly active in this regard in the European theatre as were the US and the British in the Pacific. It was estimated that 218,000 mines were sown during the war, with aircraft dropping about 85% of the total.

During the Second World War the development of rockets, particularly air-to-ground rockets, was accelerated. They were highly favoured for aircraft launching as they produced no strain on the launching plane and their installation for carriage was very simple and left little or no residual fittings. Moreover, the battery of rockets normally carried was equal in destructive power to a destroyer's main battery.

Rockets for aircraft use ranged from the 2·75-in which was about 50 in long and weighed about 20 lb, to the 5-in high velocity aircraft rocket.

As in the case of gunnery, the pilot had to adapt his flying to the rocket, for any manoeuvre in progress at the moment of firing would have an effect on the rocket's direction. Time from launch to target could be as short as three seconds.

Sea Hurricanes, an Albacore and a Swordfish preparing to take off from a British carrier en route to Malta

USS *Essex, her deck packed with Dauntlesses, Hellcats and Avengers with their wings folded*

THE LONG ARM OF THE NAVY

By the outbreak of the Second World War the aircraft carrier had replaced the battleship as the most important capital vessel. The pioneering navies of Britain and the United States had built up substantial carrier forces, Japan was not far behind, France had the *Béarn* in service and other vessels on the stocks, and even Germany and Italy were beginning to toe the line.

The Royal Navy was the first to pay the price for its pioneering efforts. All its carriers except the *Ark Royal* had been launched more than 20 years previously, and the Fleet Air Arm's aircraft were hopelessly outdated. Only two weeks after the start of hostilities the *Courageous* was sunk, and *Ark Royal* and *Hermes* were withdrawn from anti-submarine sweeps because they proved too dangerous.

The Royal Navy lost its second carrier in June 1940, when *Glorious* was sunk by the battle cruisers *Scharnhorst* and *Gneisenau*. By then, however, the first of the new carriers with armoured decks and radar—*Illustrious*—had been commissioned. Her armour prevented her from sinking after being hit by German dive-bombers in January 1941, but the old *Ark Royal* succumbed to a submarine attack in November of that year.

By this time the rapidly expanding Imperial Japanese Navy had ten carriers in service, compared with the US Navy's three in the Pacific (plus five in the Atlantic). The IJN's devastating attack on Pearl Harbor in December 1942 signalled the beginning of five months when the Japanese were invincible. The Royal Navy's *Hermes* was sunk by Japanese bombers in April 1942, but the US Navy began to fight back the following month in the first ever battle in which the opposing fleets neither saw each other nor fired a shot at the enemy's vessels.

The battle of the Coral Sea was also the IJN's first major setback. Japanese forces attacking the Solomon Islands and New Guinea were supported by two large carriers and the light carrier *Shoho*. The *Shoho* was sunk in the engagement and, although the US Navy's *Lexington* was also lost, the Americans had won a moral victory. The following month the US Navy delivered the hammer blow—at the battle of Midway the carriers *Akagi*, *Kaga*, *Soryu* and *Hiryu* were sunk for the loss of the *Yorktown*.

By June 1944 Japan was ready for the make-or-break battle—the largest carrier engagement ever—off the Marianas. On the nineteenth of that month the battle-hardened US fighter pilots tore apart the newly trained Japanese carrier air fleet at the 'Marianas turkey shoot'. Japan lost about 275 aircraft and the carriers *Shokaku*, *Taiho* and *Hiyo*. Four months later another four went to the bottom—*Chitose*, *Zuiho*, *Chiyoda* and *Zuikaku*.

In the Atlantic the convoys from North America to Europe and from Britain to Russia's Arctic ports were taking a battering from submarines, aircraft and surface raiders.

With the outbreak of war in 1939, the practice of converting existing ships was adopted, particularly in the case of escort carriers to fill gaps in the defence of convoys and to support the larger carriers and amphibious landings.

Many details of carriers require special design. For example, the cavernous hangar deck was probably the most obvious difference from conventional warships, apart from the 'flat top'. These hangar decks, while appearing large when a carrier is in

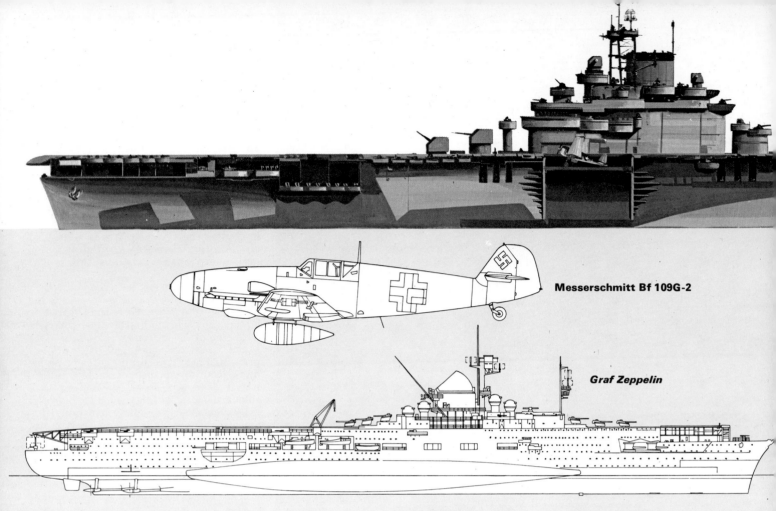

Messerschmitt Bf 109G-2

Graf Zeppelin

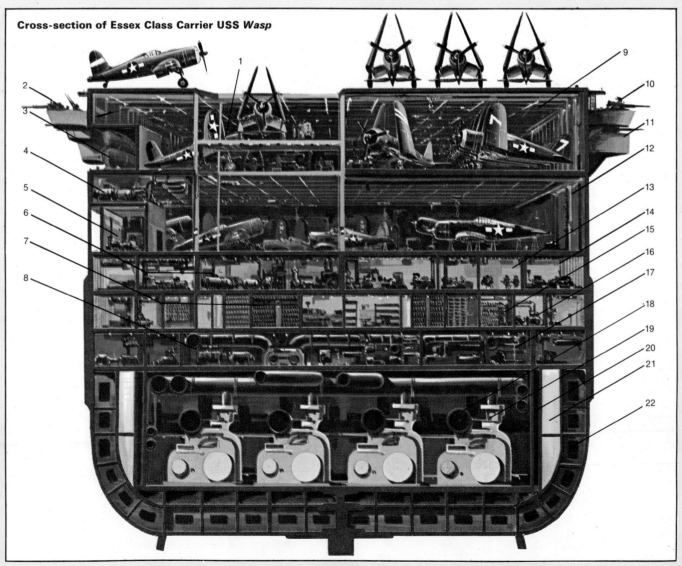

Cross-section of Essex Class Carrier USS *Wasp*

1
2
3
4
5
6
7
8
9
10
11
12
13
14
15
16
17
18
19
20
21
22

USS Wasp
The *Essex* Class (the *Wasp* is shown here) became the standard US fleet carrier of the Pacific war and made up the core of the fast carrier groups
Displacement: 27,100 tons *Length:* 872 ft overall *Max beam:* 147 ft *Max speed:* 32 knots *Armament:* 12×·5-in guns, 44 to 68 40-mm AA guns, 100 aircraft *Crew:* 3500

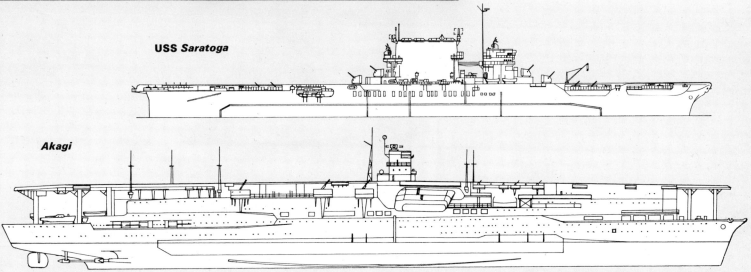

USS *Saratoga*

Akagi

USS *Wasp* cross-section
1 Lift **2** 20- & 40-mm AA guns **3** Two lifeboats **4** Fan motors **5** Airframe workshop **6** Workshop deck & lift machinery **7** Ammo & aircraft stores **8** Air conditioning plant **9** Main hangar (aft) **10** AA guns **11** AA guns **12** Servicing hangar **13** Aero engine stores **14** Engine servicing shop **15** Port ammo stores **16** Emergency lighting plant **17** Engine-cooling motor **18** Steam pipes to turbines **19** Turbines **20** Fireproof coffer dam **21** Aviation spirit tank **22** Oil fuel tanks

Flugzeugtrager *Graf Zeppelin*
Germany's only aircraft carrier, the *Graf Zeppelin's* projected complement featured 12 Bf 109Gs and 28 Ju 87 dive-bombers (see page 31). Hitler's lack of interest in the surface fleet halted the project before completion
Displacement: 23,200 tons
Armament: 16×5·9-in; 12×4·1-in AA
Complement: 1760 *Launched:* 8 December 1938

USS *Saratoga*
The *Saratoga* and her sister-ship the *Lexington* were the largest carriers in the world at the outbreak of the Second World War. Launched in 1925, the 'Old Sara' was to take a tremendous battering from Japanese submarines and Kamikazes yet survived the war.
Displacement: 33,000 tons *Length:* 888 ft overall *Beam:* 105½ ft *Speed:* 34 knots *Armament:* 8×5-in guns; 125×20- & 40-mm AA guns, 90 aircraft *Crew:* 3300

Akagi
Launched in 1927, the *Akagi* was the Japanese Navy's first big fleet carrier. She had served as Admiral Nagumo's flagship at Pearl Harbor. At Midway the *Akagi* was found by dive-bombers from the *Enterprise* with her decks crammed with planes, and she was sunk along with the *Kaga, Soryu,* and *Hiryu*
Displacement: 36,000 tons *Aircraft:* 91

port, are in fact marginally adequate in combat. Stowage of full-size aircraft, plus spares of almost every conceivable aircraft part, is in the areas overhead. Complete fuselages, propellers, wing panels as well as tail surfaces also find overhead stowage. Engines and other components find nooks and corners in which to be secured. Handling gear such as tractors, engine hoists, jacks and complete machine shop and engine overhaul facilities are all crowded into this hangar deck along with the work stands and maintenance personnel to service the planes.

High explosives are stowed much like shells in the average cruiser and get the same precautionary handling that shells might expect. However, aircraft require and get regular fuelling and oiling. The fuel, in particular, requires special handling to prevent static electricity from detonating the fumes. At sea there is the regular refuelling of the carrier with fuel for its own machinery in addition to the volatile 100 octane aviation gas.

Two distinct groups operate a carrier: the ship's crew mans the ship as it would any other naval vessel, while the second group is the air department. This consists of the air officer and assisting officers and crew whose responsibilities cover all the aviation activities. These include the operation, maintenance and storage of all aircraft, aircraft accessories, work shops and berthing and plane handling. Under the latter category are such jobs as handling crews to see that the planes are moved expeditiously and spotted either on the flight deck or hangar deck. In addition, there are plane directors, fuel squads, fire crews and ordnance men.

Under combat conditions a carrier is full to overflowing with men as well as machinery. During the long operational cruises,

space and facilities were at a premium. More often than not meals, showers and other personal necessities were taken in shifts. One consolation was the quality of food, which was usually above average, as was the cleanliness of the ship – kept that way by constant policing of crews of both the air department and ship's crew.

Structural details of the carrier are beyond the scope of this book. However, by illustration we are able to convey some of the detail and complexity of these ships, such as the machinery of the ship and its control. One of the principal features not covered previously is the aircraft elevator – or elevators – as they developed. While apparently taken for granted they are the all-important link between hangar deck and the flight deck and vice versa. Damage to the aircraft elevator could effectively silence the carrier. For this reason, modern carriers built as carriers include at least two or more elevators to preclude the possibility of restricting the expeditious handling of the aircraft.

Another fact worthy of mention is the influence that elevator size or weight limitations have on the design of the aircraft. For example, the Japanese aircraft Jill and Myrt had a distinctive forward rake to their fin and rudder and this was designed specifically to adapt to elevator size. In the case of the US Curtiss SB2C Helldiver, the designers never did completely solve the directional stability problems which were the result of designing the plane to fit the elevator rather than designing it to fly well.

The carriers were, and are, huge floating cities designed to place a potent force within combat range of anywhere in the world. They are the long arm of naval forces which enable the mailed fist, the aircraft, to strike repeated blows upon an enemy wherever he may be.

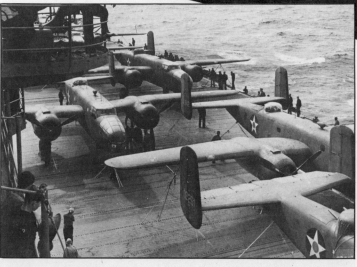

On 18 April 1942 Lt Col James H 'Jimmy' Doolittle led a raid on Tokyo flying Mitchells from the Hornet and carrying on to crash land in China. Above left he is receiving Japanese medals to be attached to the bombs – the first to fall on the home islands during the war. The flight deck of the Hornet (right) vividly illustrates the problems of flying the bulky B-25s from a carrier's deck, even with special preparations and stripped down planes

AND DOOLITTLE'S B25s

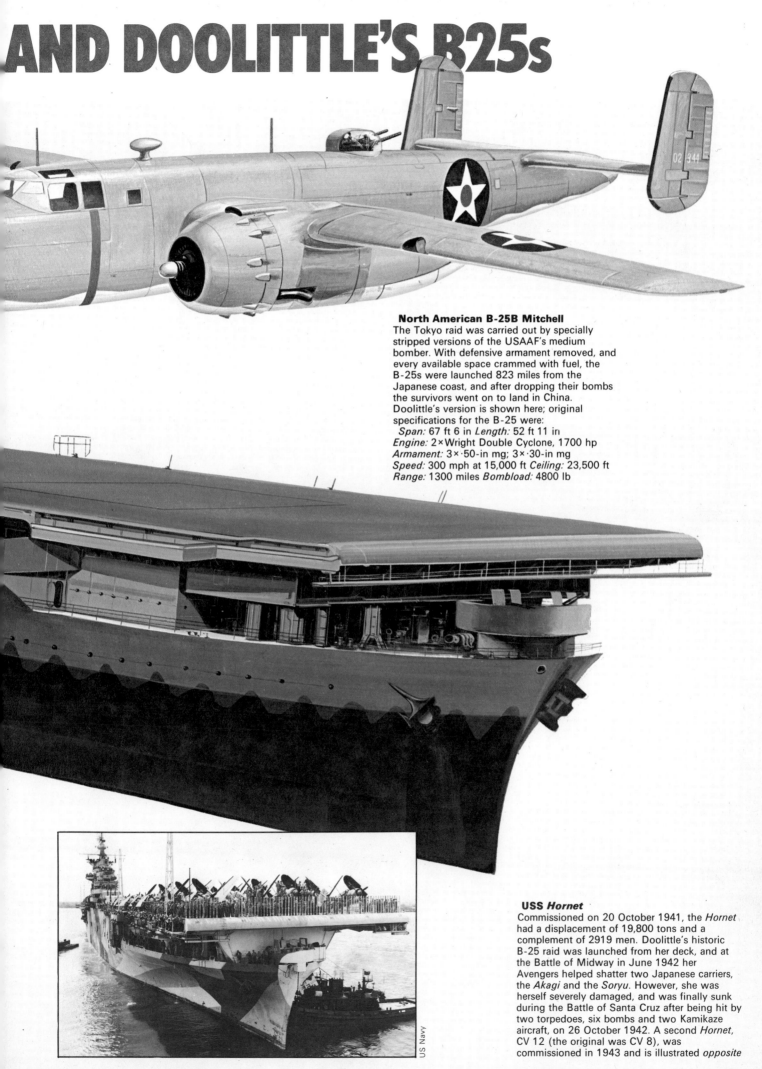

North American B-25B Mitchell
The Tokyo raid was carried out by specially stripped versions of the USAAF's medium bomber. With defensive armament removed, and every available space crammed with fuel, the B-25s were launched 823 miles from the Japanese coast, and after dropping their bombs the survivors went on to land in China. Doolittle's version is shown here; original specifications for the B-25 were:
 Span: 67 ft 6 in *Length:* 52 ft 11 in
Engine: 2×Wright Double Cyclone, 1700 hp
Armament: 3×·50-in mg; 3×·30-in mg
Speed: 300 mph at 15,000 ft *Ceiling:* 23,500 ft
Range: 1300 miles *Bombload:* 4800 lb

US Navy

USS *Hornet*
Commissioned on 20 October 1941, the *Hornet* had a displacement of 19,800 tons and a complement of 2919 men. Doolittle's historic B-25 raid was launched from her deck, and at the Battle of Midway in June 1942 her Avengers helped shatter two Japanese carriers, the *Akagi* and the *Soryu*. However, she was herself severely damaged, and was finally sunk during the Battle of Santa Cruz after being hit by two torpedoes, six bombs and two Kamikaze aircraft, on 26 October 1942. A second *Hornet*, CV 12 (the original was CV 8), was commissioned in 1943 and is illustrated *opposite*

US Navy Classification System

The USN's formula for designating an aircraft type was generally divided into four units. The first unit of either one or two letters gave the function of the aircraft. The second was a number denoting the model. The third unit, of one letter indicated the maker and modifications were indicated by a further hyphenated number. Thus in the F6F-3 Hellcat formula, F is for fighter, 6F shows it is the sixth fighter type to be produced by Grumman, and -3 shows the third modification of the design. An X prefix denotes an experimental model. If an aircraft was sub-contracted to more than one firm, that firm's code letter would be used in the formula, hence the Vought F4U Corsair when built by Goodyear became the FG. (The second, model number unit is sometimes omitted when the number is 1.)

First Unit (Function)

A	Amphibian	P	Patrol
B	Bomber	PB	Patrol Bomber
F	Fighter	R	Transport (multi-engined)
G	Transport (1 engine)	S	Scout
H	Ambulance	SB	Scout-Bomber
J	Utility	SN	Scout-Trainer
JR	Utility-Transport	SO	Scout-Observation
N	Trainer	T	Torpedo
O	Observation	TB	Torpedo-Bomber
OS	Observation-Scout	X	Experimental

Third Unit (Maker)

A	Brewster	M	Martin/General Motors
B	Beechcraft/Boeing	N	Naval Aircraft Factory
C	Curtiss	O	Lockheed
D	Douglas	P	Spartan
E	Bellanca/Piper	Q	Stinson
F	Grumman	R	Ryan
G	Goodyear	S	Stearman
H	Howard	T	Timm
J	North American	U	Vought
K	Fairchild	V	Vultee
L	Bell	Y	Consolidated

A US Navy Avenger takes off straight out of the hangar deck of an aircraft carrier